# PSALMS FOR YOU

CHRISTOPHER ASH

# PSALMS FOR YOU

**Psalms For You**

Published by:
The Good Book Company

thegoodbook.com | www.thegoodbook.co.uk
thegoodbook.com.au | thegoodbook.co.nz | thegoodbook.co.in



(Hardcover) ISBN: 9781784984168
(Paperback) ISBN: 9781784984151

Printed in India

Design by André Parker

# CONTENTS

# SERIES PREFACE

Each volume of the *God's Word For You* series takes you to the heart of a book of the Bible, and applies its truths to your heart.

The central aim of each title is to be:

- Bible centred
- Christ glorifying
- Relevantly applied
- Easily readable

You can use *Psalms For You:*

**To read.** You can simply read from cover to cover, as a book that explains and explores the themes, encouragements and challenges of this part of Scripture.

**To feed.** You can work through this book as part of your own personal regular devotions, or use it alongside a sermon or Bible-study series at your church. Each chapter is divided into two (or occasionally three) shorter sections, with questions for reflection at the end of each.

**To lead.** You can use this as a resource to help you teach God's word to others, both in small-group and whole-church settings. You'll find tricky verses or concepts explained using ordinary language, and helpful themes and illustrations along with suggested applications.

These books are not commentaries. They assume no understanding of the original Bible languages, nor a high level of biblical knowledge. Verse references are marked in **bold** so that you can refer to them easily. Any words that are used rarely or differently in everyday language outside the church are marked in **grey** when they first appear, and are explained in a glossary towards the back. There, you'll also find details of resources you can use alongside this one, in both personal and church life.

Our prayer is that as you read, you'll be struck not by the contents of this book, but by the book it's helping you open up; and that you'll praise not the author of this book, but the One he is pointing you to.

*Carl Laferton, Series Editor*

**Bible translations used:**

- NIV: New International Version, 2011 edition (this is the version being quoted unless otherwise stated)
- ESV: English Standard Version
- KJV: King James Version (also known as the Authorised Version)
- NRSV: New Revised Standard Version
- NASB: New American Standard Bible

# INTRODUCTION TO THE PSALMS

## Come, learn to pray!

In many parts of the Christian church today the Psalms are a neglected treasure: many churches are like a poverty-stricken house with incalculable riches forgotten, neglected, moth-eaten and dusty in the attic. Let us bring the Psalms out and revel in the wonder they offer—a fullness and richness of relationship with God undreamt of by so many of us half-starved Christians.

So I want to invite you to come with me on a journey to learn to pray.

This is exactly what the Psalms are in the Bible to do. The Psalms give a window into how Jesus learned to pray, in his fully human life; and they are how the people of Jesus are to pray as the Spirit of Jesus leads us in praying and praising by the Psalms.

The Psalms are in the Bible so that *all* the people of Jesus may learn to pray *all* the psalms *all* the time. What do I mean? Let's look at the opposite. Someone told me enthusiastically about a pastor who says he reads through the Psalms until a verse resonates with him; and then he dwells there for a period, until it ceases to resonate, at which point he moves on. It sounded wonderful—and yet it would be hard to find a more completely wrong approach to the Psalms! If I adopt this approach, it puts me in the driving seat; I decide what resonates with me, and then enjoy it. And the danger is that the psalms (or the verses) I select act like an echo chamber for my own desires and thoughts, amplifying my feelings, whatever they may be, and never challenging my thoughts or views.

The purpose of the Psalms is very different. In the Psalms we learn to pray corporately, with the church of Christ in every age. We learn to pray **Christocentrically***, with our prayers led by Jesus Christ, by whose Spirit we pray them. And we learn to pray empathetically, as we identify with the wider church and focus less on our individualistic

---

* Words in **grey** are defined in the Glossary (page 265).

(and often introspective) concerns. This will involve a massive **paradigm shift** for many of us, especially those of us nurtured in individualistic Western cultures, where the Christian life is a "me and God" thing, with the emphasis on "me". Learning to sing and pray the Psalms will be a challenging affair, an unsettling experience, and yet a discipline that transforms us into the image of God's Son, the Lord Jesus, whose own prayer life was shaped by these wonderful poems.

## Come, learn to feel!

I also want to invite you to come with me on a journey to learn to feel.

Do you ever wonder what we are supposed to do with our feelings in the Christian life? Since about the 1960s, when the **charismatic movement** swept much of the **evangelical** world, there has been something of a sad divorce between what we call head (thinking) and heart (feeling). Some "do" feelings with energy and enthusiasm; in reaction to this, others "do" thinking. "You just think but don't feel!" says one Christian to another. "Well, you feel but don't think!" comes the reply. Neither is helpful.

I want to invite you to come with me on a journey to learn to feel.

The Psalms are God's chosen way to engage our thinking and our feeling in a way that is passionate, thoughtful, true and authentic. The Psalms show us how to express our varied feelings; but, more than that, they reorder our disordered affections so that we feel deeper desires for what we ought to desire, more urgent aversion to that from which we need to flee, and a greater longing for the honour of God in the health of Christ's church. The Psalms form within us a richer palette of rightly-directed emotions. It is not so much that the Psalms resonate with us as that they shape us so that we most deeply resonate with the God-given yearnings they so movingly express.

## Who wrote the Psalms, when, and why?

The Psalms were written by a great variety of people over a long period of Old Testament history. The earliest psalm whose period we know is one by **Moses** (Psalm 90) from around the time of the **Exodus**. **King David**, centuries after Moses, was the pre-eminent psalmist, which is why the umbrella headline for the **Psalter** is "the Psalms of David"; about half the psalms have his name at the top. From the day the Spirit of God came upon him, when he was anointed by **Samuel** the prophet (1 Samuel 16), he began to sing songs that were inspired by the Spirit of the anointed king who was yet to come (see, for example, 2 Samuel 22, which became Psalm 18).

It was King David who made provision for societies of musicians who wrote and led Israel in psalms at the temple (see, for example, 1 Chronicles 16 and 25). From then on, right through the period of Israel's kings, through the exile in Babylon and beyond, Spirit-inspired poets wrote psalms. Many come from subsequent generations of the song-writing societies founded by David (for instance, the psalms headed "of Asaph"); many others are anonymous. But, whether named or anonymous, these psalmists "prophesied" (see 1 Chronicles 25:1-3); that is, they wrote and sang by the Spirit of God, who is the Spirit of the Christ who was to come (1 Peter 1:10-12). We do not know quite how or when the Psalms were arranged, by inspiration of the Spirit of God, into their present order. We know that the last psalms were written no earlier than the exile in Babylon (see, for instance, Psalms 74 and 137). It seems likely that Books I and II were the earliest collection, that Book III was put together during or after the exile, and that Books IV and V were arranged last of all. The study of the arrangement of the Psalms is a hot topic in biblical scholarship.

God's people sang these songs in Israel, in exile, and when they returned to the land, and were still doing so when Jesus walked in Judea. The Lord Jesus and the New Testament writers made much use of the Psalms. In Appendix 1 you will find a list of the most important Psalms quotations in the New Testament. The way they are quoted confirms that these psalms find their fulfilment on the lips of, and in the life, death, resurrection and ascension of the Lord Jesus himself. The Psalms are the God-given words by which the Lord Jesus Christ leads his church in praying to and praising the Father.

## A guided tour

Some museums offer an audio guide; this highlights and gives commentary on selected exhibits. You pause at each one for which information is provided, to have a close look and a careful listen, before moving on to the next. In the same way, we shall not look at every psalm but consider 32 psalms. We shall take these in 16 related pairs. I have chosen some well-known psalms, but also some others to illustrate the large number of less-known psalms; for it is our task to learn to pray them too. Some of my choices are arbitrary (even personal); but I have tried to include a representative sample of types of psalm from each of the five books.

It will be frustrating to walk quickly past so many psalms; and yet my prayer is that by the end of our tour you will feel better equipped to explore those we passed by; and that you will deeply desire to make all the psalms your prayers, again and again and again, for the rest of your life, and to lead others to do so.

Here are three things to bear in mind as we pause at each psalm.

1. *We will ask who is speaking.* There are different voices in the Psalms. Sometimes we hear a voice of authority speaking "down" to us from God on high. At other times we hear a human being speaking "upwards" to God on high, speaking by the Spirit of God, who is the Spirit of Christ. And then again we sometimes hear the people of God speaking together, in prayer or praise, or to one another.

   Always we will ask what it would have meant for the original psalmist to have spoken the psalm. Whether it was King David, some other named psalmist or an anonymous believer, we need to ask what the psalm originally meant for them.

2. *We will ask what the psalm meant in* **old-covenant** *times.* The Psalms have been carefully arranged in five books. We cannot always tell exactly why they are in the precise order in which we find them. But it is often significant in which book a psalm is placed. I shall comment briefly on this as we embark on each book in our walking tour. That will help us as we ask what it would have meant for an old-covenant believer (such as **Simeon** or **Anna** in Luke 2:25-38) to have said or sung this psalm before Christ came.

3. *We will ask what it meant for Jesus and now means for us in Christ.* What would it have meant for Jesus of Nazareth to have sung a psalm during his earthly life? This is arguably the most significant question of them all; again and again it opens up the meaning and force of a psalm. In his full humanity, and as the forerunner of our faith, what did it mean for him, as the perfect believer, to pray this psalm?

   This will help us as we move on to consider what difference it now makes that we sing a psalm after Christ. How does the old covenant language of the psalm translate into **new-covenant** fulfilment? How does the whole Bible help us see what the old-covenant **types and shadows** mean? I will try to help us get a feel for this.

   All this will help us to grasp what it now means for us, either individually or together, to sing a psalm as men and women in Christ.

## Joining Christ's choir

Imagine you are seated in a great concert hall. In the middle of the stage is Jesus Christ, the conductor and song-leader of the people of God. Behind him stands a huge choir: his church in every age. This choir sings the Psalms as the songs of Jesus, led by Jesus, shaped by Jesus, guided and taught by Jesus.

What do you need to do to join in? You need to understand the words of the psalms. You need to get hold of the "tune" of the psalms, by which I mean the emotions and affections they convey. You need to grasp what commitment will be required of you if you are to join the choir of Jesus and join in, for every psalm asks of us some commitment. Finally, you need to get up out of your seat in the audience and join the choir! That is the aim of this guide—to help us to do that.

**Note:**

I have written more fully about the Psalms in my two-volume book *Teaching Psalms* (Christian Focus: Volume 1, 2017; Volume 2, 2018). Volume 1 is a handbook about how to sing the Psalms in Christ, addressing the main difficulties and with chapters on the big themes of **biblical theology**. Volume 2 includes a short Christian introduction to each psalm and a chapter on the overall shape of the five books of the Psalter. These volumes would make a useful companion to this book. Material taken or adapted from these volumes is used by permission. Other resources are listed in the bibliography.

PSALMS 1 AND 2

# 1. AT THE ENTRANCE GATE

Chapters 1 to 4 feature eight examples from Book I of the Psalms (Psalms 1 – 41). Apart from Psalms 1 and 2, almost all these psalms are headed "of David". Together with Book II (Psalms 42 – 72), this forms the main "of David" collection of psalms. There is a tremendous focus on God's anointed king—at first David, then David's successors, and finally "great David's greater Son": the Lord Jesus Christ. The word "anointed one" is "Messiah" in Hebrew and then "Christ" in Greek. David and his successors were, in a manner of speaking, little "messiahs"; they show us something of the character and destiny of the final Messiah, the Lord Jesus Christ.

Psalms 1 and 2 are like two grand pillars, one on each side of the entrance gate into the books of Psalms. They introduce Book I and also head up the whole Psalter. The early **church father** Jerome (AD 342-420) described Psalm 1 as "the preface to the Psalms, as inspired by the Holy Spirit" and compared it to the great door of the building that is the Psalter (see Waltke and Houston, *The Psalms as Christian Worship*, page 118). But it is really Psalms 1 and 2 together that fulfil this introductory function. Unlike almost every other psalm in Book I, they have no heading; almost all the others have "of David" at the top. These two psalms are bracketed by blessing and conclude with warnings. Psalm 1 begins with a declaration of blessing (**1:1***, "Blessed is..."), and Psalm 2 ends with a blessing (2:12, "Blessed are..."). Each warns, near the end, of a "way" that

---

* All Psalms verse references being looked at in each chapter part are in **bold**.

"leads to destruction" (**1:6**; 2:12). Together they set the scene and put down critical markers for our whole tour.

Psalm 1 is simple, problematical and, on the face of it, patently untrue. It declares a blessing (**1:1-3**), warns of destruction (**v 4-5**) and concludes by restating both of these (the blessing, **v 6a**, and the destruction, **v 6b**), so that we are in no doubt about the double-edged thrust of the psalm.

## The blessed one

To say "Blessed is the one who..." (**v 1**) is confidently to affirm that the one to be described is under the favour of God: ultimately happy, the recipient of life, joy, peace, and delight. It is to declare that this person will be blessed and that blessing needs to be sought, and can be found, in no other place. This is an extraordinarily profound declaration. It calls for a decision of the will and heart. "Yes," I say. "I really believe that this person, and only the person who is described here, will be blessed by God." Even to join in with the first few words of this first psalm is a demanding challenge!

The blessed one is described first in terms of what they do not do. This comes in three stages, building in a crescendo.

First, this is "the one who does not walk in step with the wicked". We meet "the wicked" often in the Psalms and in other books in the **wisdom literature**, especially Proverbs. These are men and women who have sold themselves to do evil; the whole direction of their life is against God. They march with this rebellious step; and we naturally want to walk in step with them, for we hate to be seen to be different. From the school playground to the senior care home, we instinctively want to say the same things as the wicked, to laugh at the same jokes as the wicked, to share the values of the wicked, to take the same life decisions as the wicked. Whatever your age, stage of life, ethnicity or culture, this will be an insidious temptation for you. It will never be easy to march out of step with an insistent world. And yet blessing comes to the one who emphatically does not march to the beat of the world's drum.

Second, this is "the one who does not ... stand in the way that sinners take". The word "stand" suggests something more settled perhaps than "walking". Every life is a "walk" along a "way": a way shaped by choices—large choices (whom to marry, where to live, what jobs to do) and smaller choices. Sinners—those whose hearts are not right with God—walk a particular "way". They might not hurry along this way. They may "stand" as a symbol of allegiance, much as we might ask of someone, "Where do you stand on this issue?" These people have a "stance", a position, a settled determination. Many of us are by nature weak; we echo the proverbial media mogul who is supposed to have said, "These are my principles. But, if you don't like them, I have other ones." We have flexible "principles" that can be adjusted to fit in with the stance of those around us. And yet blessing comes to the one who deliberately and intentionally does not "stand" with them.

Third, here is "the one who does not ... sit in the company of mockers". This is both more settled and more **adversarial**. It is more settled because they have not only "walked" and then "stood" but now they "sit". To "sit" in the ancient world was the posture of legal deliberation; a judge would "sit" in judgment, as they do today. And it was the posture of authoritative teaching; you sat to teach, as Jesus did for the Sermon on the Mount (Matthew 5:1) and in the synagogue (Luke 4:20). So here is a settled position in which these people not only take their own decisions but claim an authority in the position they have taken. That position is emphatically adversarial; for not only do they themselves decide against God's way but they are "mockers" who jeer and sneer at the one who walks God's way. We experience this all the time from the **morally liberal** and **theologically pluralist** elite in our society. They mock us. And, as the eighteenth-century Christian William Paley lamented, "Who can resist a sneer?"

To be "the one who does not" do these things—who does not walk with these people or stand with these people—is very hard; for it results in being the object of the mockery of these people. This person may be blessed, but their blessing comes at a cost.

So, if this is what the blessed one does not do, what positively defines this person? Psalm **1:2** tells us. Their "delight is in the law of the LORD". In the deepest depths of their heart they love the LORD (the God of the covenant), and therefore they love his "law". The word "law" (Hebrew *Torah*) means instruction or teaching. Probably here it refers especially to the whole of the first five books of the Bible (the Pentateuch) and the preaching of the prophets as they proclaimed this covenant instruction. This person delights in this God-given scriptural instruction. And therefore they meditate "on [God's] law day and night". The word "meditates" in the original Hebrew means more than silent thought; it conveys the idea of vocal and declarative speaking of God's teaching, and also the conviction that what is spoken audibly expresses the innermost convictions of the heart. Here is a person who not only "talks the talk", saying what we might expect a **pious** person to say, but does so out of the deepest desire and delight of the heart. That is to say, this person genuinely believes that blessing comes from loving God and walking his way; this person both speaks and believes the declaration "Blessed is..."

In **verse 3**, we are given a beautiful picture of blessedness. In a hot climate, the only vegetation that always bears fruit is a tree with roots deep in life-giving water. Here is someone whose roots go deeply into God, the source of life; and so their "fruit" does not fail. In their life you see the fruit of their roots. They "prosper" in every way. (When we read the whole Bible, we find that "prosperity" is more deeply defined than we might think. Counterintuitively, it includes suffering, but it issues in eventual glory because it shapes a person in godliness.) They evidence love, joy, patience, kindness, unfailing faithfulness, peace and so on. And they do so consistently.

**Verses 1-3** paint a beautiful picture of the blessed one. And yet their prosperity is hard-won, for this person will necessarily be the object of cruel mockery from those who resent their refusal to walk with them in wickedness.

## Blessing comes with warning

**Verses 4-5** warn that there is no other path of blessing. There is a judgment coming. There is an "assembly", which means a church or a congregation, to which "the righteous" (those who conform to the description of **v 1-3**) belong. Those who "stand" today "in the way that sinners take" now "will not stand in the judgment". They may seem substantial, even weighty and significant; but on that day they will be seen to be insubstantial, blown away like "chaff" at harvest time. This is hard to believe, as we look at the confident assurance of those who care nothing for God's law; and yet it is true. As the sixteenth-century **Reformer** John Calvin wrote:

> "The profane despisers of God, although for a time they may reckon themselves happy, shall at length have a most miserable end." (*Commentary on the Book of Psalms*, Volume 1, page 1)

**Verse 6** gives the deep reason why both the blessing and the warning are true. "The LORD", the covenant God, is the reason. He "watches over" (in loving **providential** wisdom and care) "the way of the righteous". Here is a "way" that goes in the opposite direction from "the way that sinners take" (**v 1**); it is a narrow way that leads to life (see Jesus' words in Matthew 7:14), and God watches over those on that way. But there is another way: "the way of the wicked leads to destruction" in the coming judgment.

## How do we read this psalm today?

So here is a psalm that sets before us a simple contrast, spelled out in vivid picture language in terms of its heart motivations, its evidence in life, and its two destinies. But it is also deeply problematical—because, while you and I want to be counted among the blessed, we know that by nature we are those who are wicked through and through. We walk in step with the wicked, conforming to the pattern of this world. We stand in the way of sinners. Indeed, we so want to be affirmed in the way we have chosen that we mock anyone who goes another way; for mockery makes us feel better about our own life choices. We do not really believe that blessing comes in the way described here, and in no other way. And therefore destruction is our destiny. This is not a comfortable psalm.

Further, as we said earlier, on the face of it this psalm is patently untrue. As other psalms acknowledge, the wicked often prosper (see Psalm 73; also Job 21). One of the great tensions that runs through the Psalter is the one between the affirmation of Psalm 1 and the evidence of history which appears flatly to contradict it. How do we make sense of this tension?

The Bible teaches that there is one man, and one man only, who truly fits the description of Psalm 1 and deserves to inherit this blessing. When Jesus of Nazareth sang, "Blessed is the one who…" he believed it with every fibre of his being. He believed it, and he lived it and sought blessing in no other place. Surrounded by pressures to walk in step with the wicked, to stand in the way of sinners, to sit in the seat of mockers, he resolutely set his face against their values, their sneering, their actions. He was mocked most sharply and felt the pain of this mockery with an intensity we can scarcely comprehend. And yet he delighted in his Father's instruction and declared it day and night with unflinching determination and the heart's delight. He is the fruitful one. The **covenant** God, his Father, watched over his way. And therefore Jesus is the man upon whom the blessing of God the Father rests—the one with whom God the Father was and is well pleased (Matthew 3:17; 17:5). Bruce Waltke and James Houston are correct when they say, "Jesus Christ uniquely corresponds to the portrait of the righteous man" (*The Psalms as Christian Worship,* page 143).

To grasp that Jesus is the fulfilment of Psalm 1 preserves us from the tyranny of **moralism**. When moralism is in charge, we end up either complacently self-righteous (if we think we have succeeded) or zealously, and sooner or later hypocritically, intent on outward conformity (for outward conformity is all we can hope to achieve), or despairingly hopeless (as we realise we continually fail). Without Jesus, Psalm 1 stirs us simply to try harder to be good. Only when we see Jesus as the blessed man of Psalm 1 is there hope. For in him, and in him alone, every blessing is to be found.

Our response as we sing Psalm 1 in Christ will therefore be a fragrant gospel blend of at least two tunes. First and foremost, we rejoice that Jesus Christ is the blessed one of Psalm 1, and that all the blessing of God rests upon him, and upon us as we are in him. Sometimes we feel that a Scripture has not been properly **applied** until there is some measurable change in our outward behaviour. And yet it is not wasted time to pause and meditate on the wonder of the wholehearted commitment of Jesus of Nazareth to the belief that blessing is truly found only in a delighted obedience to the law of his Father. His righteousness is **imputed** to us by **grace** through **faith**. By his righteousness we are freed from condemnation.

> When struggling with cold legalism the Spirit will use this psalm to rekindle a delighted love of God's law.

But then, stirred by his Spirit within us, we resolve—under grace and with joy—that we too will evidence more and more the marks of this blessed person. Our resolve to turn from the pressures of a sinful world will be strengthened; our delight in the law of God will be enriched and deepened; our confidence in final blessing and fruitfulness will be emboldened. When deeply troubled by the pressures of a world that insists we conform, the Spirit of Jesus within us will use our praying of this psalm to stiffen our determination to be different. When struggling with a cold **legalism**, the Spirit of Jesus will use this psalm to rekindle a delighted love of God's law in our hearts. When anxious and tempted to "two-time"

God—professing to be Christian while hedging our bets and still worshipping the world's gods—this psalm will deepen our confidence that the way of Jesus, the Psalm 1 way, is indeed the only good and blessed way to live.

## Questions for reflection

1. In what ways are you walking, standing or sitting in the way of sin?
2. How could you use God's word to help you turn away from those ways?
3. How would you sum up from this psalm what it means to be blessed?

## PART TWO

It is often thought that the purpose of Psalm 2 is to celebrate the coronation (or anointing) of a king in David's line. Such a coronation is shadowed by intense conflict, as we shall see. If there is a calm and measured clarity about Psalm 1, Psalm 2 confronts us with an urgent intensity of contrasting truths.

The psalm begins with a shared desire (Psalm **2:1-3**); this desire is answered by a twofold declaration (**v 4-9**), which issues in a momentous choice (**v 10-12**).

### Plotting for "freedom"

The desire is for what the world calls "freedom". **Verses 1-3** tell us who shares this desire (**v 1-2a**), against whom this desire is directed (**v 2b**) and for what this desire longs (**v 3**).

"Why do the nations conspire and the peoples plot in vain?" (**v 1**). The "nations" and "peoples" are general terms for the rest of the world, apart from the people of God. These people—all of us by nature—"conspire"; we do not agree about much, but we agree about this, we all want this! And they (we) "plot"; the word translated as "plot" is the same word translated as "meditate" in Psalm 1:2. It expresses an audible whispering or murmuring. The righteous one of Psalm 1 speaks with audible meditation on the delights of God's law; these people speak in an audible conspiracy against precisely that law. This is all "in vain", and we shall see why later in the psalm. But the words "in vain" make it clear that the question "Why?" expresses not anxiety but astonishment at the folly of what will be described. How stupid can you get?!

Psalm **2:2a** sharpens the general description of "nations" and "peoples", and focuses on those who have the most power: "The kings of the earth rise up and the rulers band together". The words "kings" and "rulers" are broader than just heads of governments; they include all human beings insofar as we have power or can exert influence. Media moguls, movie directors and producers, news-channel anchors and editors, bloggers, celebrities and all those categorised as "influencers" come under this umbrella. Anyone who can make a difference in the world—and that is pretty much everyone who is alive—is included here. All these lead a shared rebellion; they "band together". Left to our own devices, we would be constantly squabbling; but faced with the authority of God, we all agree that we must rebel.

**Verse 2b** brings into the open the object of hostility for humanity's rebellion. We rise up "against the LORD and against his anointed". That is, we rebel against the covenant God in heaven ("the LORD") and his rule on earth expressed by "his anointed": his anointed king, the king in David's line, ruling from **Zion**. We will not have this king to rule over us. We believe in ourselves; we declare our autonomy, our **sovereign** individual right to make our decisions, to govern our own lives.

We define freedom as the absence of restraint; it is freedom *from* God's law. But, as this psalm will persuade us, such so-called freedom sets us on a terrible path to destruction. True freedom is not about being free *from* restraint but being set free *for* living rightly, in glad obedience to God's law. This was the vision set before us in Psalm 1.

True freedom is not about being free *from* restraint but being set free *for* living rightly.

## Meet your king

This universal human desire for freedom, expressed so energetically in **2:1-3**, is answered in **verses 4-9** by a twofold declaration. The first part (**v 4-6**) is spoken by the LORD, God in heaven, who "laughs" and "scoffs" at these rebels. There is in heaven a sound of derisive laughter. These people (who include us) may join the chorus of mockers

(1:1); but this mockery is answered by a much more terrible mockery in heaven's courts. It is a mockery that issues in a terrifying rebuke; in hot anger God says, "I have installed my king on Zion, my holy mountain" (**2:6**).

We are not simply expected to understand what this rebuke means; we are meant to feel a sense of visceral terror when we hear it. The God who made the world and in whose hands is our very breath (Acts 17:24-25) is furiously angry at our rebellion. *No!* he says. *I have made a decision*; *I have "installed"* (with no appeal, no second thoughts, no chance of reversal) *my king: the "anointed" one against whom you rebel. And I have done so "on Zion, my holy mountain."* Zion is the city of David (see 2 Samuel 5:7). Many Old Testament Scriptures associate Zion and the promises of the covenant with King David (Psalm 132 is a good example of this). Here is a king who will be quite unlike the rebellious kings of Psalm **2:1-3**, for this king will be the one who exercises the sovereign rule of God on earth, who brings in the **kingdom of God**. This king is also the blessed one of Psalm 1! The testimony to this king (as Calvin put it)...

> "... resounds through the whole world [for] the apostles first, and after them pastors and teachers, bore testimony that Christ was made King by God the Father."
>
> (*Commentary on the Book of Psalms*, Volume 1, page 16-17)

The anointed king himself gives the second part of the declaration in **2:7-9**. He tells us what God in heaven has said to him: "You are my son; today [on the day of the king's coronation/anointing] I have become your father" (**v 7**).

The king in David's line inherited the promise of 2 Samuel 7: that there would be an intimate Father–Son relationship between the king and the covenant God in heaven. The king would be the man made in the image of God in heaven who would execute God's rule on earth, much as Adam had been called to do in Genesis 1. The king would share the character of God in heaven, with the son's likeness to the father.

The most important blessing the covenant God gives to his anointed son, the king, is the privilege of prayer: "Ask me" (Psalm **2:8**). This anointed king is the one who can pray, and know that God in heaven will hear and answer him when he prays for what he is about to be invited to pray for. This is an astonishing prayer! And here is how God will answer him, in **verse 9**:

> "I will make the nations [the rebellious nations of **verses 1-3**] your inheritance, the ends of the earth your possession. You will break them [that is, break their proud rebellion] with a rod of iron [or "an iron sceptre"]; you will dash them to pieces like pottery."

The anointed king is invited to pray to conquer the world, to subdue all the rebellions of **verses 1-3**, to inherit all things, to govern creation on behalf of God his Father. When he asks this in prayer, his prayer will be fully granted.

## A momentous choice

There is, therefore, a momentous choice. In **verses 10-12**, the voice of authority in the psalm turns to speak to the "kings" and "rulers" of **verses 1-3**: that is, to all of us insofar as we have any power of agency or influence. They, and we, are urgently warned:

> "Serve the LORD [against whom you rebel, **v 2**] with fear [reverent fear] and celebrate his rule with trembling [a glad but awestruck surrender]. Kiss his son [the anointed king, with the kiss of homage]."

Because the terrible alternative is "destruction".

Here is a sobering and urgent warning. Turn right around, repent, from the proud autonomy of **verses 1-3**. From setting yourself "against" the covenant God and his anointed king, turn around and bow gladly to the rule of God in heaven, expressed in his rule on earth through his anointed king. If you do not do that, if you persist in the "way" these verses set out, you will be destroyed, just as the wicked at the end of Psalm 1 are on a "way" that "leads to destruction".

But the psalm ends with an invitation, a declaration of blessing: "Blessed are all who take refuge in him" (**2:12**—that is, in God's anointed king, the son.

The decision to sing or pray Psalm 2 begins with a deliberate distancing of ourselves from the rebellion of **verses 1-3**. For we sing of it from a distance; we watch, we listen, we consider, but we ourselves no longer want to be identified with those who speak rebellion in these verses.

We then listen, humbled and sober, to the sure and certain twofold declaration from God in heaven (**v 4-6**) and from the anointed king on earth (**v 7-9**). And when we hear the warning and the blessing pronounced in **verses 10-12**, we are moved to be warned by the warning and wooed by the blessing. By the time we end the singing of the psalm, we are kneeling at the feet of God's anointed king, to take refuge in him from the wrath to come. The effect upon us, by the Spirit of Christ, of singing Psalm 2 is to subdue our proud desires for autonomy, to persuade us more deeply that Jesus really is Lord and nothing can change that, and to move us to bow the knee to him now, in this age, before it is too late.

## The Psalm 1 man is the Psalm 2 king

As we begin the Psalms, we are looking for a Psalm 1 man who will be the Psalm 2 king—the king who is righteous, and the righteous man who is king. For Psalms 1 and 2 have set before us a good rule and a good ruler. The good rule is the law of God and the blessing that comes to the one who loves both God and his law (Psalm 1). But if the good rule of God's law is to be effective in the world, it needs a good ruler: the Psalm 2 king who is the Psalm 1 law-lover of God. This combination of a good king and a good law is central to the praying of the Psalms. We find the same combination in Deuteronomy 17:18-20, where the king is instructed to devote himself to the loving study of and obedience to God's law. This is the king we need. The reason there is blessing in taking refuge with the king of Psalm 2 (Psalm **2:12**) is that the king's rule is precisely the good law of Psalm 1. The two blessings (here and in 1:1) are inseparable. Only the righteous man of Psalm 1 can be the world ruler of Psalm 2.

The promise of Psalm 2 was foreshadowed in David and his line; it echoed down Old Testament history and must often have appeared absurd, as David's heirs fell short of the righteousness of Psalm 1 and the reign of Psalm 2. And then the man came who lived the righteousness of Psalm 1 and inherited the promises of Psalm 2. The rest of the world united to plot against Jesus the Messiah (Acts 4:25-26; Revelation 11:18). But God declared him to be his Son, both at his baptism (Matthew 3:17; Mark 1:11; Luke 3:22) and at his transfiguration (Matthew 17:5; Mark 9:7; Luke 9:35), and this declaration is echoed in Acts 13:33, and Hebrews 1:5 and 5:5. This man will inherit the nations (Psalm **2:8** is echoed in Hebrews 1:2— see "heir of all things") and rule them with an iron sceptre (Psalm **2:9** is echoed in Revelation 12:5 and 19:15).

When we sing Psalm 2, we commit ourselves to at least three decisions of the will. First and foremost, we affirm that we too believe in the universal kingship of Jesus the Messiah. One day the kingdoms of the world will become the kingdom of our Lord and of his Messiah (Revelation 11:15). We believe this and say it clearly and publicly.

Second, we affirm that, if we continue to trust in him to the end and are thereby "victorious", we too will share with him in ruling the nations. The ascended Lord Jesus says to "the one who is victorious" (that is, the man or woman who goes on in believing obedience "to the end") that he will give to them "authority over the nations", whom they will rule "with an iron sceptre" (Revelation 2:26-27). He applies the language of Psalm **2:8-9** to every believer, who will reign with him in the new heavens and new earth.

Finally, we declare that we too heed the warning that rebellion is futile and leads to inescapable destruction. We flee from the pointless pride that kicks against God and his Christ, understanding the pointlessness and inevitable failure of all proud human autonomy.

We have now stood in the entrance hall of the Psalter. We have wondered at the blessed person of Psalm 1 and the victorious king of Psalm 2. We have considered that one man, and one man alone, fits perfectly both these psalms. For Jesus Christ, the righteous One, the King in David's line, is precisely the righteous King these psalms so beautifully and powerfully portray. Blessing is poured upon him by the Father. Blessing is to be found in him, and in him alone.

## Questions for reflection

1. How do you respond to the way Jesus is described in this psalm?
2. How does Psalm 2 encourage you to pray for those you know who are actively rebelling against God?
3. What does the psalm encourage you to pray for yourself and for the world?

PSALMS 11 AND 20

# 2. THE KING'S VICTORY

As we enter the front gate to the Psalter, the twin pillars of Psalms 1 and 2 proclaim to us that the best and happiest way to live is to keep God's law with delight and zeal (Psalm 1) and that God's good king is going to rule the world (Psalm 2). But from Psalm 3 onwards, we are plunged into a world in which neither of these supposedly reassuring declarations seems to be true at all. On the contrary, the wicked do very well for themselves, and people who have no time for God's law enjoy a great deal of power and influence. This was the world in which David lived after he was anointed king by the prophet Samuel (1 Samuel 16 onwards); it was the world in which King Jesus lived; it is our world today.

I have chosen for our next pair two psalms of David which speak of the king's victory, despite opposition.

In Psalm 11, King David answers a powerful, persuasive and enduring temptation: to run away. The psalm is headed "For the director of music" (implying that it was used in the sung worship of the people of God) and "Of David" (which normally means, as here, written by David).

## A bird in the storm

King David's headline (**v 1a**) is to say, "In the LORD I take refuge". **Verses 1b-3** tell us why this matters. He goes on: "How then can you say to me…?" (**v 2**). Some people ("you" is plural) were saying something to David to which the answer was that the covenant

God is his refuge. What were they saying? "Flee like a bird to your mountain" (**v 1**). Run away! You watch a coastal bird in a storm as it flies up to some clifftop cleft in the rocks and hides there, completely safe. *Do that, King David,* they urge him. *Give up trying to be the king that God has commissioned you to be.*

Why is this a persuasive temptation? **Verses 2** and **3** tell us. In the NIV these are printed as if they are still the words of David's tempters. This is quite possible; there are no speech marks in Hebrew. Or they may be the words of David, filling in for himself the reasons why he might agree that he should run away. Whoever said them, they are true and powerful words. Here is the reason for God's king to abandon his post. *Look!* says the voice: *all around you there are archers ready to shoot deadly arrows.*

In **verse 2** we hear of a people, a preparation, an action and a target. The people are "the wicked", whom we meet often, especially in Book I of the Psalms; about half the references to "the wicked" in the Psalter come here. "The wicked" appeared first in Psalm 1 and then again, as the rebellious people who will not have God's king rule over them, in Psalm 2. In Psalm 11 they appear in **verses 2**, **5**, and **6**, having already been prominent in Psalms 9 and 10, appearing as "the wicked" or "the nations" and inflicting great suffering on the righteous. They also feature darkly in Psalms 12 and 14. The designation "the wicked" doesn't just mean people who get things wrong; it means men and women who set themselves and their whole direction of life against God.

Their preparation is described in the vivid language of archers getting ready to fire deadly arrows; there they are, arrows set against the strings, bows bent, ready to fire.

Their action is "to shoot" (well, of course, that's what archers do!) but it's worse than that, for they shoot "from the shadows". This is not open warfare; this is an ambush. There is something sobering about having archers aiming their arrows at you, but there is something utterly terrifying about these archers being hidden; you never know from what direction the deadly arrow will come.

And their target is "the upright in heart": those whose intentional life direction and determination is to act rightly before God and people. For although this is an individual prayer (**11:1**, "say to me"), it is prayed in the context of a struggle between two groups. The first of these groups is "the wicked"; the second is "the righteous" or "the upright", which means the righteous king of Psalms 1 and 2 and all who stand with him; these appear in **11:2**, **3**, **5**, and **7**.

**Verse 3** spells out what happens: "the foundations are being destroyed". When Bible poetry speaks of "the foundations", it means the moral foundations of society: what theologians sometimes call "creation order"—the pillars upon which the moral order of the world rests, the bulwarks protecting humankind from chaos, evil, disorder and death. These foundations are summed up in the Ten Commandments. The **seventh commandment**, for example, shows that one of society's moral foundations lies in keeping sexual intimacy exclusively within marriage, the strong covenant bond between one man and one woman. In our society this is perhaps the most prominent of the Ten Commandments to be dismissed and mocked. But all the others are rejected too. For example, no lottery would exist were it not for the encouragement of human covetousness. And all around David these good commandments—the law celebrated in Psalm 1—are being trashed. In his attempt to be God's king, David feels like a man trying to shore up a collapsing building in the midst of an earthquake. As the German **Lutheran** commentator Hans-Joachim Kraus writes, this is a time when "all law and order is overturned and chaos in the form of raw violence breaks out" (*Psalms,* Volume 1, page 202).

No lottery would exist were it not for the encouragement of human covetousness.

It seems a hopeless task: "What can the righteous do?" (**v 3**). David and those on the side of the king have something much worse than an uphill struggle; they have an utterly impossible task. All around David the king, and all around those who stand with him, the moral order of the world is collapsing in chaos and ruins. There is, it seems, nothing that he or they can do.

Before we sing the rest of the psalm, we must feel the force of this. David felt it acutely. King Jesus felt it with desperate intensity and strength, surrounded as he was by wickedness of every kind: evil that was **endemic** in his society, his people, his world (see Matthew 17:17). What could the king possibly do? Nothing! *Just run away, abdicate, abandon your post!* That is the temptation; it is a powerful and persuasive one, and we too feel its force. Few things demoralise us more than a sense that we are engaged in a hopeless task. We look at the statistics of church attendance: the consistent picture of a demographic in which the tide of faith is ebbing away, as believers get older and fewer young people trust Christ as Lord. If we face this honestly, it is deeply discouraging. What is the point of getting out of bed in the morning if I am doomed to failure? What can you and I possibly do in the work of God's King Jesus that can succeed against this overwhelming stream of so-called "progress" that undermines the foundations of God's law? There is a sad desperation that lies behind Psalm **11:2-3**. Only faith in the promises of God can counter this. And it does!

How wonderful that King David could assert that "In the LORD I take refuge" (**v 1**). How much more deeply wonderful that King Jesus could sing and mean these words: *In the Lord, my Father God, I take refuge. I will not run away but will persevere in the task I have been sent to accomplish*. And accomplish it he did. We too, as the King's people, need to hear the rest of the psalm, for it gives the reason why we can take refuge in our Father God and persevere with the work of our King and his gospel.

## God is on his throne

**Verses 4-7** tell us why the king, and the king's people, can safely make God their "refuge". This is given in terms of a governing presence, a universal watching, an intense hating and a passionate loving, and then finally a wonderful promise.

**Verse 4a** assures the king of the unchanging presence of God, who is "in his holy temple" and "on his heavenly throne". When the psalm was written, this did not simply mean that God was everywhere (although he is **omnipresent**). It meant he was present in relationship with his people, in a way that was somehow focused on his temple in Jerusalem, which was spoken of as his heavenly throne, the place from which he ruled the world by the government of his king in David's line, keeping the law expressed in the Ten Commandments on the tablets of stone in the **ark of the covenant** in the **Most Holy Place** in the temple. David could trust that God's governing presence on earth could not finally be destroyed by the wicked. Jesus, who was himself the fulfilment of all that the temple foreshadowed (Matthew 12:6; John 2:19-22) could trust the same, for the Father was unchangingly present with him. We too can trust in the unchanging presence of the Father with us through Jesus our King and now indwelling our hearts by his Spirit.

**Psalm 11:4b** teaches us that the God who rules also watches. The wicked think they can skulk in "the shadows": that no one sees them plot, hears them conspire or watches them shoot. They are wrong. For the God in heaven who governs the world sees every deed and hears every word.

**Verses 5** and **6** assure the tempted king that God hates the wicked intensely:

> "The LORD examines the righteous [watching over them with loving discipline] but the wicked, those who love violence, he hates with a passion."

We shy away from such strong language. But God in heaven does not just "love the sinner, but hate the sin"; no, he hates the wicked. They are described as "those who love violence", who are actively plotting against God's king and his people (**v 2**). God is passionately against them (or us)! And his passionate hatred will issue in terrible judgment. In frightening language that echoes the destruction of Sodom and Gomorrah in Genesis 19 ("fiery coals and burning sulphur"), the troubled king is assured that those who destroy the moral foundations of society will themselves be suddenly and finally destroyed.

The king may be sure of this because of the first two lines of Psalm **11:7**:

> "For the LORD is righteous [so "the righteous" are on his side!],
> he loves justice".

Set against the necessary hatred of God towards the violent wicked is the love of God for justice. God is determined that his world shall be a place of moral order, justice, goodness and fairness. And he will ensure that happens. To join with the church of Christ in speaking **verses 4-7** ought to deepen our confidence that, against all appearances, the church of Christ and the law of God are not doomed to failure, but rather they are bound to triumph in the end, as we know with even greater assurance since the bodily resurrection of the Lord Jesus and his ascension to the place of cosmic authority at the right hand of the Father.

Finally there is a promise: "the upright will see his face."

To "see" God's "face" means to stand before him as honoured servants, rather as we speak of someone having direct access (or direct report) to a president. This is the promise: that in the finally restored good government of the universe, all who stand with the king will stand before God the Father as honoured servants.

## He watches over us

David trusted this promise, took reassurance from the truths of this psalm, made his LORD his refuge, and did not give up on his task. Supremely, the Lord Jesus, our King, when he sang this psalm, pledged to entrust himself to the Father who judges justly (1 Peter 2:23) and not to abandon his task as King. He determined to walk the whole suffering path to accomplish it, until he could cry, "It is finished!" (John 19:30)—and then enter into his kingdom with joy.

The truly wonderful thing is this: we who appropriate this promise are by nature wicked and violent. Like **Saul of Tarsus**, we are by nature hostile to God. Only because our King took upon himself our punishment (Psalm **11:6**) can we hope to stand before God on the last day. Because our King stands before the Father, so shall we!

If we are Christians, we are "righteous" by faith and determined to live lives of "uprightness" by the Spirit of Christ our king. We too may take comfort from this psalm. As we sing it, we too take refuge in the God and Father of Jesus. We too feel a rising sense of desperation as the moral foundations around us are destroyed. But we too may be assured, as Jesus was, that God our Father is present with us in Jesus our "temple", by his Spirit; that God our Father watches and sees everyone; that God our Father hates violence and wickedness; and that God our Father promises that we will one day see his face.

## Questions for reflection

1. In what ways does our world seem like the situation described in Psalm 11:1-3?
2. How are you tempted to respond to such a world?
3. Which of the remaining verses is the best encouragement to you to persevere in following Jesus?

# PART TWO

A psalm that says, "May [God] give you the desire of your heart and make all your plans succeed" (Psalm **20:4**) looks set to be a popular one! I once saw this verse printed and fixed to a church wall, alongside other great promises in the Bible. It is easy to see its appeal. It would seem to suggest that the purveyors of the so-called "**prosperity gospel**" are right: that the Bible does promise that God will give us what we want. We have only to "name it" in prayer and we can "claim it". But we must be careful: can I really just substitute my name in place of "you" and "your"? Or is there something more going on? There is, and we can't! To do so would be totally to misread the psalm.

## Praying for the king's victory

Like Psalm 11, Psalm 20 is headed, "For the director of music. A psalm of David". But there is something different about it. Psalm 11, like many psalms, especially in Book I, is a prayer of David the king. Most such psalms are individual (e.g. Psalm 3); some are a mixture of individual and corporate in which King David leads his people in prayer (e.g. Psalm 4). But Psalm 20 is rather different; it is a prayer not *by* the king but *for* the king. Augustine of Hippo, the fourth-century North African bishop, rightly says that here...

> "it is not Christ who speaks; but the prophet speaks to Christ, under the form of wishing, foretelling things to come."
>
> (*Commentary on Psalm XX*, page 56)

This becomes clear in **Psalm 20:9a**: "LORD, give victory to the king!" The "you" and "your" in the psalm refer, then, not to you or me but to the king of God's people. The Hebrew **preposition** translated as "of" in "of David" has a range of possible meanings. Usually in the Psalms it means "by" and implies authorship. But it can mean "to" or "for", and one of these would seem to be the more natural meaning here. This is a psalm for David, in which the people pray for their king.

(It is, of course, possible that it is also by David, and that David wrote it to teach the people how to pray for their king.)

The psalm is opened up if we look for the word "answer". In **verse 1** the people pray that the LORD will "answer" the king. All of **verses 1-5** are a prayer that the king's prayers will be answered. Then in **verse 6** an individual—presumably a song-leader—affirms that God "answers" the king. **Verses 6-8** expand on this assurance. Then the psalm concludes in **verse 9**: the first part sums up the prayer of the psalm ("LORD, give victory to the king!"); and then in the second part the people pray, "Answer *us* when we call" (my italics). There is a connection here, and it is critical to understanding the psalm. Only when our king is the man whose prayers are answered may we, the king's people, hope that our prayers will be answered—and, even then, only when the heartbeat of our prayers is the longing that the king's prayers will be answered. This, in the end, is what it means to pray in Jesus' name: in the name of—and for the victory of—the king.

So it is best to take the psalm in those three unequal parts. First, in **verses 1-5**, the people of the king pray for the victory of the king.

> "May the LORD answer you when you are in [literally "in the day of"] distress; may the name of the God of **Jacob** protect you."
>
> (**v 1**)

The covenant God is the One who protected Jacob when he was in distress (see Genesis 32 and 35; notice Genesis 35:3—"God, who answered me in the day of my distress"). The God of Jacob is the covenant God (the LORD) who will answer his king when he too is in deep distress (such as we heard about in Psalm 11, and which runs as a strong theme through Book I of the Psalms). The people ask the LORD to help the king "from the sanctuary … from Zion" (Psalm **20:2**). The "sanctuary" (at the heart of the temple) in "Zion" is the holy mountain where God promised the kings in David's line that one day one of them would rule the world (2:6). So this prayer for the king is asking God to do what, in Psalm 2, he has promised to do.

The people pray that God will accept the king's "sacrifices ... burnt offerings". As the king, who was the representative head of his people, David was responsible for the offering of sacrifices for his and his people's sins (although the priests actually made the offerings). Here the people pray that these sacrifices will be acceptable to God, so that the king's prayers for his people may be heard.

So in **20:4**, the prayer is that God will give the king the desires of *his* heart and make all *his* plans succeed. Prayer is the overflow of the desires and plans of the heart. The king's heart and affections are to be so aligned with the purposes of God that they will all be granted, because they are precisely in tune with the will of God.

We can pray this too, because we know the only king who has ever fulfilled this description: Jesus. Our king is not a cardboard cutout; he has desires in his heart; he makes plans and wants them to succeed. When we pray this psalm, we ask God in heaven to give our king what he deeply desires.

What a king he is! When this king comes, the prayer of **verse 5** will be the climax:

> "May we shout for joy over your victory and lift up our banners in the name of our God. May the LORD grant all your requests."

We rejoice not when our individual desires are satisfied but when our king is victorious.

We, the king's loyal people, rejoice not when our individual desires are satisfied but when our king is victorious! This is what causes us to "lift up our banners" (or, we might say, wave our flags). So this is a very different psalm from the individualistic, "me first" appropriation of the promises on that church wall. My default—and it will probably be yours too—is to rejoice, to wave my cheerful flag, when I do well, when I am victorious—when I do well in an exam or am praised by other people or get a good job or make a happy marriage, and so on. This psalm reshapes my desires so that I begin genuinely to care more about the victories of King Jesus than about my own success or failure. That is a wonderful but radical change!

## Assurance of the king's victory

What is more, such desires are assured of satisfaction. I can want success for myself as much as I like, but I cannot be sure of getting it. But when I want Jesus to succeed, my longings will be granted. From **verses 6-8**, a leader of the people leads them in confident assurance that what they have asked in **verses 1-5** will indeed be granted. The prayers of their king will be answered. The speaker is sure, and assures us, that "the LORD gives victory to his **anointed**" (**v 6**). The people prayed in **verse 5** that they would shout for joy over the victory of their king, and that prayer will be answered. We too will shout with jubilation when he finally wins every battle. God will answer the king's prayers and give the king victory. The "right hand" of God (**v 6**) is a way of speaking that we can understand (an **anthropomorphism**) to convey the strong power of God. (If you are left-handed, you just have to run with this Bible idiom!)

That strong power is expanded in **verse 7**. In the ancient world (and in fact until the invention of gunpowder and motorised transport) any army that had horses and chariots was like a nuclear superpower. The horse and chariot were the unbeatable weapons of the ancient world. It was blindingly obvious that if you had those, you could put your trust in them; they would be your security, your guarantee of victory. But there is a higher power. The God who declared in Psalm 2 that his anointed king would rule the world is the supreme power in heaven and earth. Those who trust in him and align themselves with his Messiah will share the victory of the king. Jesus is Lord, and one day every knee will bow before him (Philippians 2:9-11).

## Our answered prayer

And so in **Psalm 20:9** the psalm is summed up: "LORD, give victory to the king! Answer us when we call!" All through the history of the Old Testament monarchy, from King David onwards, the people of God—if they were true believers—prayed this prayer for their king. The human successors of David all disappointed, as David himself had done. Some disappointed horribly (such as Manasseh, 2 Kings 21); others did better (such as Hezekiah, 2 Kings 18 – 20, or Josiah, 2 Kings 22 – 23); but all disappointed in the end. And yet the longing continued: that one day a king would rule in David's line whose prayers would all be answered.

A millennium or so later a great descendant of David stood at the grave of a four-day-dead corpse. He had prayed to God his Father to raise this man from the dead. And then he said, "Father, I thank you that you have heard me. I knew that *you always hear me*" (John 11:41-42, my italics). Here at last was the King whose requests are all always granted; and death itself bowed before him!

## How do we pray this today?

What will it mean for us, as men and women of King Jesus, to pray Psalm 20 today? First, it will cause us deeply to rejoice that the prayers of the man Christ Jesus were always answered: that in his deepest distress, even when the foundations of his world were being dismantled by an earthquake of evil (see Psalm 11), the Father always heard his prayers. We shout for joy at his victory (Psalm **20:5**) over death and over the one who has the power of death (Hebrews 2:14-15), when he defeated him at the cross (Colossians 2:15).

But the final victory is not here yet. And so, second, we also pray this psalm today as we cry to God our Father for the final victory of the Lord Jesus when he returns in glory and every knee bows before him.

Thematically, Psalm 21 follows closely on Psalm 20. It builds on Psalm 20 as it celebrates the king rejoicing in the LORD's strength and in the victories he gives (21:1), and in the fact that God in heaven has given this king "his heart's desire" (21:2).

The biggest **existential** challenge for us is to learn from these psalms to root our deepest desires in the victory of our King and to find our deepest joys when our King wins. By nature our strongest longings are for our own success, safety, or comfort, and so our joy is most felt when things have gone well for us (and it's extinguished when those things are threatened or lost). But what truly matters most is the people of King Jesus: the worldwide inter-generational church of Jesus, his body, in whose persecutions he is persecuted (Acts 9:4) and in whose exaltation he is exalted. When going for a job interview, I am to pray, "Father, give Jesus what he wants today". When taking an exam, I should ask, "Father, give Jesus the result he wants for me today". When belonging to a local church, I ought to pray, "Father, may the yearnings of King Jesus' heart be fulfilled in what happens in this church, even if it includes me being humbled and having a tough time". Those will be radical prayers to pray.

These psalms begin—just begin—to reshape our affections and desires, so that we long most deeply for the victory of Jesus, seen in the **vindication** of his people and ultimately in his return in glory, and so that we experience in our suffering a foretaste of the joy of our king's final victory.

## Questions for reflection

1. Why is it tempting to read this psalm as if it were addressed primarily to us?
2. How might realizing that it is addressed to God's King reshape your desires?
3. In what areas of your life do you need to put Jesus' success and victory above your own?

PSALMS 22 AND 23

# 3. THE KING'S TRUST

In chapters 3 and 4 we come to two pairs of very different psalms in which the king expresses his trust in the covenant God. In this chapter, we consider two of the most famous psalms in the Psalter. Psalm 22 is famous because it begins with the words Jesus cried on the cross: "My God, my God, why have you forsaken me?" (**22:1**). Psalm 23 is probably the most famous psalm in the Psalter, and perhaps the most famous poem in all human literature. What unites this otherwise very different pair is the theme of trust: the king trusts God.

Psalm 22 is an extreme psalm. It begins with almost unimaginable depths of suffering and concludes with an astonishing hymn of worldwide praise. One writer says that it...

> "... traverses unimaginable dimensions. From the depths of abandonment by God, the song of the rescued person rises to a worldwide hymn that draws also the dead into a great homage of God in heaven." (Kraus, *Psalms,* Volume 1, page 300)

It may surprise us that God's anointed king expresses such abandonment. After all, is kingship not a position of comfort, wealth, privilege, fame and power? Yet the first part of the psalm is frightening in the intensity of its suffering. The truth is that to be God's anointed king is to inherit a calling to suffer more deeply than we can imagine.

David experienced a foretaste of the sufferings of *the* Christ. This psalm is quoted or echoed repeatedly in the New Testament (see Matthew 27:39, 43, 56; Mark 15:29, 34; John 19:24; Romans 5:5; 2 Timothy 4:17, 18; Hebrews 2:12). By the Spirit, David voiced words that would find their fulfilment centuries later. This means that as we read the psalm, we should be thinking not only of David's suffering but of Jesus' too.

> "The fact that [Psalm 22] is quoted thirteen times in the New Testament, and nine times alone in the account of Jesus' suffering and death, points to a fuller meaning realised only in our Lord's messianic affliction."
>
> (Allan Harman, *Psalms,* Volume 1, page 215)

We do not know just what suffering in David's life drew out of him this astonishing psalm. It comes as a terrible shock after the joyful victory celebrated in Psalms 20 and 21. There is victory at the end of this psalm too (Psalm **22:22-31**); but we reach it only through the sufferings of **verses 1-21**. There was joy set before God's king; but he attained it only by enduring the cross (Hebrews 12:2).

## The suffering of the king

The psalm is headed, "For the director of music. To the tune of 'The Doe of the Morning'. A psalm of David". As with so many psalms, the designation "For the director of music" (and the naming of a tune) suggests that it was used corporately by the people of God down the centuries. By the end of it, we shall see why.

In Psalm **22:1-21**, the king prays in the context of intense suffering. Three themes are interwoven: the king describes his sufferings; the king cries out in prayer in his sufferings; and the king speaks, to the God with whom he is in covenant, about God's trustworthiness.

The king begins with a sustained cry of desperate suffering (**v 1-2**):

> "My God, my God, why have you forsaken me? [See Matthew 27:46; Mark 15:34.] Why are you so far from saving me, so far from my cries of anguish? My God, I cry out by day, but you do not answer, by night, but I find no rest."

He experiences agonising distance from the Father ("so far ... so far") and terrifying silence ("you do not answer"). The covenant God ("My God" is repeated twice in these opening verses), who never, ever "forsakes" his people (for that is the definition of covenant faithfulness) has "forsaken" him. He cannot rest, although God seems to have no difficulty resting in silent distance. We need to feel the viscerally terrifying predicament of the king, so that when we hear the Lord Jesus cry, "My God, my God, why have you forsaken me?" from the cross, we have some sense of what he was enduring for his people—for us.

After this agonised cry, the king sings of God's trustworthiness (Psalm **22:3-5**). Notice the threefold "trust ... trusted ... trusted". *We praise you,* says the king, *precisely because those who put their trust in you are always rescued. You are utterly trustworthy. No one who trusts you is put to shame in public disappointment.*

The king goes on to vividly describe his public shame (in direct contradiction of **verse 5b**, "not put to shame"). He is not like a dignified "man" but like a despised "worm". He is "scorned [and] despised". People "mock" him and "hurl insults" at him, as they would ten centuries later at the Lord Jesus (Matthew 27:39; Mark 15:29; Luke 23:35-36). They mock him because "he trusts in the LORD" (see Matthew 27:43). Notice the repetition of words indicating public disgrace in Psalm **22:6-7**: "scorned ... despised ... mock ... insults, shaking their heads". *Why am I the contradiction of everything we held to be true about your trustworthiness?* asks the king of his God. Something very deep and strange is going on here, that would later be fulfilled by the mockery directed at the Lord Jesus on the cross.

In **verses 9** and **10**, the king returns to the trustworthiness of God, saying, "You made me trust in you" (**v 9b**); all through his life God has been "my God" (**v 10**). Again, that word "trust"—further expressed as he continues, "I was cast on you ... my God"—indicates a sure faith in the covenant God who has made promises to the king. **Verse 11** brings us back to the distance of God ("far from me") and moves us on to what is "near"; God is "far" but trouble is "near".

In **verses 12-18**, we hear a spine-chilling evocation of the sufferings of the king. Notice how this expands on the second and third lines of **verse 11**. He is surrounded by wild, predatory beasts. He is desperately thirsty (fulfilled in John 19:28). His hands and feet are pierced. His clothing is divided among his executioners (fulfilled in Matthew 27:35; Mark 15:24; Luke 23:34; John 19:24). We need to read these horrifying words slowly to feel the awfulness of what the king suffers—first, King David (in anticipation) and finally, King Jesus in the horror of fulfilment.

Notice the repetition of the word "far" and the theme of "dogs" (Psalm **22:16**) and wild predatory "lions" (**v 13**). This king is being torn apart and there is no one to help. Whatever King David may have experienced, the psalm's words reached their fulfilment at the cross of Christ. No historian's physical description of Roman crucifixion comes close to the power of this poetry in helping us to feel the terror, the agony, and the shame of what our king suffered for his people.

The first part of the psalm concludes with a fresh and urgent appeal for rescue (**v 19-21**). Before we move on to the second part of the psalm, it is good to ask how we are meant to respond to **verses 1-21**. Certainly we feel an echo of the misery of the Lord Jesus as he offered himself to take away the sins of the world; that will move us to a fresh depth of gratitude for what he has endured in our place, as our substitute, for us: a sacrifice we cannot make for ourselves.

But we are also being prompted to remember that it is by sharing in his sufferings—in some manner corporately as his church—that we too are qualified to share in his glory (Romans 8:17). None of us can suffer to pay the penalty for sins; Christ has done that for us. But all of us, if we are followers of Jesus, are called to share in his sufferings. That means there may be some echo of the pain described here that comes to us, and we should not be surprised when it does.

## The vindication of the king

In the second part of the psalm (Psalm **22:22-31**) there is a tremendous change in the emotional music. The king's prayer to be rescued (**v 21**) has been wonderfully answered. We do not know what answer David experienced; we do know that ultimately the answer the Lord

Jesus experienced was bodily resurrection, public vindication, ascension, exaltation and being seated at the right hand of the Father.

In **verse 22** the vindicated king calls out:

"I will declare your name to my people; in the assembly I will praise you."

Hebrews 2:12 says that ultimately these words of King David are spoken by Jesus himself as he declares the righteous name of the Father to his church (his "assembly"). The Father, whom he trusted (1 Peter 2:23), proved himself utterly trustworthy in the end. The assembly of the people of God is another way of speaking of God's church, since the word "assembly" can equally be translated "congregation" or "church". We are to picture this great congregation gathered together as the now-vindicated king stands to declare the "name" of the Saviour God to them; that is, ultimately, to us. This "name" is the public revelation that this God truly saves; he has saved the king, and therefore we may be confident he will save the king's people.

God has saved the king, and therefore we may be confident that he will save the king's people.

Psalm **22:23-24** fills in the content of what the vindicated king declares. He exhorts all his people ("You who fear the LORD," **v 23**) to praise, honour and revere this covenant God because he has not "scorned the suffering of the afflicted one" (singular—the king God has anointed, **v 24**). He has proved himself worthy of the king's trust. The king was afflicted; he suffered terribly. In his suffering, he cried out to God; God did not mock his cries, but heard them and vindicated him. Ultimately this vindication comes by resurrection.

**Verses 25-26** move from the singular—"the afflicted one" of **verse 24**—to the plural: "the poor ... those who seek the LORD" (**v 26**). This is where we come in. Because—precisely because—God has proved himself faithful to King Jesus in his affliction, we may be absolutely confident that he will be faithful to us in ours. We too will "eat and be satisfied". We picture the whole assembly—the world-wide church of Christ through all generations—joining the king in this heartfelt praise. What a chorus of adoration that will be!

**Verses 27-31** echo both the covenant with **Abraham** (beginning in Genesis 12:1-3) and the promise of Psalm 2: that the king will rule over the nations. This gospel of rescue for the afflicted will spread to "all the ends of the earth ... all the families of the nations" (Psalm **22:27**). From those at the top ("the rich of the earth", **v 29**) to those at the bottom of the heap ("those who cannot keep themselves alive"), there will be "worship" (**v 29**) and a proclamation of God's "righteousness" (**v 31**).

It is a jubilant conclusion to a psalm that began with infinite suffering. Here, in this vision of universal praise and worldwide worship, is the joy set before the Lord Jesus when he endured the cross.

## A song for when life is hard

This psalm takes us on an emotional journey. This is why the people of God have sung it again and again down the ages. We need to taste the bitterness of the cross (**v 1-21**) before we can truly appreciate the wonder of the worldwide experience of rescue and worship that the cross brings about (**v 22-31**). The Lord Jesus must have sung this psalm many times in its entirety before he cried the first line in agony from the cross. When he cried out, "My God, my God, why have you forsaken me?" (Matthew 27:46; Mark 15:34), it was not because he did not know the answer. He knew—it was the entire purpose of his being made flesh—that he must endure the hell of God-forsakenness to pay the penalty for sinners. And yet, in the agony of separation from the Father whom he had known with loving delight for all eternity, only this psalm could begin fully to express the depth of his suffering. And yet, even as he endured the **covenant curse** of being forsaken, somehow perhaps the remainder of the psalm spoke to his suffering heart of the joy set before him, and gave him the strength to continue giving himself to the very end, when he could cry, "It is finished!" (John 19:30).

For us too, as we experience some overflow of the sufferings of Christ (see Colossians 1:24), and as we suffer with him that we may be glorified with him (Romans 8:17), this psalm helps us not to be surprised when the Christian life is hard. We shall never have to suffer to pay the penalty for the sins of others; indeed, as Christians, we shall never have to suffer for our own sins, for Jesus has done that, fully and completely, for us. But we will suffer; and so, in some measure, as the people of Jesus, we shall feel the pain of the first part of Psalm 22.

But then, as we come to the second part, we hear and rejoice as Jesus our King proclaims what the Father has done for him in his resurrection. We grasp more deeply, as we sing this psalm, that what the Father has done for Jesus he will do for us as the people of Jesus. All over the world in the age to come, men and women who know that they deserve nothing of the blessings poured out on them—who know that those who were poor have been made rich by Jesus (2 Corinthians 8:9)—will cause the new heavens and new earth to resound with glad proclamation of the righteous deeds of their God. "He has done it!" we shall sing, with joy in our hearts and exultation in our voices.

## Questions for reflection

1. How does this psalm help you to imagine what Jesus experienced on the cross?
2. Have you experienced suffering like this in your own life?
3. How does the psalm help you to be confident that God is faithful to you in such afflictions?

## PART TWO

The Bible **commentator** Peter Craigie comments:

> "There are few psalms in the Psalter which are so well loved and well known as [Psalm] 23. Its appeal lies partly in the simplicity and beauty of its poetry, strengthened by the serene confidence which it exudes." (*Psalms 1-50,* page 208)

This is true. And yet one of the problems with Psalm 23 is its anaesthetising familiarity. The words trip off the tongue of anyone who has had any kind of exposure to Christianity in their upbringing or culture. So the words might wash over us, giving us a warm religious feeling of comfort but without (necessarily) much or any understanding. In that case, need to press the intellectual and emotional "reset" button before coming afresh to this beautiful psalm. By the end of this chapter, I hope we shall delight in it with a greater depth, in Christ.

Like most of the psalms in Book I, the heading tells us that this is "A psalm of David". This should remind us that before this much-loved psalm can become ours, we must remember that it was first David's. It is a psalm of the king. David sang it; we do not know when, or prompted by what, but it was the authentic expression of his faith and experience. We need to call to mind that as with all the psalms (and the other psalmists), David spoke as a prophet, by the Spirit of the Christ, the anointed king who was yet to come. And so, before this psalm can become ours, it is first David's, and then it is the prayer of Jesus Christ, our king. As the nineteenth-century Scottish pastor Andrew Bonar points out:

> "The church has so exclusively (we might say) applied this psalm to herself, as almost to forget that her shepherd ... once needed it and was glad to use it."
>
> (*Christ and His Church in the Book of the Psalms,* page 80)

Because Jesus called himself "the good shepherd" (John 10:11), we jump too quickly to think of ourselves praying the psalm about Jesus our Lord, who is our shepherd. He is, but we must remember first the original context in David's life and the fulfilment context as Jesus our king would have prayed it. This is a psalm of our king, and must be read as such before it can properly become ours in him. So we will think of David, and then Jesus, singing this psalm; and then we shall learn to pray it ourselves!

Although the word is not used, this psalm shares with Psalm 22 the theme of trust. For the king who trusts God in the face of desperate suffering in Psalm 22 trusts this same God to be his shepherd "through the darkest valley" in Psalm **23:4**. The emotional tone also is different. Psalm 22 is a grand and intense psalm, taking us down to the depths in its first part and with trumpets playing exultant joy in the final part. But where Psalm 22 is more like a Verdi piece (in classical-music terms), here in Psalm 23 we are perhaps best to imagine that we are accompanied by the music of Vaughan Williams. There is a quiet reflectiveness here in the prayer of our king.

The psalm begins and ends with "the LORD", the covenant God (**23:1**, **6**). So the covenant that God has made with the king in David's line (2 Samuel 7:11b-14) should be uppermost in our minds. This is not a psalm about some generic "god" but about the covenant God of the Bible story, and specifically the God who has made covenant promises to the king he has appointed (see Psalm 2).

## To the place of plenty

The song begins with the confident affirmation that this covenant God leads his king to a place of full provision (**23:1-3**). God is the king's "shepherd" and therefore the king lacks "nothing" (**v 1**). David celebrates the truth that the LORD takes him where there is satisfaction. The words "makes me lie down ... leads me ... refreshes me [literally "causes me to turn"] ... guides me" in **verses 2-3** all speak of the LORD's initiative in bringing the king to where there is plenty.

Although the language here is individual ("my ... I ... me"), we can also use "shepherd" language corporately, as in Psalm 28:9: "Save your people and bless your inheritance; be their shepherd and carry them for ever". The God who is the shepherd of the king is also the shepherd of the people, for the king is the representative head of the people. The king represents God to his people. He is also our representative, speaking for us as well as mediating to us the covenant relationship that he himself has with God.

This link is reinforced by the strong echoes here of the language used in Exodus and Deuteronomy to describe what the covenant God did for the people of Israel at the exodus and in the wilderness. The psalm "is steeped in a covenantal setting, and it has many affinities with descriptions of the Exodus experience," notes Harman (*Psalms,* volume 1, page 225). So the words "I lack nothing" (**23:1**) echo the experience of Israel travelling through the wilderness, where, Moses told them, "You have not lacked anything" (Deuteronomy 2:7). The phrases "he leads me", "green pastures" and "he guides me" (Psalm **23:2-3**) are echoes of the song of Exodus 15, sung on the eastern coast of the Red Sea. Here the Israelites celebrated how…

> "in your unfailing love [covenant love, *chesed*—see Psalm **23:6**, where the same Hebrew word is translated "love" in the NIV] you will lead the people you have redeemed. In your strength you will guide them to your holy dwelling [literally pasture]".
>
> (Exodus 15:13)

The word "quiet" in "quiet waters" (Psalm **23:2**) is elsewhere translated as "rest" and used of the **promised land** in Psalm 95:11.

King David sings of how the covenant God brings him, the representative head of Israel—the one who in his own person embodied Israel—to the place of plentiful provision. This is not the song of any isolated individual; it is the song of the representative head of the people of God. What God does for him, God does (implicitly) for the whole people of God of whom the king is the leader. It seems likely that "as the king, David is viewed as personally summing up the nation's experience" (Geoffrey W. Grogan, *Psalms*, page 75). What God does for his chosen king, he does for the people of the king. So, as we also are the people of the King—men and women "in Christ"—this blessing and comfort is ours too.

All this God does "for his name's sake" (**23:3**). Because God has made a covenant promise to the king—the covenant promise that restates the promises made to Abraham and his descendants—the reputation ("name") of God depends upon his doing what he has promised. King David's confidence that God would lead him was not wishful thinking; it was a trust in the faithfulness of God to his covenant. David spoke by the Spirit of Christ. And when the Lord Jesus would have sung **23:1-3**, he would sing it as the anointed King, the Messiah, the head of the people of God, the embodiment of Israel. In this capacity he was confident that God his Father would bring him, and with him all his people, into the place of plenty—the "inheritance" that is the new heavens and new earth.

As the people of King Jesus, we may rejoice with him in this quiet confidence that, as we belong to him, we too will be led, guided, refreshed (caused to turn) and made to lie down in that place of beauty and plenty. It makes a wonderful difference, however, to pray these lovely words deeply conscious of our corporate identity in Christ our King. This will be for us a wonderful antidote to the cripplingly lonely individualism that is endemic in our Western cultures. For the "green pastures", the "quiet waters" and the "right paths" to which we are led are the pastures, river banks and ways to which our King has gone before, and to which he now—as our good shepherd—leads us, his redeemed people. Let us not picture ourselves being taken to a place of solitary satisfaction, but rather, to a pasture sufficient for all who are in Christ. Let us see ourselves as being led together, as his flock, to the place he has prepared for us to enjoy together with one another and with him.

Here is a wonderful antidote to the cripplingly lonely individualism that is endemic.

## Through valleys of darkness

**Verse 4** makes clear, however, that the pathway to these "green pastures" is the road of suffering, as it was in Psalm 22. It takes the king through the "darkest valley" or "the valley of the shadow of death" (ESV). About half the Old Testament occurrences of the word translated here as "darkest" come in the book of Job. The word speaks of a shadow behind which does indeed lie death itself. Yet even here, as the king goes into this valley (and as our King Jesus went deep into this valley on the cross), he need ultimately "fear no evil". The shepherd's "rod" fends off wild, predatory beasts; the shepherd's "staff" or crook guides and controls the sheep, to keep them going in the right paths. This king, who is the leader of God's people, goes himself into deep darkness for them.

As we follow our King, we too are called to enter the shadow of death, in small ways through trials and sickness and in deeper ways as we face death itself; and yet even in the darkest trial—in the deepest valley, the place where death itself covers our souls with a darkness so black that there seems to be no hope—even there we may trust that the Son, who is now our shepherd walks with us too, just as the shepherd Father first walked with Jesus. While we should not take comfort from **23:4** in solitary or individualistic "me and God" spirituality, we may indeed take great comfort from it when we meditate on the security we have in Jesus Christ. Our King has gone before us, into and through the deepest and darkest valley; when we enter that valley, and finally when we enter the darkness of death itself, we do so as members of the people of the King who has gone before. He will take our hands and lead us, as he himself was led by his Father. By the Holy Spirit, we now enjoy fellowship with the Father and the Son (1 John 1:1-3); that fellowship cannot be broken even by death itself.

## Towards the victory

Psalm **23:1-3** expresses the king's confidence that he will lead his people into the place of plenty, and **verse 4** supports this by affirming that even death itself cannot stop him; and then **verse 5** looks forward to the final victory of the king. There is a "table" laid up for a victory banquet. There are "enemies"—those who persist to the end in opposing God's king—but they cannot participate in the banquet; they can only watch in defeated frustration, as their hopes for freedom, which were so confidently voiced in Psalm 2:1-3, end in failure. The king's head is "anointed with oil" in preparation for the banquet, and his "cup overflows" with abundant blessing. At last the king of Psalm 2 will rule the nations! And—as we saw in Psalm 22—we will rule with him. For "the Lord's people will judge [i.e. rule] the world" (1 Corinthians 6:2).

## The place of loving delight

Psalm **23:6** is the climax. After the gentle leading (**v 1-3**), the assured presence in darkness (**v 4**) and the victory banquet (**v 5**) comes the final delight: love. The "goodness" and covenant steadfast "love" (*chesed*) of God are the king's to enjoy in intimate fellowship with God his Father for ever. This is what the king most desires; and it is what he will forever enjoy. In this "house of the LORD" he will gaze on the beauty of the LORD (Psalm 27:4). The goal of this drama is the unbroken delightful fellowship of God the Father and the king. The covenant name "the LORD" forms a bracket with **23:1**.

The King who inherits these covenant assurances is ultimately Jesus Christ. He is the singer of Psalm 23. What comfort this psalm must have brought to him in his earthly sufferings! And now it is ours, as we are "in Christ". Our King becomes, with God the Father, our good shepherd, leading us, his sheep, where he has gone before. With our King—and only with our King, never in isolated Christless spirituality—we share this deep and beautiful assurance: that as we follow him through the valley of the shadow of death, we too need fear no evil, and we too will dwell with Jesus in our Father's house for ever.

## Questions for reflection

1. What difference does it make to you personally to know that Jesus has gone through the valley of death for you?
2. How does this psalm make you feel about your future?
3. If we pray this psalm "deeply conscious of our corporate identity in Christ our King", what kinds of thing we will pray for our churches and Christian communities?

PSALMS 31 AND 40

# 4. THE ROCK OF REFUGE

We could have taken many psalms in Book I to illustrate the trust that the king places in his God and Father. I have picked Psalms 31 and 40, partly because they are among my favourites and partly because each is quoted by or of the Lord Jesus in the New Testament.

What will it take for you to trust the God and Father of Jesus at all times and even in the face of death itself? Psalm 31 will answer that question in a wonderfully gritty and deeply persuasive manner.

This is "a psalm of David"—again, we are reading a psalm that is first David's, then supremely belongs to Jesus, and only then belongs to us, "in Christ", as the people of the King.

The key to unlocking the psalm is what David says at the end of it, in **verses 23-24**. After recounting his own prayers and their answers, he turns to the people of God and exhorts us to trust as he has trusted. All of the psalm to that point is intended to motivate us to respond to the appeal of **verses 23-24**.

## A realistic repetition

**Verses 9-22** virtually recapitulate **verses 1-8**. Each section begins with urgent prayer in dire straits (**v 1-5**, **9-13**) and ends with an assurance of prayer answered (**v 7-8**, **21-22**). Are these two successive crises and their resolutions? This seems unlikely. The language is quite general, and there are other psalms with a similar oscillation between distress and praise. More likely, the longer section (**v 9-22**) expands on the whole drama already outlined more briefly in **verses 1-8**. The glad assurance voiced at the end of each section may or may not be David's testimony to deliverance already experienced; it is very likely (as in many psalms) that, rather, it expresses a confidence in a deliverance yet to be granted. This is rather like what is sometimes called the "prophetic perfect", where a past tense is used in the Bible of something that is in the future, the past tense being used to express the certainty that it is—as we say—as good as done. (The past tense "glorified" in Romans 8:30 is perhaps the most famous example of this.)

The tension between prayer, distress and praise is a normal part of the life of faith.

If this is so, then there is something deeply realistic about the repetition, for it models for us the interplay between prayer, distress and praise. This tension is a normal part of the life of faith. We do not usually just pray about something once and then get on with life, confident that our prayer has been heard; any assurance we experience comes and goes, and we need again and again to cry out in prayer and feel again that assurance in our souls. Psalm 31 both models for us and shapes in us such persistent and repeated cries for help and expressions of trust.

## "Into your hands I commit my spirit"

Psalm **31:1-5** is bracketed by parallel statements of trust:

> "In you, LORD, I have taken refuge ...
> Into your hands I commit my spirit."

The dominant images are of a place of safety. This is called "my rock of refuge, a strong fortress" (**v 2**), where the word "rock" means a high mountain cliff or crag in which a safe place of refuge may be found. David does not say much about his troubles (yet), but he refers to "the trap that is set for me" (**v 4**). Clearly he is in great danger; but he knows that the God who has made a covenant with him ("the LORD") is "my faithful God" (**v 5**): the one whose "hands" are the safe place—indeed, the only safe place—for his "spirit", his inner being.

In **verse 6**, David contrasts the two possible strategies for a human being under pressure. One is to "cling to worthless idols"; the other is to "trust in the LORD". An "idol" is any god, goddess, philosophy, thing, person or project in which or in whom we trust for what we most deeply need. It is the person or thing without which we consider that life would be a living hell. It might be something as humdrum as our savings, home or pension. It might well be a beloved man or woman upon whom all our hopes rest. Perhaps it is a project—my work, my career or my ministry—to which we look to give us a sense of being valued. Idols come in many forms, for the human heart is—as the Reformer John Calvin said—"a factory of idols"; no sooner have we abandoned one than we form or shape another. What all idols have in common is that they are "worthless". The word means empty, vain, useless; that other great Reformer, Martin Luther, called them "supervain" (John Goldingay, *Psalms,* Volume 1, page 440). They cannot ever provide a reliable place of safety. They always let us down; no one whispers on their deathbed, "I wish I had put my trust more wholeheartedly in my pension, my career, my girlfriend, my philosophical ideas." When the king says, "I hate those who cling to worthless idols", he is not expressing a personal vindictive hatred; the word "hate" means to "repudiate", to "be against", to "have nothing to do with" these people, in the sense of an absolute refusal to join them in their clinging to idols (Goldingray, *Psalms,* Volume 1, page 591). Instead, our king says emphatically about himself ("as for me"), that he "trusts" in the covenant God. This sums up what he has said in **verses 1-5**.

**Verses 7-8** voice a beautiful "glad" assurance, rooted in the "love" (the covenant love, *chesed*) of God. The image shifts from a place of safety to a place of space. The king was in "anguish": a word that conveys a sense of narrow straits, being cramped, hemmed in, confined; he is sure that the covenant God has (or will) "set my feet in a spacious [literally "uncramped"] place".

It is a moving sight to watch David pray like this, for he expresses a trust that holds fast in all the extremities of life. It is a yet more moving sight to watch the Lord Jesus bring this trust to fulfilment as he voiced the famous words "Into your hands I commit my spirit" from the cross (Luke 23:46); in that short quotation he encapsulated all the trust and assurance of Psalm **31:1-8**. He really believed that he could entrust himself to the One who judges justly, even in the face of death itself (1 Peter 2:23). **Stephen**, the first Christian **martyr**, echoed this trust as he was killed (Acts 7:59), and Peter exhorted all "who suffer according to God's will" to "commit themselves to their faithful Creator" (1 Peter 4:19).

## "My times are in your hands"

While David has only hinted at his troubles in Psalm **31:1-8**, in **verses 9-13** they are painted for us in terrible sharpness. **Verses 9-10** focus on weakness. When Bible poetry speaks of "eyes", the poet often means what we think of in terms of energy, drive, desire and ambition: all the things that get us out of bed in the morning. "Sorrow" has made David very weak, both in body ("bones") and heart. Doctors and psychiatrists emphasise that human beings are psychosomatic unities: we cannot separate our bodies (*soma*) from our minds and emotions (*psyche*). We are whole beings. Every facet of David is weakened by suffering.

The king's "enemies", first mentioned in **verse 8**, reappear with a vengeance in **verses 11-13**. These enemies have done such damage to David that he is now a pitiful and despicable figure of weakness, fit only for "contempt", "dread", and distance ("flee from me", **v 11**), and ultimately to be "forgotten", as if "dead" (**v 12**). He is like the victim of a "terror" attack; his limbs and heart have been shattered "like broken pottery". The proud powers of 2:1-3 "conspire against" him, and they seem to have done so successfully (unlike in Psalm 2), as they "plot to take my life" (**31:13**). All this happened in some measure to King David; it happened in full measure to King Jesus. And, as we sing **verses 9-13** with Jesus, we remember that the overflow of his sufferings should be what we, his people, expect in this age.

In the face of this distress, the theme of "trust" (that is so strong in **verses 1-6**) emerges again in **verses 14-18**: "But I trust in you, LORD" (**v 14a**). To say, "You are *my* God" (**v 14b**, my italics) is to reaffirm covenant loyalty, which is the same as trust. When the king says, "My times are in your hands" (**v 15**), he says effectively the same as "Into your hands I commit my spirit" (**v 5**); but the emphasis here is that all the king's "times"—every year, each day, hour by hour, second by second—are in the safe hands of the God of "unfailing love" (**v 16b**—the same word, *chesed*, as in **verse 7**). What the king values above all things is that the "face" of the God he loves might "shine" on him (**v 16a**). This echoes the priestly blessing of Numbers 6:22-27: it is the personal loving favour of God upon all who are in covenant with him, and it begins with the king. The counterpart of trust for rescue is trust that "the wicked", who are defined as those who "speak arrogantly against the righteous [singular, "the righteous one"]", will "be put to shame" and have their accusations "silenced" (Psalm **31:17-18**).

In **verses 19-20**, the king's focus begins to move from himself (in the singular) to "those [plural] who fear you" (that is, who fear God, **v 19**) with loving reverent fear. The God who keeps the king safe has "stored up ... good things" for *all* "who take refuge in you". And so, when the king voices again in **verses 21-22** the glad assurance that he sang in **verses 7-8**, he does so with an eye to those many who will be encouraged by his testimony. He was (and Jesus was, **metaphorically** speaking, when he referred to this psalm on the cross) "in a city under siege" (**v 21**), in a state of terrible alarm, "'cut off from your sight!'" (**v 22**); but he, the king, has been shown, and assured of, the wonders of God's love (the *chesed* of **verses 7** and **16**).

And so the king's song ends with an exhortation to us...

## Take heart!

The exhortation in **verses 23-24** is addressed to "all [God's] faithful people" (**v 23**). The word translated as "faithful" is derived from the word *chesed*. It is speaking about people who have first received that wonderful love and then begin to express it in their lives. That is, it is speaking of all believers: men and women who belong to God's anointed king. These people are exhorted to "love the LORD", which means being warmly and devotedly loyal to him: to "cling" to him, rather than clinging to worthless idols (**v 6**).

**Verse 23** sums up all that the psalm has affirmed about the character of the God who has stood by his chosen king. What he does for the king he will do for all "those who are true to him", which means to be humbly dependent on him and is the very opposite of "the proud", who will be paid back for their arrogant hostility.

The result of loving the LORD with this confident love is that we can "be strong and take heart" (**v 24**) when we ourselves experience some of the overflow of the pressures and sufferings of Jesus our King. We are "you who hope in the LORD". A hope that is rooted in trust in God's covenant promises fulfilled for us in Christ (2 Corinthians 1:20) is the future confidence that gives us strength to go on living each day.

What will it take for you to trust the God and Father of Jesus at all times and even in the face of death itself? It takes, first, some time to meditate on the trust that Jesus himself showed in his God and Father. Read and **meditate** on Psalm **31:1-8** and feel the force of those words "Into your hands I commit my spirit" (**v 5**). Then read and meditate on **verses 9-22** until you feel the agony of the Lord's sufferings and can grasp something of the wonder of a man under the pressures of **verses 9-13** saying, "My times are in your hands" (**v 15**). Then, when you have meditated afresh on the faith that Jesus showed in his Father, hear again his exhortation to us, his people, in **verses 23-24**. Go back, then, over the whole psalm, making the trust of Jesus your own trust as you enter into his words and heart. You may like to make the words "My times are in your hands" very specific and say not just "my times" in general but "this time" in particular: "This day—this day of pressure, this day of anxiety, this day of persecution, this day of bereavement, even this day of my death—is in your hands."

And then be ready to pray this again and again, for the pressures of following Jesus will not relent, and you will find your trust wavering. Use this psalm for the purposes for which God inspired King David to pray it, and King Jesus to fulfil it—that we may walk in Jesus' footsteps, "love the LORD" (**v 23**) and "be strong and take heart" (**v 24**) as we "hope" in the God and Father of Jesus, who is the faithful God of unfailing love.

## Questions for reflection

1. What "idols" do you or those you know cling to?
2. What would it look like for you to put your trust wholly in God instead—today?
3. How will you respond to the appeal of verses 23-24?

# PART TWO

## The one and the many

In Psalm 40, King David sings sometimes about himself ("I ... me ... my", **40:1**) and sometimes about his people ("us ... the great assembly", **v 5**, **9**). The key to understanding and singing the psalm is the relationship between the king and the king's people. Most of the psalm is intensely personal; David sings about himself and what happens between him and the covenant God. But (and this is the key) what happens to the king shapes what will happen to his people, for this one man is the key to the destiny of many. As O. Palmer Robertson has expressed it, "As it fares with the messianic king, so it fares with each member of the messianic kingdom" (*The Flow of the Psalms*, page 63). We need to remember that none of us are the king; but we must equally remember that, if we belong to Jesus, we are among the king's people, Christ's church. So let us hear, and then join in, this song.

The psalm begins with the king's story (**v 1-3**), after which the king makes a declaration about God (**v 4**, **5**) and a declaration about his own self-offering (**v 6-8**). His declaration concludes with a proclamation of God's saving greatness (**v 9-10**). After this the tone changes, and in **verses 11-17** he pleads for God to rescue him now.

## Watch the rescue

The king comes to the front of his choir and sings, "I waited patiently for the LORD" (**v 1**). The king's story begins with a long drama of trust. To wait patiently means to pray and to trust the promises of God, and to do so day after day. David knows the promises of Psalms 1 and 2, and of 2 Samuel 7. He knows that the God who made a covenant with him is committed to blessing the king who keeps that covenant law (Psalm 1); and that this king will be God's Son and will inherit the world (Psalm 2). That is what God has said. But the reality in David's experience falls far short of that. We do not know when David wrote this psalm, but when we come to **40:11-17**, it becomes very clear that he has not yet inherited the world! And yet he waits patiently because he trusts. David did that often. Jesus of Nazareth always did that. Every day he waited patiently in prayer.

The king's testimony (**v 1b-3a**) is that the God who was committed to him heard that prayer. From "the slimy pit ... mud and mire" (**v 2**)—that vivid poetic image of weakness and impending death—God has lifted him up, set his feet "on a rock" (a place of solidity) and given him "a new song" (**v 3**), in which he praises God for rescuing him. David could sing that after any of the little rescues he experienced. Now the risen and ascended king sings that after his final rescue.

We come in at the end of **verse 3**: "Many will see"—that is, see God rescue his chosen king—"and fear the LORD" with loving reverent fear. They too—and we too—will "put their trust in him". When the old-covenant people saw God rescue King David, or any of the other kings in David's line (such as Hezekiah in 2 Kings 18 – 20), they were encouraged to put their trust in God, just as their king had put his trust in God. Supremely, when we see God the Father raise Jesus his Son, our king, from the "slimy pit" of death and put his feet on a rock, we see and are moved to put our trust in the God in whom King Jesus put his trust.

And so Psalm **40:1-3** can become our story in Christ. We too are called to wait patiently in times of trial, confident that the day will come when, in Christ, we will have a new song in our mouths: a song that celebrates the way the God and Father of Jesus has rescued us from the slimy pit of death.

## Heed the blessing

By the end of **verse 3** we, the choir of the king, have heard the king's story and watched the king's rescue. We are ready to trust. Now, in **verse 4a**, the king declares what we already suspect to be the case: each and every one "who trusts in the LORD" is "blessed". If we walk in the king's footsteps of trust, we too will be blessed, just as our king is blessed.

But there is a warning also in **verse 4b**. To trust in the covenant God and Father of the king means *not* trusting in ("does *not* look to", my italics) "the proud". The "proud" are people who "turn aside to false gods". Why is it proud to do that? Because a false god is always made in "my" own image; he or she will be a god or goddess very much like "me", an extension of my own ambition or imagination. And therefore to trust in a false god is essentially the same as trusting in myself. To "look to" the proud is to follow their example: to put my trust in myself or other people—perhaps a partner, a family member, a celebrity, a rich benefactor, a company that employs me and promises me the world—or to trust in a project in which I invest my energies and all my hopes. Whatever it may be, a false god will always disappoint. Blessing is to be found only in trusting the God and Father of our king.

> A false god is always made in my own image; they will be a god or goddess very much like me.

In **verse 5** the king expands the blessing. The key word is "many". He sings of "many ... wonders ... too many to declare". Why so many? The word "wonders" is often used for exodus-like rescues—acts of **redemption**. These are "the things you planned", not just for one man, the king, but "for us". The "many" of **verse 3**, who see the king's rescue and trust the rescuer, will each be rescued. And each individual rescue—the redemption of each man and woman in the King's people—is a wonderful act of God. There are many wonders, because there are many rescued people.

## The heart of the king

In an extraordinary and intensely personal section, the king now pledges himself to do the will of God by making an offering for sins. In **verse 6** he understands that although under the old covenant God decreed that various sacrifices should be offered, ultimately what God wanted was what those sacrifices symbolised, and not the sacrifices themselves. Such sacrifices were only symbols of the true sacrifice that would be offered later. What God did not want was the sacrifices offered just as empty religious ritual with no repentance and faith involved (see Hosea 6:6).

God has "opened" the king's "ears"—that is (in the poetry), God has bored earholes into his body so that he can hear the word of God. The Greek translation of the Old Testament (sometimes called the Septuagint) reads slightly differently: "a body you have prepared for me". (This Greek translation was made two or more centuries before Christ. Sometimes the translators seem to paraphrase the Hebrew. But when the New Testament writers quote from the Septuagint, we may be confident the meaning is right.) Here the sense is the same in Greek and Hebrew. This king is given "a body" with "ears"; that is to say, he is the king who hears the word of God and obeys it.

This is why, in Psalm **40:7**, he says to God his Father, "Here I am [or "Behold!"], I have come". Here is the king about whom the "scroll" (the Law of God) says that he will do the will of God. In the Law of Moses, we are told that the king had to write out and meditate on the Law of God. That is to say, the Psalm 2 king had to be a Psalm 1 believer. He had to be able to say, with every fibre of his being, "I desire to do your will, my God; your law is within my heart" (**40:8**). It is an extraordinary prospect: a king who has the heart desire to do exactly what God wants. Many kings never got close to doing what God wanted (e.g. Manasseh, 2 Kings 21); some attempted it (e.g. Josiah, 2 Kings 22 – 23), but none succeeded until Jesus of Nazareth, the Son of David, who could say about his Father, and mean, every day of his life, "I always do what pleases" him (John 8:29).

What an astonishing king! King David foreshadowed him, but never perfectly. King Jesus offered himself as the perfect sacrifice for sins. This is why Hebrews 10:5-7 quotes this section of the psalm about Jesus. Hebrews goes on to say that by his perfect obedience Jesus has made us holy (Hebrews 10:10). Blessing for the many, the King's people, came by the sin-offering of the one, the King.

As we sing Psalm **40:6-8**, we marvel at this perfect obedient self-offering of Jesus for sinners. We take comfort in the fact that we have been set apart to belong to God ("made holy") by Jesus' obedience, that...

*His perfect obedience and blood*
*Hide all my transgressions from view.*

(Augustus Montague Toplady, "A Debtor to Mercy Alone")

And then perhaps we too, by the Spirit of Jesus, begin more and more to desire to do God's will in our own lives.

## In the great assembly

**Verses 6-8** are a poignantly personal pledge made by the king to his God, fulfilled in Jesus' lonely self-offering when he "bore my burdens to Calvary and suffered and died alone" (Charles H. Gabriel, "I Stand Amazed in the Presence"). By contrast, **verses 9-10** are a public proclamation of the king in "the great assembly"—the words which bracket the section. The "great assembly" or congregation is the gathering of the whole people of God: Israel under the old covenant, the church of Christ (Jew and Gentile) under the new.

The public nature of these verses is emphatic, both positively and negatively. Positively, "I proclaim ... I speak". Negatively, "I do not seal my lips ... I do not hide ... I do not conceal". It is important that God knows and can attest to this ("as you know"). Why this emphasis on wide publicity? Because we, the great assembly of the king's people, absolutely need to hear what the king proclaims. We cannot afford to miss out on learning this! What the king will proclaim is what God has done for the king, and what the king has done for his people.

What is it that the king proclaims? Answer: the rescue of God—that God keeps his promises by saving the king. In telling the story of his rescue, King David is not so much talking about himself as proclaiming that the covenant God rescues his chosen king. King Jesus made this final proclamation after his resurrection and ascension.

We need to hear this proclamation because the God who rescues the king is the God who will rescue, with him, all his people. Our hope depends entirely on the resurrection and ascension of Jesus our King. As we join our King in singing **verses 9-10**, our hearts lift with joy, knowing that the God and Father of Jesus is indeed the God of unchanging love and faithfulness, in whom we can safely trust.

## Back in trouble

After the high drama and grand resolution of **verses 1-10**, culminating in the magnificent declaration of the saving power of God (**v 9-10**), the sudden change to a **minor key** in **verses 11-17** comes as a surprise. Suddenly David seems to be back in dire straits. The "love and ... faithfulness" he has so confidently proclaimed in **verse 10** are now most urgently needed in **verse 11** ("may your love and faithfulness always protect me"). **Verse 12** is an intense **cameo** of suffering. The king is surrounded by countless "troubles": more than the hairs on his head. These troubles he equates with "my sins", for he understands that there are wages to be paid for sins, and that all troubles are ultimately the result of sin (although they are not necessarily the result of specific sins—see John 9 v 1-3). As a result, he is close to despair ("my heart fails within me").

What are we to make of this? For King David, there were plenty of his own sins that help us make sense of this. But, even with David, we are faced with the paradox that the one who speaks of "my sins" in **verse 12** is the one who has pledged, "I desire to do your will" in **verse 8**. David was speaking prophetically of a future king who would be perfectly obedient to God and, at the same time, the bearer of many sins. The sins which that greater king would count as his own ("my sins") would be the sins of all his people, so that he would become their sin-bearing sacrifice: the one who does the will of God by taking upon his own shoulders the weight and burden of his people's sins, being made sin for them (2 Corinthians 5:21).

Whether Psalm **40:11-17** represents a later time of trouble into which David plunged after the rescue celebrated in **verses 1-10**, or whether—as seems more likely—it is revisiting and reliving the troubles from which he has been rescued, the point seems to be that the king's troubles arise out of the king's self-offering as the sacrifice for the sins of his people.

**Verses 13-17** can stand on their own as a prayer, which is why they have been taken and reused as Psalm 70. The section is bracketed by a petition to God to save the king himself. **40:13** asks for this, and at the end **verse 17** repeats it with urgency.

Between these two prayers for deliverance, however, **verses 14-16** contain two further pleas. First, the king prays for God's just punishment upon those who want to kill him and long for his ruin (**v 14-15**); for impenitent hostility towards God's chosen king is enmity towards God. Second, in **verse 16** the king prays for his people. They are described as "all who seek you" or "those who long for your saving help"; he asks that they may have joy and gladness and "always say, 'The LORD is great!'" This—for us—is the climax of the psalm: that we, as the King's people, rejoice in the God and Father of Jesus, and celebrate his greatness as we see it in the resurrection and ascension of our King.

But note the very final note of the psalm in **verse 17**. The king prays for urgent rescue: "Do not delay". What might this mean as a prayer today? In one sense, Jesus has no need to pray this, for he himself is seated at the right hand of God. And yet, those who persecute his church persecute him (Acts 9:4); there is, therefore, a real sense in which the Lord Jesus leads his persecuted church in this final plea. Cast your mind around to those parts of the world where you know the church of Christ to be bitterly persecuted. Pray for these brothers and sisters thoughtfully as you pray Psalm **40:17**. One of the blessings of praying these psalms corporately in Christ, rather than simply individually, is that we consciously identify with the persecuted church and we pray with them.

## Questions for reflection

1. If Jesus is ultimately the "I" and "me" of this psalm, how does it help us to understand the cross better?
2. How could you become someone who says "The Lord is great!" more often?
3. Who do you know of who needs deliverance and help?

PSALMS 42 - 43 AND 44

# 5. LAMENTS OF A LEADER AND PEOPLE

Book II (Psalms 42 – 72) begins with a group of psalms authored by the "**sons of Korah**" (42 – 49). 42/43 and 44, at the start of the book and the start of this group, are both laments. Psalms 42/43 are the laments of an individual, while Psalm 44 is a lament of the whole people.

From Psalm 42 right through to Psalm 83—that is, in all of Book II and more than half of Book III—the psalms have a general preference for the word "God" rather than "the LORD". (A comparison of Psalm 14, in Book I, and the almost identical Psalm 53, in Book II, illustrates this well.) The words translated as "God" (Hebrew *El* or *Elohim*) are universal words that would be understood by anybody knowing the language, or other related languages of the ancient Near East. The word translated as "the LORD" (often written "Yahweh", although we do not know how it was pronounced) is the particular covenant name of the God of Israel. The two refer to the same God, but the former is perhaps more readily accessible to a wider audience. We do not know why this section of the Psalter prefers the more general name "God"; it may be especially targeted at a slightly wider audience, but we cannot be sure. (For more on this, see Robertson, *The Flow of the Psalms,* pages 95-102.)

Although Psalm 42 and Psalm 43 are separate in the original manuscripts, there are good reasons for studying them, and praying them, together. The most obvious is the (almost) identical refrain in **42:5**,

**42:11** and **43:5**, beginning "Why, my soul, are you downcast?" and each closing a preceding little section, so that we have four verses followed by a refrain, another five verses, another refrain, and then (at the start of 43) a further four verses and a final refrain. Another link is the words "Why must I go about mourning, oppressed by the enemy?" in **42:9b**, echoed in **43:2b**. A third is that all the psalms from 42 to 49 are headed "Of the sons of Korah" except for 43, which suggests it is closely connected with 42 and comes under its heading. Feel free to pray them separately; but I will take them together.

## Talking to yourself

Most of us talk to ourselves from time to time. Many of us have said, "I need to give myself a good talking-to!" Talking to yourself is not necessarily, in fact, a sign of madness, but is very probably an expression of sanity: asking yourself questions, reasoning with yourself, talking yourself out of one emotional state and into another, better frame of mind. It's a good idea. Psalms 42 and 43 show us how to do it! Indeed, they show us how Jesus of Nazareth would have done it, and there can be no better example than him.

The question asked at the start of each refrain is expressed in two parallel ways. First, "Why, my soul, are you downcast?" (**42:5**, **11**; **43:5**). The word for "soul" (Hebrew *nephesh*) does not mean the soul as the non-material part of me—my soul as opposed to my body; that idea was popularised centuries later in some Greek (**Platonic**) philosophies, but it is not a biblical concept. This is illustrated in the psalm as the psalmist refers to his "bones" (**42:10**), which are emphatically bodily. No, we are psychosomatic unities; the *psyche* (soul) and *soma* (body) are united in one whole person. The expression "my soul" in Hebrew means something like "the whole of me with a focus on my desires or needs". So the "soul" can thirst or hunger; it can be elated, satisfied, downcast or whatever. Here in **42:5**, **11** and **43:5**, "my soul" is "downcast", which is what in our age we call depression, or in low spirits. In other ages it might have been called melancholy. It is the opposite of having one's tail up, like a bright, motivated, energetic puppy. This is the song of one whose inner being is struggling to get out of bed in the morning.

The second way the question is asked is this: "Why so disturbed within me?" The word "disturbed" means something like "in turmoil, all unsettled, churned up inside". The writer does not sleep; when he lies down, his anxious thoughts trouble him. Depression and turmoil are the presenting symptoms in these psalms. They are closely related and very common experiences today, as they have been in every age (although our age is perhaps more self-absorbed in our insistent focus upon them). As James Mays points out:

> "When facing the suffering of his passion, Jesus echoed the language of these psalms in speaking of his own downcast, disquieted soul (Matthew 26:38; John 12:27)." (*Psalms,* page 176)

The basic structure of these two psalms is very simple, as we have seen. There are three sections, each consisting of four or five verses followed by a repeated one-verse refrain (Psalm **42:1-5**, **6-11**; **43:1-5**). Although the three sections have their distinctives, they also overlap. We have seen that the words "Why must I go about mourning, oppressed by the enemy?" in the second section (**42:9b**) reappear in the third section (**43:2b**). Also, the pain of people saying to the psalmist, "Where is your God?" appears in the first section (**42:3b**) and is repeated almost verbatim in the second section (**42:10b**). So, although I will suggest different headings for the three sections, it is important not to forget that they are closely interwoven.

## When you're lonely

The psalm begins with an intense image of a deer panting desperately for life-giving waters (**v 1-2**). The word translated as "pants" is used elsewhere in the Old Testament only in Joel 1:20, in a terrible scene of dried up streams. There can be no more urgent desire than this. It is the only way the psalmist can describe his desperate longing for God, who is "the living God" and the only source of life. (Notice how often "God" is mentioned in these psalms.)

Far from finding "streams of water", the only water the psalmist knows is his "tears" (Psalm **42:3**). Instead of eating, he weeps. Notice the theme of time: in **verse 2**, he asks "When?"; in **verse 3a**, he weeps "day and night"; in **verse 3b**, the taunting question "Where is your God?" comes to him "all day long", and he has no answer to give that will be persuasive to people who look for sensory evidence—for what may be seen or touched (an image or idol). For the God he knows has chosen to reveal himself in one place and in one way, and the psalmist is far from that place.

**Verse 4** tells us about that place and that revelation. The psalmist chooses to "remember" (for to "remember" in biblical thought means more than cognitive recall; it means a deliberate act of calling to mind). He pours out his soul, which is a strange expression; it is as if his inner being pours out of him with his tears. What he remembers is "the house of God"—the temple in Jerusalem—and the people of God gathering for one of the great Old Testament covenant festivals, like **Passover** ("the festive throng"). He used to "go" there; indeed, the word used to describe his going may mean that he was a leader, leading the people in that joyful praising multitude. He remembers "the swirl of the festival hymns" (Kraus, *Psalms*, Volume 1, page 440).

What he misses is not some solitary mystical experience of God but the corporate throng of enthusiastic temple worship, of which he may have been a leader. When Jesus of Nazareth would have sung this, he would be longing not only for the immediate presence of his Father but for his place as the joyful leader of the assembled people of God. When we sing this, we express and deepen an intense longing for the immediate presence of God the Father, and for the joy of being in the new heavens and new earth, led by Jesus our worship-leader as we sing songs of exultant praise and joy. This longing is partially sated in the joyful corporate worship of the church here on earth.

Hans-Joachim Kraus comments perceptively:

> "All the longing of the thirsty and languishing petitioner is directed to Zion, to the place **Yahweh** has chosen to bear witness to his presence there ... The election of Zion as the place of God's presence has in the NT been transferred to Jesus Christ and his community. In the light of fulfilment we recognise anew that only in the place of God's presence and the assembled congregation are life and salvation to be found. Apart from this reality a consuming sadness operates." (*Psalms,* Volume 1, page 441)

And so the psalmist (and later Jesus, and now each of us) talks to himself in **verse 5**. He asks the question "Why?" and exhorts himself to continue to "hope in God", confident that the time will come when he will again "praise him" because he is God "my Saviour" (or "my salvation"). In speaking to himself, Calvin says, he "represents himself as if he formed two opposing parties" (*Commentary on the Book of Psalms*, Volume 2, page 134). It is a moving thought to consider Jesus speaking these words to himself when troubled by anxious thoughts and a downcast spirit. We too can follow where he has led.

> It is a moving thought to consider Jesus speaking these words to himself when troubled by a downcast spirit.

## When you're under pressure

One talking-to is not enough. It is clear in **verse 6** that the psalmist's soul is still downcast within him. And so again (as in **verse 4**) he engages in a deliberate intentional remembering: "Therefore I will remember you". For now, he is, either literally or metaphorically, in "the land of the Jordan, the heights of Hermon". Mount Hermon was a multi-peaked mountain in the far north of the promised land.

The Mount Mizar mentioned in **verse 6** may be one of those peaks, although we do not know. The headwaters of the Jordan formed in the Hermon range. Whether or not the writer was literally there, these images speak of a very great distance from the temple in Jerusalem.

The River Jordan conjures up a third water image. In **verse 1**, the psalmist longs for streams of life-giving water. In **verse 3**, he weeps watery tears. Now, in **verse 7**, there are terrifying roaring waterfalls—huge waves are breaking over him. There is a double play on words in the Hebrew: the "sound" (NIV "shouts", **v 4**) of the joyful crowds are replaced by the "sound" (NIV "roar", **v 7**) of the waterfalls; and instead of the prospect of "passing" (NIV "go", **v 4**) into the temple, he now faces the waters that are "passing" (NIV "swept", **v 7**) over him. The sound of overwhelming waters replaces the joyful sound of thronging crowds. The expression "deep calls to deep" is not reassuring but frightening. This is Bible poetry for chaos and terror. Not only is he far from the people of God rejoicing in the presence of God; he is under overwhelming pressure.

The parallelism in the first two lines of **verse 8** does not mean that one thing happens "by day" and a different thing "by night"; rather it means that throughout both day and night these two things happen: the LORD, the covenant God (the only use of this name in these psalms), directs or commands his covenant "love" (*chesed*) towards him, and he responds with a "song" of praise. Even in the midst of troubles, these fixed points of God's love and his song remain.

In **verses 9** and **10** we learn what is causing the terrifying "waters": enemies. Again, this is not an individualistic psalm. The writer longs for the corporate joy of the people of God; he is surrounded by hostility that inflicts suffering ("My bones suffer mortal agony") and mockery ("my foes taunt me"). And again there comes that haunting question: "Where is your God?"

The refrain (**v 11**) is very slightly different from its first occurrence in **verse 5**. In the final line of **verse 5** the words translated as "my Saviour" are literally "the salvation of [that is, from] *his* face"; in

**verse 11** it is "the salvation of [that is, to] *my* face". Perhaps there is a movement from God's face of blessing to the psalmist's face of need. Salvation begins with God's "face" and comes from there to the "face" of the psalmist.

Again, just as we considered the Lord Jesus singing **verses 1-5**, it is wonderful to think of him praying **verses 6-11**, as he faced the terrifying floodwaters of human hostility, the concrete expression of the Father's wrath pouring over him, drowning his soul in sorrows as they swept over him. And yet in the midst of it all, the Father's love was unchanging (**v 8a**). As we face the pressures and troubles that come with following Jesus, we too can talk to ourselves with the words of realistic faith that we find in this section.

## When you're rejected

**43:1** is the first explicit prayer in the two psalms. The language switches to that of the law court, with the words "vindicate … plead my cause". Here is one who is falsely accused. Literally he is accused both by "an unfaithful nation" and by an individual who is "deceitful and wicked" (the NIV makes this individual plural). This individual is perhaps the ringleader of the opposition, a kind of **Judas Iscariot** figure. The word translated "unfaithful" means the opposite of showing the covenant love (*chesed*) of God. The psalmist is still "mourning, oppressed by the enemy" (**43:2**, echoing **42:9**), but he prays to God his Father, who will be his "stronghold".

In **43:3** the psalmist cries for God to send out his "light" and "faithful care" (literally "truthfulness"; that is, truthfulness to his covenant promises), as messengers or agents to bring light where there is darkness and promise-fulfilment where at present there seems to be rejection. These wonderful embodiments of the love of God will "lead" this believer to Zion, the "holy mountain" (see 2:6) where God dwells. When the glad day of his arrival there comes, he will again lead the worship of the people of God at God's "altar" (**43:4**) and praise with glad songs.

But for the moment, it is time to sing the troubled refrain a third time (**v 5**). Still he is downcast and troubled. Still he hopes, waits and prays, confident that the day will come when he will lead the people of God in the praise of God. This "son of Korah", the psalmist, wept, waited, hoped, talked to himself and reassured himself with the promises of God; he did so by the Spirit of a greater believer, Jesus of Nazareth, who hoped, waited, prayed, and encouraged his own troubled heart with these same promises. His heart was fired with a pure longing, not only for his Father's immediate presence but also—wonderfully—for the joy of leading the cheerful throng of all his people in praise of his Father. That hope took him through deep darkness. "For the joy set before him he endured the cross" (Hebrews 12:2).

We too, fixing our eyes on Jesus, can pray this psalm as we learn to talk to ourselves when troubled and downcast. This anonymous psalmist talked to himself. He told himself things that he knew were true; the very action of telling them again to himself strengthened his faith. In some extraordinary and utterly sinless way, the Lord Jesus, in his earthly life, talked these same truths to his own heart that his faith might not waver. And now, all these centuries later, we who belong to Jesus may walk in his footsteps as we too talk these precious truths to ourselves in our trials.

## Questions for reflection

1. Which of the images and emotions in these psalms do you find most familiar?
2. What difference does it make to know that Jesus echoed the language of these psalms?
3. How could these psalms help you next time you are lonely, pressured or rejected?

## PART TWO

"But I don't deserve it!" says a suffering friend. What do you say?

If they are not a Christian, Jesus tells us the answer in Luke 13:1-4. "Did these people deserve it?" people ask Jesus. Shockingly, Jesus says, "Unless you repent, you will all perish". When an unrepentant person suffers, that suffering is not the worst that they face—for as sinners, they are deserving of far worse. To claim, "I don't deserve it!" is to be self-deceived.

But what about for the repentant person? The great surprise of this psalm is that the correct answer is "No, you are right. You don't deserve it!"

We do not know what prompted Psalm 44 in Old Testament history. As in so many psalms, the sufferings are not specified. Perhaps it is placed alongside Psalms 42 and 43 at the start of Book II to set the tone, rather as Psalms 1 and 2 set the tone for Book I (and indeed for the whole Psalter).

Although it is mostly corporate, to be sung by the people of God together, from time to time it suddenly becomes singular. We need to consider why this happens. It will be the key to unlocking the psalm.

### Trust for victory

The word "victory" appears four times in the first eight verses of Psalm 44 (**v 3**, **4**, **6**, **7**). **Verses 1-3** look back to a good tradition from the "ancestors" (the forefathers of Israel, from the days of the exodus). The news that the promised land was a gift from God had been passed down from parent to child through the generations. It was God who "drove out the nations" and "planted" them in the land (**v 2**). The word "planted" is a beautiful image that is developed in Psalm 80, where Israel is a fruitful vine (80:8-11). The point, made repeatedly and emphatically, was that it was not Israel's strength that achieved this, but God's "right hand" (the image of strength) and, above all, his "love" (**44:3b**).

**Verses 4-8** say, in effect, *We heard this and we still believe it. Every victory we have ever known is your gift to us. We boast in your love towards us; we will not trust our own resources; we "praise your name" and not our own.* But notice that the voice in **verse 4** becomes singular: "You are *my* King and *my* God". An individual comes to the front of the choir and claims a covenant relationship with God. To say that God is "my God" does not imply that God belongs to me but that I belong to him in covenant relationship. Whoever this is, he speaks and sings as a leader of the people of God. Perhaps he is the "son of Korah" who wrote the psalm. But he speaks and sings as a prophet, by the Spirit of God, who is the Spirit of Christ. And therefore we begin, even now, to hear in this psalm the voice of the great leader of the people of God as he leads his choir.

**Verse 5** returns to the plural: *We follow our leader in trusting you, God, for victory today, just as our ancestors trusted you for victory when they entered the promised land.* Then in **verse 6** the individual speaks again; he voices his personal "trust" in God, not in himself. The people join in again in **verse 7**. **Verse 8** is the climax. *We do not praise ourselves; we boast in God.*

If the psalm stopped here, it would be a simple and cheerful song! The praise of God would simply be this: *They trusted you and you gave them the land; I trust you and the people I lead trust you. You gave them victory; you will give us victory.*

So **verse 9** is a shock. The music changes sharply.

## Expect defeat

The words "But now" at the start of **verse 9** echo a similar contrast in 89:38. Now God appears to be absent, the armies of Israel have retreated, and the people have been plundered (**44:9-10**). And it gets worse. Not only are their precious possessions plundered but they themselves are "devoured like sheep" and "scattered" (**v 11**). It feels as though God cares little or nothing for them (**v 12**), for he has sold them off cheap, like an unloved piece of furniture put up on eBay for a negligible price. It was as if God just said yes to the first derisory low bid because he wanted to get rid of them and would almost pay someone to take them away. *It feels as if we really don't matter very much to you,* says the psalmist, *and that hurts.*

An absent God, a defeated army, a plundered people, a devoured people, a scattered people. What a sorry sight. And these are the people led by the leader who trusts God for victory! And yet in some way this is the typical experience of the people of God; it's to be expected. For the pattern of Bible expectation shapes the church of God not to be surprised when those who follow God's leader experience suffering. Perhaps Romans 8:17 is one of the most concise verses where this truth is expressed in its New Testament clarity: "If we are children, then we are heirs—heirs of God and co-heirs with Christ, if indeed we share in his sufferings in order that we may also share in his glory."

And it gets still worse. If Psalm **44:9-12** focuses on defeat, **verses 13-16** sharpen the misery with a depiction of shame.

## Anticipate shame

With defeat goes shame. **Verses 13-15** say one thing in six ways, once in each half line. And then **verse 16** expands on the reason.

God's people are taunted by those close to them (**v 13a**), derided by those "around us" (**v 13b**). We need to feel the misery of those words "scorn" and "derision"; and these come from the people we can't avoid. They are our "neighbours" (close to us), those "around us". We can't go to work without seeing them; we can't go home without hearing their derisive laughter. *Oh, look, here's that stupid believer; what a moron!*

When people want to insult someone, they use our name as a shorthand for ridicule (**v 14a**), a "byword", a proverbial saying of mockery. They "shake their heads at us" (**v 14b**); the knowing wink or raised eyebrow says, *What a fool!*

And it is not only in all places (**v 13**); it is "all day long" (**v 15a**). There is no escape at any time, just as there is no way out in any place. Notice the singular voice again in **verses 15-16**: "*I* live in disgrace" (my italic). This individual, the leader or representative of the people, is disgraced and covered with shame (**v 15b**).

The reason (**v 16**) is the "taunts"—the mockery—"of those who reproach and revile me". The focus of this shame is the representative leader of this defeated people.

We trust for victory, following the example of our leader's trust; but our leader experiences defeat and the misery of shame. We too taste it with him.

So how will he (the individual) and they (his people) respond? Next comes the surprise.

## Pledge loyalty

The surprising thrust of **verses 17-22** is this: it wasn't their fault! When **Nehemiah** prayed, he identified himself with his people in their guilt (Nehemiah 9:33, 37). When **Daniel** prayed, he did the same (Daniel 9:5-7). When Psalm 106 recounted the history of the people of God, it did so as a history of the people's recurrent sinfulness.

But not here! No: in **44:17** "all this came upon us, though we had not forgotten you; we had not been false to your covenant". The "covenant" is the key. The defeat they are experiencing is an outworking of the covenant promises and curses, for example in Deuteronomy 28, which promise victory to the faithful people and disaster to the unfaithful. This is what happened when the northern kingdom (Israel) "sinned against the LORD" and broke the covenant, as is described in 2 Kings 17 (see especially v 7).

And yet in Psalm 44, the people have been faithful! They were "not … false to your covenant". This leader and the people who sing the song with him were faithful. **Verse 18** emphasises this. They didn't turn back from faithfulness, either in their hearts (intentions and desires) or with their feet (actions).

And yet, as **verse 19** laments, despite their faithfulness, "you crushed us". Their beautiful land became "a haunt for jackals": just a ruin, a wasteland, with wild predators roaming its desolation. The faithful covenant God covered them with "deep darkness" (the shadow of death).

And it's not fair! As **verses 20** and **21** insist, if they had abandoned the path of covenant loyalty—if they had prayed ("spread out our hands" in prayer) to false gods, then God would have known and have been just to punish them. They would have deserved it. But—and this is the clear implication—they didn't, and so they didn't deserve it!

God's people can speak openly before God, who knows our hearts. And their consciences are clear. God can look deep in the recesses of their hearts, and he will find no disloyalty to the covenant. This is a remarkable claim! No wonder one sceptical commentator says we have "the beginnings" here "of **Pharisaical** piety" (Gerhard Kittel, quoted in Kraus, *Psalms*, Volume 1, page 448). But he is wrong. **Verse 22** is the key to understanding this psalm: "Yet for your sake we face death all day long; we are considered as sheep to be slaughtered". They are suffering "for your sake": for the sake of God's honour. We shall come back to that. It will show us this is a far cry from Pharisaical self-righteousness. They are right; they do not deserve it!

But first let us finish our tour of the psalm:

## Pray urgently

In **verse 23**, they cry to God *Wake up!* for it seems he has fallen asleep. In **verse 24**, they say that he is hiding his face—the face whose light had given past victories (**v 3**)—and that he seems to have forgotten their "misery and oppression". The people are creatures of dust. They were, in Bible language, made by God's creative activity as disconnected atoms and molecules were woven together in their mothers' wombs. Cell was joined to cell, blood vessel to blood vessel, sinew to sinew, neural pathway to neural pathway. And then they were joined together as a people. But now this wonderfully interconnected people, consisting of marvellously organic individuals, is heading back "down to the dust" (**v 25**); they are heading for disintegration.

And so they pray, "Rise up" (**v 26**), in an echo of the cry that went up when the ark of the covenant was carried into battle in those old days (for instance Numbers 10). The final word of the psalm is "unfailing love" (*chesed*), covenant love (Psalm 29:26). On this they finally rely.

So what is going on? I want to unpack this in two stages.

First, let us focus on the individual who comes to the front of the choir and sings in the singular at certain points. Who is this? We don't know. But he prays with the voice of a prophet (as do all the psalmists), and therefore by the Spirit of the Christ to come.

Here is a man who knows in his experience a steady trust for victory with no dependence upon his own strength, the bitter experience of defeat in a failed ministry, the deeper misery of shame, when mocked and taunted; and yet it was not his fault. He could quite rightly say he did not deserve it. And so he prays, with loud cries and tears, to the God who can save him from death (Hebrews 5:7).

Here is a leader of the people of God whose loyalty never falters and who casts himself on the covenant love of his Father in heaven, because he knows that his sufferings are not deserved—that it is for the sake of the reputation of God his Father that he must suffer these things. What a leader!

But, second, what about the plurals? Most of the psalm is corporate: "we ... our ... us". Romans 8:36 quotes Psalm **44:22**, in the context of those who "share in [Christ's] sufferings in order that we may also share in his glory" (Romans 8:17). These people "face death all day long" and do so "for your sake"—that is, for Christ's sake.

So Psalm **44:22** is the key to this psalm. No doubt there were forerunners of the **Pharisees** who sang this psalm in the Old Testament period, just as there were Pharisees who sang it in Jesus' day. But for real believers, the **remnant** in Israel all through the old-covenant period, this was not Pharisaism. And for Christian believers today, this is not Pharisaism. For this psalm expresses Christian experience.

As we pray **verses 1-8**, we too go on trusting the God and Father of Jesus for final victory. We renounce dependency on ourselves. We are confident that the God who gave the people the promised land as an inheritance has an inheritance kept in heaven for us (1 Peter 1:4): an inheritance which will one day come down from heaven to earth and be our resting place, the new creation. We long for that day. There is to be in our discipleship a wistfulness for glory.

> There is to be in our discipleship a wistfulness for glory.

When we sing Psalm **44:9-12**, it reminds us not to be surprised when we too taste defeat as Jesus our leader did. For, as Hans-Joachim Kraus writes, "The signs of the cross already rest on the Old Testament people of God". They rest now on us. We know what it is to be retreating, as churches struggle; to be plundered, as the Christian moral framework is eroded; to be scattered and sold cheap.

**Verses 13-16** help us feel the misery of shame: what it is to be mocked and laughed at. We need to understand shame as seen through biblical spectacles, so that when we take up the cross and experience something of this as followers of Jesus, we understand what is happening to us.

And yet it is not our fault! Since **verse 22** is the punchline and Romans 8 tells us that this is us, presumably we are to sing Psalm **44:17-22**. But how? Romans 8:1 gives us the answer: "There is no condemnation". We have a leader, our representative head, who has indeed faced death on our behalf, to pay the penalty for our sins as our substitute. If we are in him and covered by his atoning death, our sins have been paid for. Nothing we suffer now is a punishment for our sins, for Jesus paid it all. And yet we do expect to suffer—to "face death all day long".

So we take comfort, as we sing Psalm **44:17-22**, in the truth that this is not a punishment for our sins. The psalm teaches us "the revolutionary thought that suffering may be a battle-scar rather than a punishment, the price of loyalty in a world which is at war with God" (Derek Kidner, *Psalms*, Volume 1, page 170).

Furthermore, we resolve that by the Spirit of Jesus, we will have hearts increasingly aligned with what we are in Christ; we remember that we walk and serve in the presence of the one who "knows the secrets of the heart".

And, as the psalm closes, we pray and pray. Our struggles cannot be the end of the story. The story of Jesus ends with resurrection and glory; our story will end with bodily resurrection and life in his glory. The "steadfast love" that closes the psalm is fulfilled, it is guaranteed, and it finds its "Yes!" to us in Jesus (2 Corinthians 1:20).

## Questions for reflection

1. Have you ever experienced suffering or shame for the sake of God's honour?
2. Do you know anyone experiencing that now with whom you could share this psalm?
3. How could you affirm your loyalty to the God of unfailing love this week?

PSALMS 57 AND 59

# 6. THE KING UNDER PRESSURE

After the group of songs from "sons of Korah" (Psalms 42 – 49) followed by one from "Asaph" (Psalm 50), almost all the others in Book II are "of David" (Psalms 51 – 70). All but one of these are also headed "For the director of music". Within this larger group, some smaller groups may be indicated: for example, each of 52 – 55 is called "a maskil" and each of 56 – 60 is called "a miktam". Three of this last group—Psalms 57 – 59—and Psalm 75 share a tune called "Do not destroy". (This may be an allusion to the prayer of Moses after the episode of the **golden calf**: "Sovereign Lord, do not destroy your people" (Deuteronomy 9:26). If so, the survival of the anointed king is implicitly linked to the survival of his people.)

Another link between some of these psalms is that five of them are explicitly connected, in their heading, with events in the early part of King David's life—the long period when he was pursued by **King Saul**. Saul was rejected by God in 1 Samuel 15:23, and David was anointed king (the "anointed one"—"messiah" in Hebrew, "Christ" in Greek) in 1 Samuel 16. But from 1 Samuel 18 to 1 Samuel 31, David was a fugitive—the anointed but unacknowledged king, rather like Aragorn ("Strider") in *The Lord of The Rings*, who is the rightful king of Gondor, but unrecognised until near the end of the drama. There is a sense in which the Lord Jesus is today, in this period between his ascension and his return, the true but unacknowledged King—unacknowledged, that is, except by his church.

The five psalms explicitly connected with this dark period in David's life are:

- Psalm 52 (linked to Doeg in 1 Samuel 22:9)
- Psalm 54 (linked to the Ziphites in 1 Samuel 23:19)
- Psalm 56 (from when David was with the Philistines in 1 Samuel 21:10-15)
- Psalm 57 (probably from David's time in the cave of Adullam, 1 Samuel 22:1-2, although it might be the cave in Engedi in 1 Samuel 24)
- Psalm 59 (from 1 Samuel 19:11)

In this chapter, we consider two of these psalms of the anointed king under pressure. First is Psalm 57: the psalm of the king in the cave.

## But is it true?

"When [David] had fled from Saul into the cave", he knew God had anointed him as king; but now he was a fugitive. Did he wonder if it was all true? Do you ever wonder if the things of God are true? You know—or you are supposed to know—that God is in heaven and supreme; that God is love; that in Jesus you have been given every spiritual blessing; that your sins are forgiven; that you are safe for eternity; that nothing in this life can threaten your eternal safety; that God the Holy Spirit dwells within you. All this you know. And you sing about it. And you rejoice in it. But is it true? On a dark sleepless night when fears crowd in—fears about your health, anxieties about your family, questions about your career or issues in your church—you worry, and it feels so dark. So is it true, in a crowded week when the pressure squeezes you and you wonder how you can possibly get it all done, when financial pressures threaten to break you? Is it true, in a normal secular workplace, as your colleagues have no

> The gap between heavenly realities and earthly pressures can be very wide.

interest in your faith, or mock it, or regard you as odd or—worse—bigoted, and say things to your face or behind your back that hurt? So is it true?

The gap between heaven and earth can be very wide. We know heavenly realities; we experience earthly pressures. Writing about this psalm, James Mays speaks of "the times of trouble, when the distance between the **transcendental** truth of God's rule and the actuality of present history is experienced" (Mays, *Psalms*, page 210). The heavenly reality was signified to King David by the anointing oil in 1 Samuel 16; but his earthly experience as he wrote this psalm was to be hated, hunted and a refugee in a cave.

Three strands are interwoven in David's psalm: the promises of God, the pressures David experiences, and the prayer for glory.

## Trust the promises

The pressures are in the background at the start, as David turns his heart urgently to God. He is in a cave for safety, but it is to "my God" (the God in covenant with him) that he turns for "refuge", and specifically to "the shadow of your wings" (Psalm **57:1**). This may well be an allusion to the wings of the **cherubim** over the ark of the covenant (1 Kings 8:6), symbolising the safety of God's covenant faithfulness (Marvin Tate, *Psalms 51-100*, page 77). He speaks of God as "God Most High" (Psalm **57:2**). (This title was first used of God by **Melchizedek** in Genesis 14:18. The Melchizedek story in Genesis 14 is strongly tied to Jerusalem and also to the covenant with Abraham.) Indeed, there is quite an emphasis in this psalm on the highness of God. It is "from heaven" (Psalm **57:3**) that he must send to save David.

Specifically, David is confident that God will send "his love" (*chesed*, covenant love) and "his faithfulness" (faithfulness to covenant promises) as his agents of rescue sent from high heaven into David's low cave. Mays again: "God ... will send his steadfast love and faithfulness out like agents of a king to do his will" (*Psalms*, page 210). David trusts that that heavenly reality will impact earthly pressure.

It is worth pausing to think about those words "steadfast love" and "faithfulness". The Hebrew word translated as "steadfast love" (here and often in the Old Testament) is often translated into "grace" in the Greek version of the Old Testament, the Septuagint. The words mean the same: God's covenant kindness. And the word "faithfulness" is often translated by the Greek word for "truth" (that is, truthfulness, which is the same as faithfulness). So, when you read "steadfast love and faithfulness", think about "grace and truth". We shall meet this pair of words again in **verse 10**; they are important for understanding this psalm.

## Feel the pressures

The pressures David is facing are intense. Here, they are compared to ravenous predators ("lions ... ravenous beasts", **v 4**), and the psalm focuses especially on what people say, which is life-threatening for it attacks not only David's body but his person, his reputation. People are saying, effectively, *You say you are God's anointed king, but you are not.*

It is worth reflecting on why words can be so dangerous. It is because words affect people's beliefs and therefore their behaviour. What people *said* about David might only have been words; but as those words spread and were believed, any chance of popular support for David evaporated. Perhaps there had been, at the beginning (and especially when David slew **Goliath** and was a successful fighter in Saul's army), a groundswell of support that believed the stories that told of Samuel's anointing of him, and that he was indeed the king of God's own choice. That groundswell of support might have led to David being acclaimed as king. But the more David suffered and the more things went badly for him, the more the rumour mill would surely have put the word around that he was just an unsuccessful imposter. And as people believed that, his support would have rapidly evaporated and his position have become dangerously exposed.

## Pray for glory

The refrain, which comes in **verse 5** and again in **verse 11**, prays first that God will "be exalted ... above the heavens", which means above the sky, to the highest place (notice the emphasis again on God's highness). The second line prays that God's "glory" (the visible manifestation of the invisible God) may "be over all the earth". This is much the same as what we pray in the Lord's Prayer: "Your will be done, on earth as it is in heaven" (Matthew 6:10). David prays that the God who is invisible will make his invisible presence felt on earth, all over the earth. By the end of the psalm we shall see how God will do this.

## Feel, trust, pray (again)

We are back to the pressures in Psalm **57:6**, which are compared now to a hunter's trap, a pit and a net. David is deeply distressed ("bowed down"). But somehow he is confident that by the end of the story, his enemies will "have fallen into it themselves". This is probably the anticipation of faith rather than the recounting of what has already happened.

The confidence of **verse 6b** spills over into an exultant believing response to God's promises. Trusting the unseen reality of the Most High God, David's heart is "steadfast" (**verse 7**), and his mouth sings joyfully (**verse 7-8**). The dawn does not wake him up; no, he is so joyful that he (metaphorically) wakes up the dawn with his glad singing!

David is confident that the day will come when he, the anointed king, will sing the praises of the unseen God "among the nations" (all over the world, **v 9**), because—and here we come back to the wonderful pair of words we met in **verse 3**—his "love" is great, "reaching to the heavens" (notice God's highness again), and his "faithfulness reaches to the skies" (**v 10**). The "grace and truth" of God has reached down from the highest heaven and rests upon the anointed king, hiding out in the cave!

So next, David prays again for the invisible God to make his presence felt all over the earth. Ultimately that can only happen when the anointed king sings the praises of God "among the nations" (**verse 9**).

## Words too big for David

David's words are—not for the first or last time—too big for David's life. He sings of a day when the anointed King will sing the praises of God all over the world. He celebrates the King upon whom "love and faithfulness" (aka "grace and truth") from the highest heaven rest on earth. He sings by the Spirit of the Christ who was to come, the King who would be "full of grace and truth" (John 1:14,17); the King on earth, upon whom the covenant love and faithfulness of God would rest in all its fullness, and in whom all the promises of the covenant would be "Yes!"

This King would know on earth the "cave" experience; indeed, finally the "cave tomb" experience, if that is not pressing the imagery too far. He would be the true anointed King, the Son of God, and yet he would be unrecognised, hated and hunted. Men would use their tongues like "spears and arrows" against him, saying he was an agent of the devil (Matthew 12:24) and an imposter (Matthew 27:41-43). They would set their traps for him (for instance, Matthew 22:15). But he too would trust the promises even as he felt the terrible pressures. He too would pray for the glory of God the Father; he would make the Father known (John 1:18).

But how would he praise God "among the nations"? Romans 15 gives us the answer. Speaking of the worldwide mission of the church of Christ, Romans 15:9-12 quotes various Old Testament texts. The first of these is from Psalm 18:49, where David says, "Therefore I will praise you among the nations; I will sing the praises of your name" (Romans 15:9). This is very similar to Psalm **57:9**: "I will praise you, Lord, among the nations; I will sing of you among the peoples." It is by the missionary lips of his worldwide church that the Lord Jesus, the anointed king, makes the Father known all over the world.

## The roller-coaster of the life of faith

You and I are not David the anointed king; we are certainly not Jesus the Christ! But here is where we fit in. Back in 1 Samuel 22, there was a group of people with David in the cave of Adullam: "All those in distress or in debt or discontented gathered round him, and he became their commander. About four hundred men were with him" (1 Samuel 22:2). What an unimpressive group: a rabble of no-hopers! But they were the friends of the king, and in that lay their hope—and in that lies our hope too. You and I are not the king; but we are friends of the king, with him (as it were) in the cave. We too are no-hopers: unimpressive men and women whose only hope for this life and for eternity is our connection to the king.

We believe that Jesus is the one upon whom the "love and faithfulness" of God rests in all its fullness; to know that love and faithfulness, that grace and truth, we must be joined to the king, for it is in him, and in him alone, that these things are to be known upon earth. We too, as his church under pressure, feel with him; the troubles of Psalm **57:4** and **6**. We too trust that the covenant promises of the Father to the Son are ours in Christ. We too pray that the Father's will may be done on earth even as it is done in heaven. Like **Paul and Silas** singing hymns in their prison "cave" (Acts 16:25—Geoffrey Grogan makes this connection in *Psalms,* page 113), we may sing as we look forward to the day when the king, through his church, will have proclaimed the praise of God the Father in all the earth.

One thing this psalm reveals to us (or reminds us of) is that the life of faith is something of a roller-coaster. As we sing Psalm **57:1-5**, we may feel a sense that the pressures of **verse 4** have been poured out to God in the believing prayers of **verses 1-3** and the climactic prayer for the glory of God in **verse 5**. We might even think that there has been a resolution. And yet in **verse 6** we are immediately plunged back into the darkest pressures of the king in the cave. Although there is perhaps some progress—there is a stronger sense of joyful confidence in **verses 7-10** than there has been in the first half of the psalm—nonetheless the prayer of **verse 5** has to be prayed again in **verse 11**, and no doubt will be prayed again and again until the Lord Jesus returns. The strange paradoxical mix of dark pressures and confident faith is a tension of Christian experience which we should be careful not to allow to dissolve, resulting either in despair (the pressures without the faith) or in triumphalism (the confidence without the pressures). No—dark pressures and confident faith can co-exist, and we should expect them to, until the King returns in all his glory to erase the former and vindicate the latter.

## Questions for reflection

1. What makes you doubt whether what you believe is true?
2. What helps you to have faith in God's grace and truth?
3. "Dark pressures and confident faith can co-exist, and we should expect them to, until the King returns in all his glory". How do you respond to this idea?

## PART TWO

What do you expect the life of faith to feel like? You may be someone who thinks feelings are irrelevant to a mature Christian life; or you may be someone who worries a lot about how you feel. For both "types", this is a necessary and important question.

It matters for the person who is very wary of their feelings. It is possible to have what passes for "faith" but which is actually just cognitive processes—an intellectual understanding or assent that does not engage the whole person. (In church history, this happened with a curious group called the Sandemanians.)

It is also important for the assurance of those of us who rely too much on our feelings. The "wrong" feelings may lead us to worry that we are not true believers. It is significant for our stability, lest we be unsettled by some of the feelings that assail us. It matters for evangelism, so that we "put on the tin" only what is to be found in the realistic experience of following Jesus.

Psalm 59, the psalm of the king under threat of death, will help us both know and feel for ourselves the strangely paradoxical experience of following Jesus our king. This psalm shares with Psalms 57 and 58 the same author (David), the same designation ("a miktam") and the same tune ("Do not destroy"). Psalms 57 and 59 each have a heading linking them to the period when David was anointed king but was still hunted by King Saul. It may well be that Psalm 58 also comes from that period, although we cannot be sure.

Psalm 59 comes from the time when "Saul had sent men to watch David's house in order to kill him". A short version of the story is found in 1 Samuel 19:11-17. It is worth meditating on just how terrifying this must have been. Being used to thrillers in which the hero is trapped in a house by heavily armed men determined to kill him, we take it for granted that David will survive. And indeed we can read on and see how he would escape. But this was real life. Saul's men knew where David was; he had nowhere to run and no place to hide. They did not want to arrest him; they were determined "to kill him". He was in mortal danger. He did not know he would escape. It was all very well to have been anointed king by the prophet Samuel (1 Samuel 16); but at any moment it could have all ended in tears, before his reign had even begun.

Before we sing the psalm with David, it is important, as so often, to remember that this is a song of the king. At least three features of the psalm highlight this. First, there are references to "the nations" (the rest of the world) in **Psalm 59:5** and **8**, and to "the ends of the earth" in **verse 13**; this grand scale of drama makes sense for the king, but it is an overstatement for "my" personal experience. Second, in **verse 8**, the laughter of God echoes the mocking laughter of God in Psalm 2, directed there—as here—against the enemies of the king. Third, in **verse 5** the enemies are called "traitors", and treachery applies supremely to a betrayal of God's king, since betrayal of the king threatens the whole order and security of the people. Although those who do this are called "the nations", and are therefore outsiders to the people of God, we know from Psalm 2 that God's chosen king has been given authority over the whole world. There is a sense in which hostility to God's king is always a form of treachery, both to God and to his king.

## An oscillating structure

Unusually, this psalm has two contrasting refrains. In **59:9-10a** and again in **verse 17**, there is an expression of confidence. In **verse 6** and **verse 14** there is a repetition of threat. Although the themes of the psalm are interwoven, it is probably simplest to let these refrains shape our perception of the structure.

**Verses 1-10** are punctuated by threat (**v 6-7**) and conclude with confidence (**v 9-10**). **Verses 11-17** are substantially parallel to **verses 1-10**, being again punctuated by threat (**v 14-15**) and concluding with confidence (**v 17**).

As we go through these, I think the psalm will teach us two things:

- We will learn to shiver at the lurking threat of evil. This will help us feel more deeply the harder part of walking in the footsteps of Jesus our King.
- We will be taught to pray confidently for the visible victory of God's King. Following Jesus is a paradoxical experience: it is hard now, but it will end with his victory and ours!

## Threat and confidence

There is an urgent crescendo of intensity in David's prayer in the four lines of **verses 1** and **2**. In **verse 1a**, there are "enemies"; in **verse 1b**, these enemies are actively "attacking" him; in **verse 2a**, they are characterised as morally evil; and in **verse 2b**, we learn again what the superscription has told us—that they are "after [his] blood". This prayer gets more and more urgent. The stakes could not be higher. If they kill the king, then evil triumphs (for they are "evildoers"), and how then will God govern the world as he has promised?

The intensity continues in **verses 3** and **4**. These mortally hostile evildoers "lie in wait for me" (**v 3**). Not only do they attack (**v 1b**) with intent to kill (**v 2b**); they are lurking in the shadows, waiting to ambush David, to catch him the moment he tries to escape. These who watch for King David are, he says, "fierce men" (**v 3**)—very powerful and violent, and they are plural (there are many men against one man). He is surrounded. There is no way out.

This has been the regular experience of the anointed king and the king's loyal people. From the beginning to the end of his public ministry, the Lord Jesus knew what it was to have enemies who "watched him closely" and "were looking for a reason to accuse" him (Mark 3:2): who were "keeping a close watch on him" and "hoped to catch Jesus in something he said, so that they might hand him over to the power and authority of the governor" (Luke 20:20). His **apostle** Paul was trapped inside the walls of Damascus because "day and night" his enemies "kept close watch on the city gates in order to kill him" (Acts 9:24).

The new truth that David introduces in **Psalm 59:3-4** is his own innocence. Like the Lord Jesus after him, he is guilty of "no offence or sin ... no wrong". His cry, that God will "arise", is the cry that accompanied God leading his people into battle with the ark of the covenant (Numbers 10:35). David can plead "Arise!" because he is in covenant with this God, and he is righteous. He is not asking God to do something arbitrary; he calls upon God to do justice.

Although Psalm **59:5** seems to reiterate the same themes, the canvas has broadened. The God upon whom David calls is addressed (unusually for Book II) as the "LORD God Almighty", which means "the covenant God who is the God of very large armies" (in older translations, "the LORD God of hosts"). What David needs is not a little local help; he needs all the armies of heaven to intervene for him. The reason he needs this is that "all the nations" are involved in this plot to kill him, in the sense that Saul's plot to kill David is a manifestation in time and space of the cosmic hostility of all powerful people on earth towards the covenant God and his anointed king—the plotting described so vividly in Psalm 2:1-3. This may look like the local drama of one hunted man; it is in fact a cosmic battle.

Psalm **59:6-7** ought to arouse in us a visceral sense of terror. As the light fades, "at evening" these evildoers "return"; we picture them taking up their hidden guard posts around the house. They are human, but they behave like "snarling ... dogs" which "prowl" (**v 6**). Centuries later, Jesus would say to his enemies, "This is your hour—when darkness reigns" (Luke 22:53).

There is something subhuman, inhumane, beastly and terrifying about David's enemies. And—as we saw in Psalm 57—what David finds particularly frightening is what they say (**59:7**). Their foaming, quasi-canine mouths spew words that are as "sharp as swords" in their destructive power. And they are so confident: "Who can hear us?" they taunt, like muggers saying to a victim, "We have your phone; there is no point calling for help; no one is listening." *There is no God who sees or hears*. Like **Cain** after murdering **Abel**, they have no idea that the blood of their innocent victims will cry out for justice (Genesis 4:10).

And yet David knows that this is a Psalm 2 battle. Which is why, in Psalm **59:8**, he can assert with quiet confidence that God in heaven "laugh[s] at them" and scoffs at "those nations"—the worldwide rebellion against God's king of which they are the local and time-bound representatives.

And so the first cycle concludes (**v 9-10**) with the first confident refrain. David may be trapped and surrounded in his house; but—since he is the covenant king—that house is like a "fortress" for him so long as God is with him. The word "fortress" occurs in **verses 1**, **9**, **16** and **17**. His house may feel like a prison, but God is his fortress. He can rely on his God, who will give him the victory.

The second cycle begins with a surprising prayer (**v 11-13**). The king asks that God will "not kill them" (**v 11**)—which, as we shall see, means to not kill them quietly or discreetly. Suppose David's enemies were just to "disappear": what then? No one would know just why their threat was ended. People would "forget". *No,* David says to God: *Will you "uproot them … bring them down … consume them in your wrath", so that "it will be known to the ends of the earth that God rules over Jacob"* (**v 13**)*?* Somehow the defeat of the king's enemies needs to be clear, public and unambiguous. The conclusion that onlookers must draw is "that God rules"—that Psalm 2 is true. And this must become known "to the ends of the earth"; there must be such a public defeat that all the world can understand it (see Willem A. VanGemeren, *Psalms: Expositor's Bible Commentary,* Volume 5, page 474).

The defeat of the king's enemies needs to be clear, public and unambiguous, such that all the world can understand it.

We naturally respond with horror to the strength of this language. It seems bloodthirsty and shocking. It is important to remember that this is not talking about personal revenge. What is at stake here is the rule of God's king. When David first prayed this, we must trust that what mattered to him, as a man filled with the Holy Spirit, was not his personal success, let alone the defeat of people he happened not to like. No, he cared supremely about the victory of God's king, because the victory of the God he loved was inseparably concerned with the victory of the king. This concern of David finds its pure fulfilment in the yearning of Jesus, who is God's final King, that in his victory his Father's glory will be lifted high. If we pray these words, we need to have firmly in our minds the final victory of Jesus in the conversion of many, yes, but also in the judgment of God upon those who will not finally repent.

The death of King Saul, the unification of the kingdom under King David, and the subsequent victories of King David, would all have gone some way to achieving this public defeat of the enemies of God's anointed king, in a provisional sense. But the New Testament teaches us that the final public victory was achieved at the cross of Jesus Christ. It was there that Jesus "disarmed the powers and authorities [and] made a public spectacle of them, triumphing over them by the cross" (Colossians 2:15). When the perfect King is surrounded, hounded, done to death and then raised bodily from the dead, the whole universe can know that sin and death have lost their sting, and all the powers of evil have been defeated.

But back in our psalm, it is sobering to reflect that the lurking threat returns in Psalm **59:14-15**. By the end of **verse 13**, the tone has become quite upbeat: there is a steady confidence that "God rules over Jacob" and will make his rule visible in the vindication of the king and the defeat of the king's enemies. But now, again, "they return at evening" (**v 14**), just as before. The short account in 1 Samuel 19:11-12 suggests that the drama lasted only one night. It may be that this abbreviates the full story, or it may be that the psalm reflects the psychological reality that threat is rarely removed in one fell swoop in the world in which David lived, and in which we still live, before the dawn of the age to come. The roller-coaster of fear and faith must go up to the heights and then down to the depths more than once in the life of faith.

There is a slightly different angle on the nature of the threat in Psalm **59:15**. In **verse 7**, the sharp words of David's enemies were the focus. Here in **verse 15** it is their insatiability. Like ever-hungry dogs, they "howl if not satisfied". And they never will be satisfied until they have David dead. Nothing less will do. So long as God's king lives, their rebellious hearts can never be quiet; they will always have the appetite for more hostility. It was the same with Jesus: "Crucify him!" was the only demand that his enemies made. It is the same today with the persecuted church of Christ; nothing less than the removal of all things truly Christian will satisfy a hostile world. Of course, when the church is not truly Christian, the world may be very satisfied, for they need not oppose a church that is assimilated to their own values. But when the church follows their king faithfully, mortal hostility is assured.

Just as the first cycle ended with confidence (**v 8-10**), so the second concludes with a song of God's "love" (covenant love) and the security of being in his "fortress" (twice in **verses 16-17**). The final words, "my God on whom I can rely", echo precisely the first line of **verse 10**. They were words spoken and believed by Jesus, who truly believed that he could rely on the saving power of God his Father. They are words that we, his people, may echo with great confidence in him. Whatever the lurking pressures of evil threatening us, God our Father is for us in Jesus; he is the God upon whom we can most surely rely.

## For days of darkness

As we sing this psalm, we too follow our King in learning to shiver at the lurking threat of evil. There are days of darkness: times of "evening" when the powers of evil are especially near—when the evil one, or the world that shares his values, or our own troubled **fleshly nature** "return[s] at evening" to threaten us afresh. We hear in this psalm their snarls; we see them prowling around; we shiver with fear, and we are right to do so. For not to shiver is to take evil lightly, and we must never do that. The Lord Jesus knew what it was to have a "troubled" soul (for instance, John 12:27) and to sweat drops of blood in the shadow of the cross (Luke 22:44).

But Jesus did not stop there, and we must never stop there. For, just as we sing the dark refrain of threat (Psalm **59:6-7**, **14-15**), so we must sing the believing refrain of confidence (**v 9-10**, **16-17**). Jesus our King was right to trust the covenant promises, to entrust himself to the One who judges justly (1 Peter 2:23), just as David his forefather had trusted. In union with Christ our King, we too may trust that every one of those promises guarantees that God will be a "fortress" to us, as he was to David, and to Jesus.

## Questions for reflection

1. How much do you think and speak about the difficulties of following Jesus? Do you think you should do so more or less often?
2. While being honest about days of darkness, how can you also make sure you are clear about the confidence you have in Christ?
3. Do you think you are as passionate as the psalmist about the rule of God's King?

PSALMS 65 AND 67

# 7. SONGS OF CREATION

Each of Psalms 65 – 68 is headed both "a psalm" and "a song". Whatever these designations mean precisely (and we don't know), the fact that they share these in their headings may indicate that they are in some way to be read together. Something else they share is at least a partial focus on universality. For example, Psalm 65 speaks of "the whole earth" (**v 8**), Psalm 66 begins, "Shout for joy to God, all the earth!" (66:1), Psalm 67 speaks of God's salvation becoming known "among all nations" (67:2) and Psalm 68 appeals to "the kingdoms of the earth" to sing to God (68:32). I have chosen two of this group to illustrate some of the ways in which the Psalms relate the **doctrine** of redemption to the doctrine of creation. Other psalms that engage particularly with creation include Psalms 8, 19, 74, 104 and 148.

## A contemporary challenge

What possible relevance does the gospel of Christ have to a generation who care about saving the planet? Many people are commendably idealistic about responsible **stewardship** of the earth, but they cannot see how the very particular message about Christ can have anything of importance to say to them. How do we speak to them? Psalm 65 will help us.

The psalm divides naturally into three parts, each of which concludes with something about the response to the things described. So **65:1-4** ends with a satisfied people; **verses 5-8** result in the whole earth being filled with awe; and the end of **verses 9-13** closes the psalm with an idyllic picture of harvest blessing.

But here is the puzzle: by the time we reach **verses 9-13**, this psalm feels like a simple harvest festival song, rather like those old hymns "All things bright and beautiful" and "We plough the fields and scatter". It is about creation blessings. And yet **verses 1-4** are very particular—they focus on Zion, prayer, forgiveness of sins and the temple. They concern a redeemed people. So what is the connection between a good harvest and matters of redemption? Did not other nations sometimes enjoy good harvests? Presumably they did, for God "causes his sun to rise on the evil and the good, and sends rain on the righteous and the unrighteous" (Matthew 5:45). We shall grapple with this important question as we read the psalm.

## A satisfied people

"Zion"—the place of God's king and God's presence in the temple—is where "praise *awaits*" God (**Psalm 65:1**, my italics). This (not easily translatable) phrase probably means either that "praise is *due* to you" (NRSV)—that is, this is where people *ought* to praise God—or that Zion is the place where God's people are always looking for any opportunity to praise him for his goodness. Old-covenant believers made "vows", pledges to offer sacrifices of thanksgiving when prayer was answered, and these would be "fulfilled" precisely because the God to whom they prayed was the one "who answers prayer". I*t is because you answer prayer,* the psalmist says, *that "all [kinds of] people … come" to you* (**v 2**).

The obstacle to prayers is never the unwillingness of God, for God is gracious and kind; it is our unforgiven sins. As Isaiah expressed it:

"Surely the arm of the LORD is not too short to save,
nor his ear too dull to hear.
But your iniquities have separated
you from your God;

your sins have hidden his face from you,
so that he will not hear." (Isaiah 59:1-2)

Psalm **65:3** therefore faces the obstacle ("we were overwhelmed with sins") and rejoices in the removal of the obstacle ("you forgave our transgressions"). Sin is described as overwhelming, for it is a heavy burden, both of guilt and of misery. As a result of forgiven sins, God will hear and answer prayers. These people account themselves so very blessed (**v 4a**) because they are those whom the covenant God has graciously chosen to "bring near", giving them access to him in the temple ("your courts").

**Verse 4b** sums up the response of the people of God to the kindness of God in forgiving sins, hearing prayer and bringing them near to him: "We are filled [satisfied] with the good things"—all the blessings signified and promised to the people of God in the old covenant through the temple. Here is a celebration of glad fullness, of deep satisfaction given by the covenant blessings of forgiven sins, heard prayer, and access into the presence of God.

King David leads his people in glad words of satisfaction in all that the old covenant promises to the believing people of God. Yet all this joy, real as it was, is but a foretaste of the joys granted to the people of the King under the new covenant. All that Zion foreshadowed is fulfilled in Christ the King, the Son of David (for the strong connection between King David and Zion, see 2 Samuel 5:7-9; for Christ as the Son of David, see Romans 1:3; Matthew 1:1, 9:27; and in many other places in the Gospels), Christ the "temple" (John 2:19-22) who, literally, "**tabernacled** among us" (John 1:14), Christ the sacrifice (Hebrews 7:27), and Christ the priest (Hebrews 5:1-10). When new-covenant believers sing Psalm 57:1-4, our hearts are filled with joyful satisfaction in all the blessings given to us through Christ. Christ is the King whose prayers are always heard (John 11:41-42), and in whose name the prayers of his followers are to be prayed. He is the one who brings his people near to God (1 Peter 3:18). In him dwells all the fullness of **deity**, and his people are brought into the blessings of that fullness in him (Colossians 1:19; 2:9-10).

The words "all people" (literally "all flesh", Psalm **65:2b**) give a hint of a worldwide blessing. And so the horizon of the song widens.

## Calling to a troubled world

The music transitions from redemption towards creation in a remarkable way. The "answer" to prayers celebrated in **verse 2** is expanded from **verse 5**: "You answer us with awesome and righteous deeds"—that is, with deeds which replace disorder with order. These are deeds performed on a grand scale, for they bring "hope" to "all the ends of the earth and ... the farthest seas". They are creation-wide deeds.

These works of God are spoken of positively in **verse 6** and negatively in **verse 7**. The "awesome and righteous deeds" of **verse 5** focus in **verse 6** on the formation or establishment of the "mountains". In biblical imagery, mountains speak of strength, solidity, unshakeability; they picture not only the material stability of creation but the underlying moral order: what **theologians** sometimes call "creation order". The formation of the mountains in this wide symbolic sense is the necessary flip side of **verse 7**. This Creator "stilled the roaring of the seas". Just as the mountains symbolise moral order, the seas speak of chaos, instability, evil, threat and ultimately death. All this is expressed in history in "the turmoil of the nations":the chaos and evil that run amok in human affairs.

What God is doing in redemption is inseparably connected with what he was doing in creation.

The drama of Genesis 1, in which dry land is established between the waters above the sky and the waters beneath—a place in which human and animal life can survive—is the drama of life in the midst of danger, of stability in the midst of chaos. To say that God answers prayer (Psalm **65:2**, **5**) by forming the mountains and stilling the roaring seas is a vivid creation-wide way of affirming that the Creator will not allow his good creation finally to be overrun by evil. What he is doing in redemption (**v 1-4**)—calling out a people, forgiving their sins, answering their prayers, drawing them close to him in Zion, and all of this fulfilled in Christ—is inseparably connected with what he was doing in creation; for he is redeeming the whole created order in Christ. There is a profound link between creation and redemption. The redemption of the people of God in Christ will find its ultimate fulfilment in the redemption of the whole created order (see, for example, Romans 8:19-21).

It is because of this magnificent scope of redemption that Psalm **65:8** can rejoice that "the whole earth" is filled with awe [literally "fear"—reverent awe] at your wonders". What God is doing through his people, who are now the church of Christ, is not a little local or personal rescue mission, confined to some ghetto; it is the beginning of the restoration of order in a broken world. The expression "where morning dawns, where evening fades" is literally "the outgoing of the morning and evening". At one level it speaks of the far east (from where the sunrise comes out) to the far west (where the sun goes out when it sets) and is a poetic way of reinforcing the first line of **verse 8** ("The whole earth"). But the words "morning" and "evening" carry associations that are more evocative than that. "Morning" has associations with happy times and "evening" with sad times. In whatever place, and in whatever state, whether it be a "morning" time of joy or an "evening" time of sadness, the good news of the Creator, who is also the Redeemer, can "call forth" from our hearts "songs of joy". In **verses 5-8** the people of God, who are satisfied by all the covenant mercies fulfilled in Christ (**v 1-4**), call out to a troubled world with a message of the good Creator, who sets limits to evil and will finally overcome evil with good through the Saviour, who has made atonement for sins and forgives sinners.

This helps us put the harvest song at the end of the psalm into its wider biblical perspective.

## Creation will be restored

**Verses 9-13** paint an idyllic picture of **harvest home**. The chaotic waters of evil are changed into life-giving waters of rainfall and irrigation, which lead to an abundance of food (**v 9**). Water now appears as "the streams of God"—like the rivers in Genesis 2 around the garden in Eden, or the river flowing out of **Ezekiel**'s visionary temple (Ezekiel 47). Together with Psalm **65:10**, **verse 9** fills our sights with such an abundance of life-giving water that the harvest then described in **verses 11-13** is overwhelmingly wonderful.

The whole "year" is "crown[ed]" with God's "bounty" (**v 11**). The "carts" (or wagon tracks of the harvesting wagons) are strewn with the superabundance of grain that seems to overflow everywhere (**v 10b**). There is corn all over the place—too much to collect it all! Even the "grasslands" of the usually barren "wilderness" areas, the higher ground of the "hills", "overflow" with crops (**v 12**). The "flocks" of sheep (**v 13a**) are so numerous that they look like a garment clothing the meadows. What a beautiful picture: you look out over a meadow and it seems to have a thick woollen coat over it! In the same way "the valleys are mantled with corn", wearing corn all over them like a dress (**v 13b**)—no wonder there is "joy" and singing all over the world (**v 13c**)! As the old hymn "To thee, O Lord, our hearts we raise" puts it:

*Bright robes of gold the fields adorn,*
*The hills with joy are ringing,*
*The valleys stand so thick with corn*
*That even they are singing.*

The picture has an aesthetic wonder. But it is more deeply providential. It is not just that it *looks* lovely; the main joy is that it will provide food to sustain life. This is more about the Department of Agriculture than the National Trust or National Park Service.

Here are three appropriate responses from the people of God to this beautiful psalm.

## Appreciation, anticipation and proclamation

Zion is the place where the psalmists praise the good Creator (**v 1**). Since Zion is so closely associated with King David, there is a sense in which Zion finds its fulfilment in Christ and the church of Christ. We do not take creation blessings for granted. We are thankful. We acknowledge and we appreciate that all these things come from the kind hand of God. We will give thanks to him (Romans 1:21).

The opposite attitude occurs at least twice on the lips of proud kings in the Old Testament. One of the Pharaohs of ancient Egypt says, "The Nile belongs to me; I made it for myself" (Ezekiel 29:3): *It is mine to use as and how I please. Put me first; make me great.* The Assyrian king says something very similar when he declares that all the trees of Lebanon and its waters and natural resources are his to use (and abuse) (2 Kings 19:23-24). Again, it is an attitude of "Put me first; make me great." By contrast, the people of God will steward the created order with loving care and thankful hearts.

The promised land in the old covenant, whose harvest is celebrated here, was called the "inheritance" of the people of God. The New Testament takes that "inheritance" language and shows us that it points forward to the new Jerusalem, the new heavens and new earth, the new creation (for example, Acts 20:32; 1 Peter 1:4). As a believer thanks God for a good harvest, he or she grasps that it will never be perfect in this age. Always it is in "bondage to decay" (Romans 8:21). It is a foretaste of a greater restored creation yet to be given us—the appetising whiff of delicious cooking that speaks of a wonderful meal yet to be enjoyed. As we sing this psalm, we thank God for material blessings in this age; but we have our eyes and hearts fixed on the blessings of the age to come. The Christian life is one of anticipation of great glories to come.

When we join in singing or saying this psalm, we proclaim the great truths of which it speaks. And we sing of these truths as they have found their fulfilment in Jesus Christ. We declare that all the blessings of God come to us through Christ, who is foreshadowed in the things of Zion (Psalm **65:1-4**). We sing that it is by Christ that sins are forgiven, prayer is heard, and we are given access to God. Men and women enjoy many blessings of God's **common grace** in this age, whether or not they trust in Christ. The heavenly Father causes his sun to rise on the evil and the good, and sends rain on the righteous and the unrighteous (Matthew 5:45). Sometimes indeed the wicked do prosper. But their prosperity will always be spoiled. Life "under the sun" will always be tainted by the frustration of which Ecclesiastes speaks, and be in bondage to decay (Romans 8:21). When we say this psalm, we declare that only in Christ will we find atonement for sins, answered prayer, every spiritual blessing, and finally a place in the new heavens and new earth. In Christ, and only in Christ, all things in heaven and earth will be brought to unity (Ephesians 1:10). He is the **second Adam**. He is the Lamb who died for sinners. He is for us "wisdom from God—that is, our righteousness, holiness and redemption" (1 Corinthians 1:30). The "Zion" of Psalm **65:1-4** is fulfilled in Christ; for the Christ whom Zion foreshadows is the only hope for a troubled world (as in **verses 5-8**), and for the joyful prospect of unspoiled abundance (as in **verses 9-13**).

## Questions for reflection

1. How does this psalm help you to relate the message about Christ to friends' concern about the planet and environment?
2. What things in God's creation fill you with awe?
3. How have you seen God restoring order and blessing to the world around you?

## PART TWO

Psalm 67 celebrates the attractive power of grace. When God works in his kindness to bless a people, others will see the beauty of God's kindness; some of them will be stirred to desire what they see. The purpose of the psalm is stated and repeated: "... *so that* your ways may be known on earth ... *so that* all the ends of the earth will fear him" (**67:2**, **7**, my italics). The whole purpose of this psalm is that there will be praise of God's saving grace from men and women all over the world. In this way the promise to Abraham (Genesis 12:1-3) will be fulfilled.

Just as Psalm 65 was a harvest song, so is Psalm 67 ("The land yields its harvest", **v 6**). In Psalms 65 and 66 the logic of grace has been sung: that when the rest of the earth see the covenant people rejoicing in the covenant kindness of God, some of them will be attracted to what they see.

Psalm 67 has a nicely balanced symmetrical A-B-C-B'-A' structure (see VanGemeren, *Psalms*, Volume 5, page 510). At either end of the psalm, **verses 1-2** and then **verses 6-7** are prayers that God will bless his people in order that the rest of the world may come to know his ways (**v 2**) and be drawn to fear him with reverent worship (**v 7**). Inside this come the refrains in **verse 3** and **verse 5**. **Verse 4** is the heart of the psalm, and the only three-line verse.

### Bless us so as to bless the world

The prayer in **verses 1-2** begins with a request ("May God...") and ends with a reason ("so that..."). The prayer is for the grace (undeserved favour) and blessing that is given to people upon whom God's "face" shines—that is, a people who are in right relationship with him. This echoes the blessing God gave Moses, which he was to instruct the priests to use over the people of Israel. I have indicated in italics the words echoed in **verse 1** of this psalm:

"The LORD *bless* you and keep you;
the LORD *make his face shine on* you and *be gracious* to you;

the LORD turn *his face* towards you and give you peace."

(Numbers 6:24-26)

It matters that this is the priestly blessing. It is given to a covenant people whose sins have been covered by the atoning sacrifice offered by a mediator (the priest). This is not just asking God to be generally nice and kind to us; it is pleading for the blessings given to those in covenant relationship with God. Many of us know in human relationships the terrible experience of someone who will not look us in the eye, who will not look at us at all, who averts their face, and in whose expression towards us we never see anything other than a frown or a scowl. All that speaks eloquently of a troubled or broken relationship. How wonderful when there is a smile, a glad look into the eyes, a warm embrace. That is what is being prayed for here. This is not a request for blessings for the sake of blessings, but blessings in the context of a delightful relationship with the God who loves us.

The reason for praying for these blessings is not—rather surprisingly—so that we will feel good, enjoy life or have joy and happiness. It is so that the "ways" of God may be "known on earth". His "ways" mean his character expressed in his actions: what he does because of who he is. As Paul will later write, it means "love, joy, peace, forbearance, kindness, goodness, faithfulness, gentleness and self-control" (Galatians 5:22); for these are the ways of God. These ways are the evidence of his "salvation" being at work in a people. A people who are experiencing the saving grace of God will have all their relationships shaped by these beautiful virtues, because their hearts are filled with God's kindness.

It is important to grasp the logic: the grace of God poured out on us in blessing makes us a people in whom the gracious ways of God become visible to all the world. In the old covenant, there was a lovely vision that Israel would be the visible image of the invisible God, so that when the **Moabites, Edomites, Hittites, Philistines** and so on looked at Israel, they would see the gracious ways of the true God writ large and beautiful in the character and national life of God's people.

The reality, sadly, was different. But this logic lies behind the promise in the covenant to Abraham: that "all peoples on earth will be blessed through you" (Genesis 12:3). It perhaps becomes more evident when that promise is repeated in Genesis 18: "Abraham will surely become a great and powerful nation, and all nations on earth will be blessed through him. For I have chosen him, so that he will direct his children and his household after him to keep the *way* of the LORD by *doing what is right and just*, so that the LORD will bring about for Abraham what he has promised him" (Genesis 18:18-19, my italics). The other nations will be blessed when the family of Abraham "keep the way of the LORD by doing what is right and just." It is this logic of overflowing blessing that lies behind this psalm.

## May the world respond with praise

That the cry of Psalm **67:1-2** is not a self-centred prayer of "please bless us to make us feel good" is made clear by the longing expressed in the refrain of **verse 3**. What we most deeply desire—or the yearning that this psalm plants in our hearts—is that "the peoples" (shorthand for all the nations or ethnic groups on earth) will "praise you, God". The reason the world is so desperately out of joint is because men and women offer disordered worship to idols; this is why moral disorder spoils the world so sadly and pervasively (Romans 1:18-32). At root is the terrible diagnosis that by nature human beings "neither glorified [God] as God nor gave thanks to him" (Romans 1:21). The yearning expressed in Psalm **67:3** is that "the peoples" will at last praise the good Creator who made them.

> We must never be satisfied—never cease singing this song—until *all* the peoples praise our king.

The second half of the verse intensifies our desire. Not only do we long that "the peoples" will praise God; we must never be satisfied—

never cease singing this song—until "*all* the peoples" (my italics) praise him. We shall never be content with the praise from the hearts of the church of Christ until, all over the world, there is a countless multitude of every tribe and tongue, "every creature in heaven and on earth and under the earth and on the sea" joining in that praise (Revelation 5:13). That day will come in the new heavens and new earth, when impenitent sinners will be no more, for they will be finally excluded and banished to outer darkness.

## He rules, he guides

Psalm **67:4** lies at the heart and the centre of the psalm. It is the only three-line verse. The key word is "for". This verse gives the reason why the rest of the world should praise God: because ("for") the reality is that he governs the world with "equity" (justice) and guides the nations. That is, he is the God who is sovereign (he "guides") and fair ("equity"). We pray that the nations will understand this and so "be glad and sing for joy".

In some way God's blessing of Israel had to demonstrate this. Israel had to be the living visual aid for the rest of the world that exhibited the beautiful providential sovereignty and government of God that brings moral order and life to a needy world. When the rest of the world looked at the people of God—the way they cared for their land, the way they cared for the poor, the way they loved one another, the overflowing love they had for the immigrant, the moral order in their respect for marriage, the contentedness that was so different from the covetousness all around—then the rest of the world would grasp that there is a good, just, kind, moral, ordered God who is sovereign and working out his purposes in a disordered world.

## The harvest

**Verse 5** repeats the refrain of **verse 3**, emphasising in our hearts, as we sing it, that the goal and longing of this psalm is worldwide praise of our good God. As Mays puts it, "The blessing of the church is for the salvation of the nations" (*Psalms,* page 225).

**Verses 6-7** reiterate the logic introduced in **verses 1-2**. But they do so specifically with reference to "harvest": "The [promised] land yields its harvest". This is the particular way that "God ... blesses us". In the old covenant, the blessings given to the people who were faithful to the covenant are often expressed in terms of harvest. Perhaps Deuteronomy 28:1-14 is the clearest place in which we see how these blessings were promised. They included "the crops of your land and the young of your livestock—the calves of your herds and the lambs of your flocks" (Deuteronomy 28:4, see also verses 5, 8, 11, 12); as a consequence, "all the peoples on earth will see that you are called by the name of the LORD" (v 10). Covenant faithfulness resulted in covenant harvest blessings that would lead to worldwide visibility for the covenant graciousness of the Creator God, who was the covenant God of Israel.

The people of God therefore prayed for such covenant blessings "*so that* all the ends of the earth [would] fear him" (Psalm **67:7**, my italics). There is a play on the word translated "earth" (**v 2**, **7**) and "land" (**v 6**); what was to happen in the "land" (the promised land) demonstrated something that applies in all the "earth". It shows that when a people live in faithful covenant with the good Creator, they will be blessed. This psalm is a celebration of the blessings of covenant faithfulness.

And therein lies a problem—for Israel was not faithful.

## He did what they did not

To pray Psalm 67 in a Christian way, it is vital to grasp that the blessings being prayed for ("bless us", **v 1**; "blesses us", **v 6**; "bless us", **v 7**), and celebrated, are covenant blessings. The old-covenant logic is that when "the peoples" (**v 3**) or "the nations" (**v 4**: that is, the rest of the world) saw the people of Israel, the old-covenant "church" or "congregation" or "assembly" (for example Acts 7:38) being blessed with rich harvests in the promised land, they too would join in the praise of the God of Israel.

The problem is that this beautiful ideal is not at all what Old Testament history records for us when it comes to the life of the old-covenant people. Sadly, they were just like us—greedy, unjust, lustful and so on. It becomes clear by the time we reach the end of the Old Testament that these were no more than foreshadowings of a better covenant yet to be given. These promises could reach their fulfilment only when an anointed man did what Israel was called but failed to do: to live in consistent faithfulness to the God of the covenant and to make the ways of God the Father known on earth (Psalm **67:2a**; see John 1:18; Luke 2:29-32). In this man—and this man alone—all the covenant blessings are to be found. All blessings—"every spiritual blessing"—is found in Christ (Ephesians 1:3). The expression "spiritual blessing" does not mean some kind of floaty immaterial blessing, but rather, all the blessings that come to us by the Holy Spirit. They include, in the end, all the material and substantial blessings of the new creation, foreshadowed for us in Old Testament Israel's harvests. Derek Kidner writes that this psalm looks outwards "to the distant peoples and to what awaits them when the blessing that has reached 'us' reaches all" (*Psalms,* Volume 1, page 236).

When we pray this psalm in Christ, we long that God will so bless us his people in Christ, with these spiritual blessings—and above all with the godliness that is consistent with God's "equity"—that others, as they see the beauty of this blessing, will be moved to join in the praise of this great God. We sing our repeated and passionate petition: that we shall be so soaked in the kindness of God that all the world will see in our lives the "ways" of this good God.

John Calvin said this psalm is…

"… a prayer for a blessing upon the church, that besides being preserved in a state of safety in Judea, it might be enlarged to a new and unprecedented extent."

(*Commentary on the Book of Psalms*, Volume 3, page 1)

The answer to that prayer has begun to be seen over past centuries as the church has spread throughout the world. May it continue to be seen in our churches, and our lives, today.

## Questions for reflection

1. How might this psalm change your understanding of what blessing and praise are?
2. How could you and your church community live in a way that points to "a good, just, kind, moral, ordered God who is sovereign and working out his purposes in a disordered world"?
3. How might this psalm help you to pray for the church and for the world?

PSALMS 45 AND 72

# 8. CELEBRATING GOD'S KING

For our final pair from Book II, I have chosen two psalms that celebrate the beauty and wonder of the promised king in David's line. One comes immediately after the two laments at the start of the book (Psalms 42/43 and 44) and the other right at the end.

We start with Psalm 45: a psalm of the beauty of the king.

## A noble theme

The king in David's line has not been explicitly present in Psalms 42 – 44. He reappears in Psalm 45 in a unique psalm, sung (as for all of Psalms 42 – 49) by one of the "sons of Korah". It is headed "A wedding song" (literally "a love song"), although it becomes clear that it is for the wedding of a king. In Psalm **45:1** the singer, who seems to be rather like a **poet laureate** commissioned to write for the occasion ("as I recite my verses for the king"), declares that his "heart is stirred by a noble theme". He is not writing under human compulsion—just doing what he has been told to by the authorities—but under divine compulsion. The Spirit of God has stirred his heart so that when he speaks ("my tongue") and writes ("a skilful writer"), it is from a heart full of the wonder of his theme.

His is indeed a wonderful theme—for the man whose praises he will sing is a wonderful king and an excellent bridegroom. The poet will give us here "a vision of incomparable perfection" (Kraus, *Psalms*, Volume 1, page 454). It is a most unusual wedding song, though, for the bride does not appear until more than halfway through (**v 10**), and then only briefly and to be given a firm talking-to! No, the burden—the "noble theme" of the song—is the bridegroom-king. He is "the most excellent" (literally something like "beautiful of beautiful") "of men" (**v 2**). He is, as we shall learn, the most beautiful man the world has ever seen, with a strong radiant masculine beauty.

## The beauty of his words

Before describing anything else about this man, the poet sings that "your *lips* have been anointed with grace" (**v 2**, my italics). It is what he says and how he says it that marks him first as pre-eminent in beauty. *We love to hear you speak and teach,* says the poet. *We hang on your every word. Your words give us fresh life; they are words in season—just the right words for each moment.*

"Who is he?" we may ask. King **Solomon** spoke many wise words, although not all the time. A few other kings in David's line spoke well some of the time, men such as **Hezekiah** and **Josiah**. But when the faithful sang this at some of the Old Testament royal weddings (supposing that they did), it must have been the triumph of faith over experience. Imagine singing this, for example, at the wedding of the evil King **Manasseh** (read 2 Kings 21:1-18)! And yet they went on singing it, even when there was no king at all from the time of the **Babylonian exile** onwards. Perhaps they knew that this song only made sense if one day a king greater than Solomon, greater even than David, would walk the earth. And then one day he did (Matthew 12:42)—a man who spoke as no man had spoken before, and as no man has spoken since (John 7:46). As the Victorian preacher C.H. Spurgeon said of Jesus:

> "Often a sentence from his lips has turned our midnight into morning, our winter into spring." (*Psalms*, Volume 1, page 187)

But we must return to the original old-covenant context of this wedding song.

## The beauty of his war

The second feature of this man celebrated by our poet is (perhaps very surprisingly at a wedding!) his beautiful warfare. That is a strange adjective to use of warfare, and in any other context it would be horribly inappropriate—but not here. This bridegroom is a warrior-king who girds on his sword and dresses in a powerful uniform of "splendour and majesty" (Psalm **45:3**). He rides forth to war and victory (**v 4a**). But the war he fights is "in the cause of truth, humility and justice" (**v 4b**). We agonise over whether and when a human war may be dubbed a "just war"; it is never totally unambiguous. But here is warfare that is entirely just. The king is not fighting for his own honour; he campaigns consistently for truth, humility (a strange word to find here!) and justice. What a strange warrior! He defeats lies with truth, conquers pride with humility, vanquishes wickedness with justice. He never seeks to overcome evil with evil, but overcomes evil with good.

What is more, his victory is on a cosmic scale, for "the king's enemies" are called "the nations"—Bible shorthand for the rest of the world (**v 5**). This is the Psalm 2 king who will conquer the world.

The singers would not know for many years, of course, when and how this victory would be won: at the cross of Christ, when he "disarmed the powers and authorities" and "made a public spectacle of them" (Colossians 2:15). The old Palm Sunday hymn "Ride on, ride on, in majesty" was inspired by Psalm **45:4**.

## The beauty of his reign

After winning his victory, this bridegroom-king will reign on his "throne" (**v 6**). Astonishingly, he is addressed now as "O God"! Although the NIV footnote explains that "here the king is addressed as God's representative", the letter to the Hebrews tells us otherwise; for in Hebrews 1:8-9, Psalm **45:6-7** is quoted to support the full divinity of Jesus Christ. He is more than God's representative; he is a fully divine person in his own right.

And yet, because he loves "righteousness" and hates "wickedness", "therefore God, your God" has given him a position of unique honour (**v 7**). And so we have a strange **paradox**: here is God, who has God as his God! Only when Jesus Christ, who is fully God—God the Son—came to David's throne could this paradox be resolved.

His reign is a beautiful reign, for under his government right behaviour (righteousness) is consistently upheld and wrong actions (wickedness) are consistently punished. It is the kind of government we long for, in our better moments, and the reign we so badly need.

The portrayal of a beautiful reign is closely accompanied in **verses 7b-8** by the fragrance of beautiful robes—the oil of joy and all the fragrances of life—and the music that accompanies them.

What a beautiful Bridegroom-King who, for this joy that was set before him, endured the cross (Hebrews 12:2), won the victory and is now enthroned in the place of all authority.

## A wise word to the beautiful bride

Were we listening to this song for the first time, we would be bound to be asking ourselves, "So who is the lucky girl who gets this man for a husband?!" She is certainly adorned with beauty, "in gold of Ophir" (Psalm **45;9**)—the proverbially wonderful gold of the ancient East—and with a wedding "gown ... interwoven with gold" and with "embroidered garments" (**v 13-14**). She has a train of bridesmaids in her wedding procession (**v 15**). And yet it is interesting that here—in the place where we might expect it—there is no description of her physical beauty, her pretty face or her attractive figure. The beauty of which we are told is a beauty that has been given to her. Perhaps we wonder who has adorned her with that gold of Ophir; we might be supposed to guess that her bridegroom-king is the giver.

In **verses 10-12**, the poet speaks to the bride. He does not praise her; his praise is focused entirely on the bridegroom. He exhorts her: "Listen, daughter, and pay careful attention" (**v 10**). It is almost, but not quite, a ticking-off! This is an urgent word to which this young woman must pay careful attention. She must do one negative thing and one positive. She must first "forget" her childhood family, her upbringing, her culture—all that she otherwise would bring with her into her marriage from her past (**v 10**). Perhaps she is a foreign princess; we do not know. But all her old allegiances—perhaps in our culture we would say her old boyfriends—must be jettisoned on this, her wedding day. She must offer her "beauty" entirely and only to her husband, who is "the king" and who is "enthralled" by her beauty (**v 11**). It is a beauty he has given her, but nevertheless he is entranced, like a wide-eyed bridegroom who, in our loose way of speaking, "cannot believe his luck"! He adores her; and she must give him her loyal adoring love, and brook no rivals in her own affections.

In doing so, she need not fear that she will lose out—that she (as we sometimes say) "might have done better" to find another, better husband. No, the wedding gifts showered on her will include those from "the city of Tyre" (**v 12**), the legendary repository of astonishing wealth. She will be so astonished at the blessings that come to her that she need never regret marrying this royal bridegroom.

## The bride and the family

This is disguised in our English translations, but the Hebrew in **verses 16-17** makes it clear, by its use of the **masculine**, that these final verses are again addressed to the king. The king will, through this wonderful marriage, have a dynasty of "sons ... princes" (**v 16**), who will rule "through all generations" and cause him to be praised by all "the nations" (**v 17**). And so the promise to Abraham—that his offspring would inherit the world (Romans 4:13)—will be fulfilled, as the family of this great king governs the new creation: the new heavens and new earth.

No princess in Israel's history matches this description. Just as we have to wait for Jesus Christ, the Son of David, before we meet this king, so we have to wait for the bride of Jesus before we meet this queen. This bride, made beautiful by grace, is fulfilled in the people of God, who are ultimately seen to be the church of Jesus Christ, made up of both Jew and Gentile. Corporately, we are his bride (see 2 Corinthians 11:2; Ephesians 5:32; Revelation 19:7-8; 21:11).

The metaphorical language is stretched of course, since we are also his family, his brethren and those who inherit the blessings of his sonship. We are both Christ's bride and we are his family.

How should we respond?

## A marriage offer

Preaching to a society of young women in London in the eighteenth century, the great preacher George Whitefield said this to those who would refuse Christ:

> "Hereby you choose rags before [instead of] robes, dross before gold, pebbles before jewels, guilt before a pardon, wounds before healing, defilement before cleansing, deformity before comeliness, trouble before peace, slavery before liberty, the service of the devil before the service of Christ. Hereby you choose dishonour before a crown, death before life, hell before heaven, eternal misery and torment before everlasting joy and glory. And need there be any further evidence of your folly and madness, in refusing and neglecting Christ to be your spouse?"
>
> (*Sermons*, volume 1, page 117-18)

This exhortation should be heeded by all of us, female or male. It is the utmost folly to refuse to be incorporated by faith into the bride of such a bridegroom!

"Forget your people and your father's house" (Psalm **45:10**). Each of us comes to Christ with a history. Our history includes the culture in which we were educated, the family in which we were nurtured, the thoughts, imaginations, and desires of our hearts, the habits of thought and action to which we have become accustomed—all that shapes us, not just in our actions but in our words and our inmost thoughts and desires. To be in the bride of Christ means deliberately, intentionally, thoughtfully to leave all that behind. Centuries later, John would put it like this in his first letter:

> "Do not love the world or anything in the world. If anyone loves the world, love for the Father is not in them. For everything in the world—the lust of the flesh, the lust of the eyes, and the pride of life—comes not from the Father but from the world. The world and its desires pass away, but whoever does the will of God lives for ever." (1 John 2:15-17)

Jesus calls it saying no to "self", taking up the cross and following him (Mark 8:34). This is not asceticism; it is not the refusal to enjoy the good gifts of this creation (1 Timothy 4:1-5). It is saying no to the evil desires of this world. This saying no will not happen only in one great moment of decision. Some Christian movements have been naïve in encouraging that hope. No, we shall need to hear and heed Psalm **45:10** again and again.

But we also need to hear the wonderful words of **verse 11a**: "Let the king be enthralled by your beauty". Our outward appearance will fade, sooner or later, no matter how many anti-ageing creams we may use or how much cosmetic surgery we may try. Our faculties of mind and body will decay. But—and this is a truly wonderful thing!—our bridegroom is working within us an inward beauty that will go from one degree of glory to another until, on the day of his wedding, we shall be, corporately, without spot or blemish. The world may despise you, and the church; but Jesus is working in you, and in all of us, qualities of beautiful character that will shine for eternity. Rejoice in that!

> He is richer, wiser, stronger, better—and he loves us and will always love us.

Perhaps, though, the greatest effect this psalm should have on us is to fill our minds and hearts with the beauty of Jesus. He is richer than any other we could wish for, wiser than any we could find elsewhere, stronger than any others we might trust for security, and better in character than the morally best person we know; and he loves us and will always love us with the kind of love that moved him to give himself for us on the cross (Galatians 2:20). What a bride-groom! What a King!

## Questions for reflection

1. Does the description of the bridegroom in verses 2-9 fit with the way you tend to picture Jesus? Why or why not?
2. What have you left behind, or what do you need to leave behind, to become part of the bride of Christ?
3. How does it feel to imagine yourself in the place of the bride in this psalm?

## PART TWO

Psalm 72 is a prayer for desperate people who feel there is "no one to help" them (Psalm **72:12**), and for those who care for such people. There are many such people, longing with an urgent desperation for someone strong to reach down to them in their affliction and help them. As I write this (in 2017), the people of Zimbabwe are celebrating the downfall of a cruel and tyrannical ruler who has oppressed their country for more than three decades; they hope—understandably, if perhaps unrealistically—for better things. Time will tell.

Almost uniquely in the Psalter, Psalm 72 is headed "Of Solomon" (Psalm 127 is the only other). Since the psalm ends by telling us that it "concludes the prayers of David" (**72:20**), and since the word translated "of" can mean "for", some take this to be a prayer written by King David for the benefit of his son Solomon and his successors; so, for example, Geoffrey Grogan suggests that this was "written by David for his son and successor" (*Psalms,* page 131). But it could equally be written by Solomon to show his people what to pray for him and then for his successors. (**Verse 20** is a concluding summary for Books I and II, since the majority of the psalms in these books are by David; but there are other psalms not by David included in this generalised summary, and there is no reason why Psalm 72 should not be one of them.) Perhaps it doesn't much matter; what is clear is that it provides a wonderfully appropriate final psalm at the end of Books I and II, with their overwhelming focus on the king. It may have been used at coronations of subsequent kings in David's line; if so, it would have been a very good choice. Here, if you like, is the kind of king for whom God says the people of God should pray.

The themes of the psalm are to some extent interwoven. But, for the sake of simplicity, we will take the main psalm in three parts, followed by a brief consideration of the final three verses, which form the conclusion to Book II.

## A king of eternal justice

**Verse 1** is the only explicit prayer (an **imperative** in the Hebrew) in the psalm: "Endow the king ... O God". From then on, there is often uncertainty about whether the Hebrew verbs should be translated as wishes (please "may" this or that happen) or as prophecies (this or that "will" happen). This uncertainty is sometimes reflected in our English translations. Not a lot hinges on this; for, underlying the psalm, there is a confidence that what the people of God long to see happening here will happen. We shall revisit this question when considering **verses 18-20**.

**Verses 1-2** introduce the psalm. The words "justice" (right decisions) and "righteousness" mean much the same thing. Notice how they appear in a balanced way: **v 1a** "justice", **v 1b** "righteousness"; and then **v 2a** "righteousness", **v 2b** "justice" reinforce this. Blessing through righteous government is the theme of the psalm.

Further, where **verse 1** asks that the king may have justice and righteousness ("the king" of **v 1a** is the same person as "the royal son" of **v 1b** for the king is to be the legitimate heir of his father), **verse 2** considers the effect on the people. These are not ultimately the king's people, but "your [God's] people". The particular focus is on God's "afflicted ones"; this is sometimes translated "poor" or "weak". It means primarily their objective state, as those in need of help and with few resources; but it can also mean those who acknowledge their dependent state and are "humble" in heart as well as in status (see Matthew 5:3; Luke 6:20). This psalm speaks urgently and with comfort to such desperate people. The responsibility of God's king is to care for God's people, and most especially for the lowest, weakest and most vulnerable of these people.

Psalm **72:3-7** is bracketed by the word "prosperity" or "peace" (Hebrew *shalom*). When the king defends the afflicted and saves the children (those who need a protector), he must "crush the oppressor" (**v 4**). It is sobering to grasp that there must needs be coercion to bring about these good ends. The oppressor must be crushed. Rulers ought to "hold ... terror" for those who do wrong (Romans 13:3) for they are "sent by [God] to punish those who do wrong" (1 Peter 2:14). The reason God gives power is so that those with power will "speak up for those who cannot speak for themselves, for the rights of those who are destitute" (Proverbs 31:8).

One of the themes in Psalm **72:3-7** is the long-lasting nature of this just government. It will be carried on day and night, as long as the sun and moon endure (**v 5**, **7**). So often a good ruler brings a measure of justice, only to die and be followed by a much worse ruler, as will the terrible King Manasseh, who succeeded his righteous father King Hezekiah (2 Kings 21). But here, long-lasting rule is associated with "the mountains ... the hills" (Psalm **72:3**), suggesting that this reign will in some way uphold the proper order of creation so that the world can flourish and abound with life (as in Genesis 1). Such a king will be "like rain falling on a mown field" (Psalm **72:6**), his kingdom fulfilling the longings of a creation subjected to frustration (Romans 8:22-25). Desperate people will find comfort for ever in this king.

## A king of universal justice

The theme of just government continues in Psalm **72:8-14**, but the focus moves from its duration in time to its extent in space. The expression "from sea to sea" (**v 8**) probably refers to the ideal boundaries of the promised land in the Old Testament: from the Red Sea to the Mediterranean Sea. The "River" in this context is the Euphrates. But even if the original reference was to do with the promised land, the language here stretches it so that it becomes "the nucleus of an empire that is world-wide" (Kidner, *Psalms,* Volume 1, page 256). **Verses 8-11** spread before us a vision of a kingdom that truly stretches across the world. The word translated "desert tribes" (**v 9**) probably refers not just to distant nomads but also to "those desert creatures often associated with demonic elements" (Philip Eveson, *Psalms*, Volume 1, page 441), hinting perhaps that the king's rule extends to the supernatural spirit world. "Tarshish" (**v 10a**) is in the far west (modern Spain); "Sheba and Seba" (**v 10b**) are probably in the far south, perhaps Arabia and Ethiopia. Whatever the precise locations denoted there, **verse 11** makes it clear that Psalm 72 is describing a universal rule: "all kings ... all nations". This is the reign of the Psalm 2 king fulfilled.

The significance of this universality is that there will no longer be any external threat. Here is a kingdom that doesn't just have secure borders that need to be guarded; it has no borders because there is nothing outside of its scope!

**Verses 12-14** are a reality check for us after the grand vista of **verses 8-11**, for in the present, God's people are still "needy" and "afflicted"; they spend much of their time "crying out", and they know that without God's king they "have no one to help" (**v 12**). God's king will rescue these desperately needy men and women; he will hear their cry. In his heart there is a wonderful "pity" (**v 13**). They suffer "from oppression and violence" (**v 14**) all over the world and all through the centuries of time, for the normal state of the people of God is to be persecuted. Those of us who live in the shelter of centuries of Christianised history in our countries find it easy to forget this; but the more our Christian-influenced heritage disintegrates, the closer we shall draw to the normal Christian life, which is one of enduring suffering for God's sake (44:22; see Romans 8:36).

> The more our Christian-influenced heritage disintegrates, the closer we shall draw to the normal Christian life of enduring suffering.

The words "precious is their blood in his sight" (Psalm **72:14b**) mean that the life and death of each one of God's faithful people, though it may be counted cheap by their persecutors, is wonderfully valuable in the sight of the God who loves us. The life of his Son, Jesus, was precious in the Father's eyes; the life of every one of our King's people—of every Christian—is as precious to the Father as is the blood of Jesus, the beloved Son.

By the time we reach **verse 14**, we truly feel the wonder of the prospect of a kingdom that will, in the words of Isaac Watts, "stretch from shore to shore" (**v 8-11**) "till moons shall wax and wane no more" (**v 3-7**). Watts' hymn "Jesus shall reign where'er the sun" was inspired by this psalm:

*Jesus shall reign where'er the sun*
*Doth his successive journeys run;*
*His Kingdom stretch from shore to shore,*
*Till moons shall wax and wane no more.*

*Blessings abound where'er He reigns:*
*The prisoner leaps to lose his chains,*
*The weary find eternal rest,*
*And all the sons of want are blest.* (verses 1, 4)

## Blessing comes to the world

In some ways, **verses 15-17** reiterate themes we have already heard and prayed about. But there is a difference. In **verse 15**, we pray *for* the king himself: "Long may he live!" The cry "Long live the king!" is a familiar one in countries that are monarchies. In the UK, a formal dinner might include "the royal toast" in which we stand, raise our glasses and say, "To the Queen!" I attended a school where we sang a rousing old school song at the end of each term the refrain of which included the wonderful words, "Vivat Rex Eduardus Sextus! Vivat! Vivat! Vivat!" ("Long live King Edward the Sixth"). It was fun to sing it but something of a forlorn hope, since that king died in 1553 and showed no signs of coming to life again in response to our voices! And yet we pray in this psalm for a king who will live long and go on living—and it is, of course, no forlorn hope.

Next, this is to be a king to whom the finest treasures in the world are brought as tribute ("gold from Sheba"), and for whom people "pray" because they recognise that he is the only hope for otherwise hopeless people. They will "bless him all day long" because of the wonderful justice he brings to the needy. **Job** remembered that, in his heyday, he had been this kind of powerful figure who had "rescued the poor who cried for help" and had been "blessed" by such needy people for his goodness (Job 29, especially verses 12-17, which echo Psalm 72 in many ways).

Psalm **72:16** brings us back to the blessing overflowing to the whole created order through this king. The language is wonderfully **hyperbolic**, depicting shoots of corn so strong that each one seems like a cedar tree in Lebanon. This king will win for himself a reputation (**v 17**, "his name") that will last until time is no more.

The punchline of the psalm is **verse 17b**: "all nations will be blessed through him". This echoes the foundational covenant promise to Abraham in Genesis 12:1-3. The Israelites expected that promise to be fulfilled through the family of Abraham; but here it is focused on the king; for this king will be Abraham's "seed", in whom all the blessings of the covenant are focused, like light passing through a prism before spreading out in beauty beyond. The New Testament unlocks for us the puzzle of how a blessing given to a people may be focused in one individual—the "seed" of Abraham is both individual (the anointed king, the Messiah, Galatians 3:16) and corporate (a people joined to him by faith, Galatians 3:29). All the blessing of God is focused in this king and flows out from him into a world in desperate need of blessing.

## Answered prayers

Each of the five Books of the Psalms concludes with an ascription of praise. Book I ends with Psalm 41:13, Book III with 89:52, Book Four with 106:48, and Book V with the "Hallelujah Chorus" of Psalms 146 – 150 (see chapter 16 of this book). Book II ends with

Psalm **72:18-20**. Why praise the covenant God ("the LORD God") for his "marvellous deeds" and celebrate the longing that "the whole earth" should be "filled with his glory" if you do not believe that the yearnings of Psalm 72 will be fulfilled? It is precisely because believers through the old-covenant era did believe that the Psalm 1 man, who would be the Psalm 2 king of which Psalms 45 and 72 spoke, would come that they sang these praises at the end of Book II.

The words "Amen and Amen" (**72:19**) are more than religious wallpaper. To say or sing the word "Amen" with conviction is to sign up to a confident belief that these things are true; it is to align myself, with all my desires and yearnings, with the longings expressed in these psalms, and perhaps especially in Psalm 72. The repeated "Amen" leaves no room for doubt: this is not the feeble, tentative, scarcely audible "amen" of some prayer meetings; it is a jubilant, convinced "AMEN"!

No Old Testament king of Israel was fully the answer to the prayer of Psalm 72. All disappointed: some utterly and some partially, but every one of them fell short. Only great David's greater Son can be the answer to this prayer. We thank God for his just, eternal, unbounded rule, and pray with fervour for his return in glory to govern the new creation so that it will be "a new heaven and a new earth, where righteousness dwells" (2 Peter 3:13), because it will be governed by the righteous king of Psalm 72.

## Questions for reflection

1. How do you think believers in Old Testament times felt to sing this song about their king?
2. Why do you think it is so wonderful that Jesus' reign is over the whole world?
3. How might the psalms of Book II inform or change your own prayers?

PSALMS 73 AND 74

# 9. PAIN IN EXILE

Book III (Psalms 73 – 89) has a very different tone to Books I and II. It smells of exile. The first eleven of the seventeen psalms are from the Asaphite school (Psalm 73 – 83); "Asaph" is probably shorthand for a song-writing society, taking their name from one of the Levites who led the music in David's day (1 Chronicles 15:17, 19; 16:4-6; 2 Chronicles 29:30). The context that dominates the book is Judah-in-exile, in Babylon. Two examples where this is most clearly seen are Psalm 79:1 ("The nations have invaded your inheritance; they have defiled your holy temple, they have reduced Jerusalem to rubble") and Psalm 83:4 ("'Come,' they say, 'let us destroy them as a nation, so that Israel's name is remembered no more.'").

In 587 BC the neo-Babylonian emperor Nebuchadnezzar conquered what was left of Judah, razed Jerusalem to the ground, ended the Davidic monarchy and burned the temple Solomon had built (2 Kings 25; Jeremiah 52; 2 Chronicles 36:15-21). For about 70 years that was how it remained, until under religious teachers like Ezra, prophets like Haggai and Zechariah, and political leaders like Nehemiah it began to be rebuilt from 520 BC onwards.

Not all the psalms in Book III were necessarily written during this period (indeed, Psalm 86 is "of David"). But they are appropriate to the experience, and seem to have been collected together with the exile as the dominant background.

As our examples from this book, I have taken, in this chapter, two psalms of lament; and then, in chapter 10, two psalms that express a continuing delight in Zion, expressing faith that the story has not ended.

Book III begins with an individual lament (Psalm 73) and a corporate lament (Psalm 74).

## When God doesn't seem good

Every Christian should pray Psalm 73 and make it a regular ingredient in the ongoing diet of their prayers. If we do not, then an unhelpful train of thought will take us by surprise and knock us off the straight and narrow road of discipleship. The central question asked and answered in the psalm is this: is God good, moral and fair? There can be few if any more important questions. "Well, yes, of course he is," we nod piously. But the answer of our experience is often "No, he doesn't seem to be". And, if he isn't, the rug is pulled from under all the motivations for godly living. So it's a very serious question. It is the question asked, implicitly and subversively, by the serpent in the garden in Eden, in Genesis 3; and it was their implicit answer to that question that undermined the lives and destinies of Adam and Eve, and through them the whole human race (Romans 5:12-21).

We do not know who wrote this psalm, why, or when. There is no explicit link to the exile, although the general context of Book III might suggest that we are hearing the anguished voice of a believer in those terrible days. But the exile only raised in an acute form the question facing the people of God in every age when they struggle or suffer: is God good?

In an affirmation that would have resounded at the terrible time of exile, and continues to at all times of suffering, the psalm begins by crying out, "Surely [or "Truly", emphatically] God is good to Israel" (Psalm **73:1**)! God shows his common grace or kindness to all kinds of men and women; but he directs his covenant faithful goodness, his steadfast love, to the people with whom he is in covenant. This is the headline.

But it is nuanced in the second half of the verse, where "Israel" is defined not by ethnicity but by faith: "those who are pure in heart". There is a tremendous emphasis on the "heart" in this psalm (see also **v 7**, **13**, **21**, **26**). Purity of heart—a single desire and yearning to love God—is the necessary definition of Israel. The covenant goodness of God is directed to this true Israel, which is in every age a remnant of the outward people of God, and to this remnant alone. How vital, therefore, is purity of heart!

In **verses 2-14**, this believer brings out into the open a train of thought and feeling that has troubled him deeply. He sums it up first in **verses 2-3**. He describes its result in **verse 2**, in terms of (almost) slipping, losing his grip on solid ground, saying goodbye to reality. And he tells us its root cause in **verse 3**: envy. He looked at the "arrogant", watched their "prosperity" (literally their "shalom"—peace, wholeness), and he began to wish that he could be like them. He started to lose his gladness in belonging to the God of Israel and to look over the fence at this "better" life of wickedness: *if only I could eat the delicious fruit that they eat; my whole being yearns for what they enjoy.* And so the seed of disaster is sown that, if allowed to grow, will untie this man from reality and place him on a slippery slope to ruin.

**Verses 4** and **5** expand on the "prosperity" of the "wicked". They have no "struggles" (**v 4a**, literally "pangs until death"); that is, they live a whole life without struggles or pain. They enjoy good health (**v 4b**); they are not weighed down by impossible pressures at work or in their family, neighbourhood or land (**v 5a**). All the "ills" that afflict the rest of us seem to pass them by. What charmed lives they lead!

And then, in **verses 6-11**, the psalmist's focus shifts subtly in a way that will unlock a way of escape from his peril. He observes not only what the wicked do *not* have (troubles) but what—as a consequence of having no troubles—they *do* have: pride! Because all is going well for them, they begin to believe they can navigate this life entirely by their own wits and resources—that within them is all that they need (rather like Buddhism). So they become proud (**v 6a**); and the next step from pride is to trample on those who get in their way, which is why pride leads to "violence" (**v 6b**), hard hearts (**v 7**), scoffing and malice (**v 8**), and speaking words that "lay claim to heaven ... take possession of the earth" (**v 9**). The limit of their horizon is themselves; the universe revolves around them. They speak in a way that betrays a belief that there is no limit, in principle, to what they and their fellow human-beings can achieve.

**Verse 10** is difficult to translate. Probably it should read "*his* [that is, God's] people" rather than "*their* people" (NIV); and the sense is that God's people are seduced by the success of the wicked and "turn back to them" (ESV). If this is right, then, as Tate puts it, "The Israelites are seen to be so impressed with the prosperity of the wicked and their impunity that they 'turn to' them" (Tate, *Psalms 51-100*, page 229). Psalm **73:11** returns to their arrogant confidence; they are sure that God knows nothing, does not see their actions, and certainly won't do anything to punish them.

In **verse 12** the psalmist sums up his observations. He looks over the fence at the wicked and sees them "always free of care" and getting richer and richer. This is of course, as we all know, a generalisation. Those who are proud and care nothing for God do get ill and have all manner of troubles. But it is nevertheless generally true that they might have longer life-expectancy and the financial means to stave off many of the pressures to which poorer godly people are subject. Job 21 contains a longer and eloquent description, from the honest but disillusioned mouth of suffering Job, of the prosperity of the wicked.

Though the ESV misses it, Psalm **73:13** repeats the emphatic word "surely" or "truly" (used at the start of **verse 1**). *Let me tell you,* the psalmist says, *what I concluded after following this train of thought about the prosperity of the wicked. I decided—or very nearly decided—that all my efforts to keep "my heart pure" were pointless: "in vain". I know I said in verse 1 that God is good to the pure in heart, but at this stage I wasn't sure I really believed that true goodness was to be found this way. I "washed my hands in innocence": I worked hard*—as the apostle Paul would later say—*to keep a clear conscience*

*(Acts 24:16). But there doesn't seem to have been any point in doing so. For "all day long I have been afflicted" (Psalm* ***73:14a****), and life consists of one "punishment" after another (****v 14b****). All I have to show for my heart's desire for purity and godliness is a life in which one misery is piled upon another. But those who care nothing for God are enjoying all the "good" things of life. If God is really "good", then he will surely bless with good things those who are pure in heart. But he doesn't.*

And so this troubled man feels he has come to decision time. He is on the very edge of giving up on the life of faith.

Is it irreverent to think of the Lord Jesus travelling, in his mind and heart, through the frightening journey of **verses 2-14**? I think not. For he felt temptation in all its intensity. "Asaph, as a representative of the Israel of God, points us to the Lord Jesus Christ, who is the true Israel (Isaiah 49:3), who, as the Suffering Servant, knew what it was to feel the temptation to give up (see Isaiah 49:4a), yet shook it off" (Eveson, *Psalms,* Volume 2, page 21). All the kingdoms of the world, with their prosperity and comfort, were offered to him by the tempter (Matthew 4:8-9); surely he felt their allure and began to wonder if he would not be better off accepting them. And yet he did not. He was without sin.

If we pretend we do not feel what this believer felt, then we are playing with fire.

We need to follow in the footsteps of the Asaphite writer of Psalm 73, and of the Lord Jesus Christ in his temptations, to trace this journey of honest anguish. We need to bring these thoughts and desires out into the open: to place them—as they are placed in this psalm—under the banner headline of **verse 1** and in the presence of God. If we pretend we do not feel what this believer felt, then we are playing with fire, for these desires lurk in all of us. Better to bring them out and look at them in the clear light of truth—which is what the psalmist now does.

## Then I understood

**Verse 15** is, in some ways, the key to reading this psalm rightly in Christ. This believing representative of the people of God, speaking by the Spirit of God who is the Spirit of Christ, reflects that "If I had spoken out like that"—like **verses 13 and 14**—"I would have betrayed your children". Why "betrayed"? Betrayal endangers a people, which is why treachery is uniquely serious. In some way the faithfulness of this man matters for the destiny of the people of God. For some reason it matters tremendously that he should not tip over the edge of unbelief and into the scepticism of **verse 13**. For if he does continue down that slippery slope, it will not only be him who suffers; the destiny of others somehow rests on his continuing faithfulness.

And so we watch with bated breath as he tries to understand (**v 16**) the prosperity of the wicked and the sufferings of the believer (**v 14**). He enters "the **sanctuary**" (**v 17a**), the temple, in which are the two tablets of the law in the ark of the covenant, the altar of sacrifice, the **mercy seat**, and all the signs of God's covenant promises and faithfulness. Perhaps he is (as Asaph himself was) a Levite with temple duties. It is when he sees, and meditates, on the covenant that he says, "I understood their final destiny" (**v 17b**). He hears afresh, perhaps, the covenant blessings and curses (see, for instance, Deuteronomy 28).

Then he grasps that it is these arrogant wicked who are "on slippery ground" and facing imminent "ruin" (Psalm **73:18**). The reason his own feet had "almost slipped" (**v 2**) was that he was on the point of identifying himself with the wicked. Although the wicked seem so secure and peaceful, very "suddenly" everything will come crashing down around them, and they will be "swept away" as if by a flash flood (**v 19**). The "terrors" of God's judgment will come upon them: a terrible fear of a guilty conscience; the realisation that they are most horribly in the wrong; all the violent, malicious things they have said and done coming up before their terrified eyes as they face the righteous judgment of God and grasp that they have no defence.

These people who seem so solid, so weighty and so secure will be like "a dream" or "fantasy"—something that quickly fades, that is weightless, that just blows away (**v 20**). God will "arise" (**v 20**), as he did when the ark of the covenant went before his people in the old days of battle (Numbers 10:35); and when he does, these prosperous wicked will prosper no more.

This is not wishful thinking on the part of this believer. He does not just hope the wicked will be blown away. The covenant law declares this (for instance, Leviticus 26:14-39; Deuteronomy 28:15-68), and he believes it. It is by the written Law of Moses that this Asaphite could affirm Psalm **73:18-20**; it is by the written Law of Moses that Jesus of Nazareth could know and believe these same truths; and it is by the law of God that we too can share the same confidence.

It is because this is clearly revealed in the Law of Moses that this believer can describe his previous train of thought as stupid in **verses 21-22**. We feel sorry for him that his heart was "grieved" (**v 21a**) and "embittered" (**v 21b**). The first word (NIV "grieved"; ESV "embittered") comes from a word linked to "sourdough and vinegar" (Goldingay, *Psalms,* Volume 1, page 411); the second (NIV "embittered"; ESV "pricked in heart") speaks literally of the piercing of the kidneys: "a metaphor for deep internal anguish" (Tate, *Psalms 51-100*, page 230). And yet he describes this way of thinking as "senseless and ignorant": no better than the thinking of cattle (Psalm **73:22**). This way of thinking is folly because it ignores the revealed law of God, which solemnly declares that the one who fits the description of **verses 6-11** will meet a terrible end, and that the one who is pure in heart will enjoy wonderful blessings.

It is those blessings to which this believer turns in **verses 23-26**. He turns from his natural focus on the good things of this age to the wonderful good things that come to all who are in covenant loving relationship with God—to be "always with you", held by God's "right hand" of strength (**v 23**), guided through this life (**v 24a**) and taken "into glory" in the age to come (**v 24b**). There can be nothing better than this. Indeed, although the wicked lay claim to "heaven" and "earth" (**v 9**), to have God is to have all that is needful in "heaven" and "earth" (**v 25**). In this age there will be suffering (**v 14**)—"My flesh and my heart may fail", he says—*but God is all I need, for this life and for eternity* (**v 26**).

## It is good to be near him

We have followed this believer from an honest grappling with the prosperity of the wicked into the sanctuary; there he has been reminded of the great and unchanging truths of the covenant blessings for obedience and the covenant curses for unfaithfulness.

As he foreshadows the tempted but triumphant faith of the Lord Jesus and models such faith for us, he concludes with a confident affirmation that the wicked are not to be envied (**v 27**) and that—in the great final echo of the word "good" from **verse 1**—"As for me, it is good to be near God", who is his "refuge" in times of trouble (**v 28**).

We too begin with what we can see. Our senses tell us very forcibly that people who care nothing for God can do very well in life. Only when we come to Jesus, who is the fulfilment of the temple—the sanctuary—are we reminded of the great gospel truths that we must hold dear: that what is seen is not what is final, that we live by faith and not by sight, and that the day will come when all who trust the living God will be vindicated, and the apparent prosperity of the wicked will come to a terrible end.

The final word from this representative believer—this leader of the people of God—is the declaration that he will "tell of all your deeds" (**v 28c**). Had he not done so, he would have betrayed his people (**v 15**); but his faith has not failed. Jesus, our forerunner in faith, has spearheaded the way, resisting these overwhelmingly powerful temptations for us (Hebrews 12:2). As we sing this psalm with him, we too are strengthened to see the folly of envying the wicked and to end up with a glad delight in the goodness of the God to whom we are "near" in Jesus Christ.

## Questions for reflection

1. Is your faith in God ever shaken by injustices?
2. Does the psalmist's description of that feeling resonate with you?
3. How does the psalm help you and strengthen your faith?

## PART TWO

If Psalm 73 is the voice of one significant individual believer who is concerned not to betray the people of God by unbelief (73:15), Psalm 74 is the corporate voice of the people of God who cry together (apart from one individual who sings in **verse 12** and perhaps through **verses 12-17**). Hope comes to a desolate church from a most surprising direction in this psalm.

This—like Psalm 50 and all of Psalms 73 – 83—is an Asaphite psalm. While there is no explicit allusion to exile in Psalm 73, the trauma of the destruction of Jerusalem could not be clearer in Psalm 74.

The psalm has three clear sections, each marked by its characteristic and contrasting musical tone. It begins with deep and anguished lament (**v 1-11**), which is then interrupted by a most surprising section of gladness and confidence (**v 12-17**), before concluding with urgent prayer (**v 18-23**).

### Grieve for a ruined church

We begin with two agonised questions: "O God, why have you rejected us for ever? Why does your anger smoulder?" (**v 1**) The word translated "for ever" can mean "totally" or "completely". *Why have you completely rejected us? Why is your anger unrelenting?* the psalm asks. *Why do we seem to be the objects of unrelenting, unassuagable anger?* As Mays puts it, "Is the humiliating present the shape of the future?" (*Psalms*, page 247). Is this what it's always going to be like?

In this lament, the song-leader remembers the promises (**v 1-2**), feels the pain (**v 3-8**) and voices deep perplexity (**v 9-11**).

First the song-leader remembers the wonders of what God had promised (**v 1-2**). These suffering people are, the psalm tells God, "the sheep of your pasture", "the nation you purchased", who lived in "Zion, where you dwelt". *We are your flock, your redeemed people, the people brought near to your presence,* the psalm points out. *But* *"your anger" has smouldered "against us", like a volcano erupting.* All this speaks of wonderful promises, now lying in ruins.

The word translated "nation" is literally "assembly" or "congregation" and is the word that refers to the old-covenant people of God; it finds its fulfilment in the new-covenant people: Jew and Gentile in Christ. John Calvin is right to say that "the people of God in this psalm bewail the desolate condition of the church" (*Commentary on the Book of Psalms,* Volume 3, page 158).

Next, the psalmist expresses pain at what the enemies of God have done. As we read **verses 3-8** ,we must travel back, in our minds and hearts, to that terrible day about which we are hearing these eyewitness accounts. Perhaps we can imagine how we would have felt had this been our childhood home. How much worse, though, when this was the only place on earth where the living God was to be found. In **verse 3**, the writer cries to God to come and have a look ("turn your steps towards") at the ruins of the temple: ruins that seem to be "everlasting"—for it seems that the exile has been going on for some time at the time of writing, and there is no sign of an end. In particular, grief is focused on "the sanctuary" at the heart of the temple—the place where the writer of Psalm 73 learned such significant truths (73:17).

Next, the psalmist remembers God's enemies ("*your* foes") as they roared or bellowed like drunken vandals, cursing, scrawling graffiti, urinating and desecrating "the place where you met with us" (**74:4**). On that terrible day, they were like drunken lumberjacks in a forest, smashing the beautiful carvings that evoked the Garden of Eden and symbolised the only hope of a re-entry into Eden (**v 5-6**; see 1 Kings 6:23-35). This was where God dwelt on earth; and they destroyed it (Psalm **74:7**). Behind it was a chilling malice: "We will crush them completely" (**v 8**). This is the world's satanic hatred of God and his people.

This Asaphite cannot forget that terrible day. It has cast a shadow over the rest of his life.

Finally, in **verses 9-11**, he voices his agonising perplexity as he asks the questions "How long?" (**v 10**) and "Why?" (**v 11**). In the ruins of the temple there are Babylonian "signs"—perhaps military symbols or dedications to the Babylonian gods and goddesses (**v 4b**)—but "we", the people of God, have "no signs" (**v 9**)—no visible indications of the covenant faithfulness of God. The altar is gone, the ark of the covenant is no more and the mercy seat has been destroyed. And "we" have "no prophets" to tell us why or what or how long. Perhaps by this stage Jeremiah had long since been taken off to Egypt (Jeremiah 41:16 – 43:7), and Ezekiel was no more. There was only a terrible silence (see Lamentations 2:19).

How should we respond to Psalm **74:1-11**? We ought to feel sad about the discouraging state of Christ's church. We see ungodliness where there ought to be holiness, false teaching in pulpits that ought to beacons of truth, and division where there should be unity in biblical truth. It is not so much that the church is small, although in places it is; the most grievous aspect is its lack of purity. And yet the truth is that we feel sadder when our own health is poor, or our family unhappy, or our circumstances hard. One of the functions of the psalms is to reorder our disordered affections, so that we truly grieve over what we ought most deeply to grieve over, and long from the heart for what we ought to desire. We are not here simply to listen in to the grief of believers long ago and far away. As we join in the psalm, we begin to share that grief and feel it welling up within our own hearts.

## Believe in the Creator's power

In **verse 12**, there is a sudden and surprising change of tone, from pain and perplexity to confidence and faith. The doctrine of creation is about to break in upon the drama of redemption.

The headline is in this verse. One individual song-leader sings out that "God is *my* King" and that he "brings salvation". (It may well be that this individual continues to speak through **verses 13-17**.)

But how does he know that God rules ("my King") and God rescues ("salvation")? The answer comes here and it is expressed in poetic imagery, first in terms of the sea and an ancient sea-monster (**v 13-15**). The "sea" is Old Testament language for the place of chaos, darkness, danger, evil and ultimately death. To "split open the sea" (**v 13a**) is to overcome that evil power, as God did in creation, when he separated the waters in order that there might be dry land on which people could live (Genesis 1:6-10), and as he later did in redemption when he split the Red Sea (Exodus 14) and later the River Jordan (Joshua 3). A parallel way of speaking of overcoming the evil power of "the sea" is to speak of defeating a sea-monster: "the monster in the waters" (Psalm **74:13b**) or "Leviathan" (**v 14a**; see Job 41; Revelation 12:9). So the taming of evil is vividly portrayed as a part of what the Creator did at the very beginning by drying up the waters and draining them away (Psalm **74:15**). When God created the world, proclaims our believing singer, he made a world in which evil was his servant and could never be a rival god—in which, in a sense, it would always be a creature and never a match for the Creator.

This believing voice speaks to God in the hearing of the people of God, troubled as they are by monstrous forces of wickedness, supernatural forces of evil, made concrete in this believer's memory by the malice and violence of the Babylonian soldiers. That voice speaks to us still; for there are monsters at work in our churches: supernatural forces of evil bringing disorder, trampling on God's moral order, going in with axes to destroy the people of God, bringing disorder from inside through false teaching and moral compromise, and prompting hostility from outside, from a Western culture whose antagonism to Jesus Christ is increasingly open.

In **verses 16-17** the creation language of boundaries is developed. Just as in Genesis 1 the destructive waters were given boundaries beyond which they could not cross, so in all of creation there are boundaries to maintain an order that is both material and moral. Day and night, sun and moon, like the waters, clearly echo Genesis 1 (see Genesis 1:3-5, 14-19). There are boundaries between day and night, between light and darkness; there are limits to darkness, limits to the sea, limits to evil and disorder; there are boundaries to stop the stable, ordered creation being overrun with disorder, instability and limitless evil. There is a distinction—a created, non-negotiable distinction—between right and wrong.

The words "established" (Psalm **74:16b**) and "set" (**v 17a**) highlight the moral role of boundaries (see Deuteronomy 32:8 for fixing borders, or Proverbs 15:25 for maintaining a widow's boundaries). In creation, God established a moral order with boundaries. Because they are given in creation (what theologians call the "created order"), they cannot be destroyed, neither by Babylonian vandals nor by today's destroyers of Christ's church. Similar language about how creation order guarantees redemption is used in Jeremiah 33:19-26.

The order in creation assures us that the God who put order into creation (and sustains order in creation) will re-establish order in creation fully when he rescues his people in the end. This is why, however perplexed this psalmist may feel, he knows that there is an answer to "Why?" and that there is a limit to "How long?" (see Michael Wilcock, *The Message of Psalms*, Volume 2, page 13).

## Plead for restoration

If we only had the lament of Psalm **74:1-11**, we might despair. If we simply heard the confidence of **verses 12-17**, we might become complacent. But because we have both, in the final section of the psalm we pray.

These final verses are full of urgent appeals to God. They are prayer in poetry. "Remember" (**v 18**); "Do not hand over ... do not forget" (**v 19**); "Have regard for" (**v 20**); "Do not let ... may the poor and needy praise" (**v 21**); "Rise up ... remember" (**v 22**); "Do not ignore" (**v 23**).

What is at stake is not our comfort as members of Christ's church but the honour of God, whose "name" is being mocked (**v 18**). Jesus echoed this when he wept over Jerusalem (Luke 19:41-44) and prayed "Father, glorify your name" (John 12:28). The church of God is like a defenceless "dove" in a world of "wild beasts" (Psalm **74:19**). There is a "covenant" to be upheld; there are "dark places" in the land, where violent deeds are committed and the perpetrators think no one can see them (**v 20**). This is a frightening picture, and it is a picture not of our society (dark though that is) but of a troubled church, haunted by evil within as well as without. When we hear ministers of the church advocating sexual immorality or learn of pastors perpetrating abuse, we feel the darkness. Jesus could have prayed this prayer for the people of God in his day, given they were so deeply compromised and led by ungodly men. We too can pray it in him today.

In **verses 22-23** there is a double uprising. The "uproar of the enemies ... rises continually"; against this we pray that God will "rise up [to] defend [his] cause".

And so as we pray this final section of the psalm, we put together a keen feeling of grief with a strong confidence in rescue, and we pray urgently that the rescuing Creator will do what he has promised to do—that he will restore his ruined church so that it shows forth his glory for ever. Believers in the old-covenant era prayed for the restoration of God's church—for instance, Simeon and Anna in Luke 2:25, 38. And then one day Simeon held a small boy in his arms and knew their prayers had not been in vain.

And yet that boy, as a man, said of his own body that others would "destroy this temple"—this place where men and women can see and meet with God: the place where God meets with us—and "I will raise it again" (John 2:19). For the person of Jesus fulfils all that the temple foreshadowed. He is the place of sacrifice; he is the sacrifice. So he is the "place"—and the only place—where sinners may meet with God. Men did destroy that temple on the first Good Friday. And it would have been appropriate for the disciples to sing this psalm on the Saturday. *Why has the enemy roared and mocked* ("Crucify him!") *and destroyed the place where we met with God, where we saw the*

*Father?* they could have sung. But the next day, they saw that same temple, rebuilt on the third day.

We too can sing this psalm as we await our Lord's glorious return and as we lament the ruined state of his church in our time. The persecuted church the world over sings this psalm; and we must sing it with them. Closer to home, we should grieve at **liberal theology** eroding a confidence in truth. We should grieve at **prosperity theology** eroding a willingness to accept sacrifice. We should grieve at materialism eroding a willingness to give. We should grieve at sexual compromise eroding the boundaries of family life. We should grieve at a culture of celebrity and entertainment eroding humility and maturity. We should grieve at **party spirit** breaking churches. We should grieve at broken lives, broken churches, broken nations, and we should grieve at the darkness and disorder of our own hearts. All around we look at the ruins of what ought to be a glorious church.

The persecuted church the world over sings this psalm; and we must sing it with them.

Five centuries after this psalm was first sung, what would it have meant for Jesus of Nazareth to sing Psalm **74:12-17**? Surely this: on the throne of the universe there is one who judges justly, who created a world of moral order, who will restore that order in the end. Jesus believed that, in his humanity; he staked his life and eternity upon it, and it proved true. In my pain and grief at the broken state of God's church, I too may entrust myself to him who judges justly (1 Peter 2:23) because he is the "faithful Creator" (1 Peter 4:19). After Jesus was crucified, the fact that the sun rose on the Saturday after Good Friday was evidence to encourage the faithful that Easter Sunday would come.

2,000 years after that, the fact that the sun rose this morning, and the fact that autumn has again followed summer, assures us that the

Lord Jesus will return, order will be re-established in creation and the ruined church will be restored. And so we should grieve; but we can also do far more than grieve.

## Questions for reflection

1. Where do you see reasons for discouragement in the church?
2. In what senses do you long for God to rescue his people today?
3. How does this psalm help you to pray about these things?

PSALMS 84 AND 87

# 10. DELIGHT IN HOME

In chapter 9, we considered the two psalms of lament that begin Book III of the Psalms. Now we consider two contrasting psalms, still in the same book, in which we express our delight in "Zion".

Though Psalm 84 does not mention it by name, both it and Psalm 87 are emphatically songs of Zion, the city founded "on the holy mountain" (87:1; see 2:6). In biblical imagery, this means all that the old-covenant Jerusalem foreshadowed: the place where the assembly of God's people gather under God's anointed King and enjoy access to God through sacrifice. The New Testament clearly shows us that all this is fulfilled in the Lord Jesus Christ and his people; in Hebrews 12:22-24 the writer demonstrates that "Mount Zion" is fulfilled in the assembly of Christ's church. When John Newton, inspired by Psalm 87, wrote his famous hymn "Glorious things of thee are spoken, Zion, city of our God", he rightly understood that Zion today means the church of Jesus Christ, Jew and Gentile, gathered around God's Christ and enjoying access to the Father through his sacrifice.

So, despite the later destruction of the Zion towards which the pilgrims who most likely first sang Psalm 84 were walking, we believe that the promises of God attached to "Zion" will be fulfilled.

## A song to stir our hearts

"Longing is written all over this psalm" (Kidner, *Psalms*, Volume 2, page 302). Psalm 84 speaks to us not so much of facts (although there are facts) as of affections. To join in the singing of this psalm will cause a warmth and delight to well up in us; it will not only inform our minds but warm our hearts. When writing the **articles** for the conduct of worship in Geneva in the sixteenth century, John Calvin wrote:

> "Certainly at present the prayers of the faithful are so cold that we should be greatly ashamed and confused. The Psalms can stimulate us to raise our hearts to God and arouse us to an ardour in invoking as well as in exalting with praises the glory of His name." (Quoted in William L. Holladay, *The Psalms through Three Thousand Years*, page 199)

Our need for warmth is no less than that of the church in sixteenth-century Geneva.

We do not know when this member of the "Sons of Korah" wrote the psalm. It may have been written before the Babylonian exile when the temple of Solomon was standing and pilgrims went up there for the old-covenant festivals; perhaps the reference to "autumn rains" (**v 6**) suggests the **Feast of Tabernacles**. There seems to be an "anointed one" on the throne (**v 9**)—a king in David's line. But it continued to be sung during and after the exile when there was no king in David's line (even if, after the exile, there was a second temple). It is placed now in Book III, which suggests a special appropriateness at a time of exile. Here is a song for believers of every age who are living as "exiles" (1 Peter 1:1), far from their final home.

It is simplest to take the psalm in three parts (**v 1-4**, **5-7** and **8-12**), each of which contains a reference to blessing (**v 4**, **5**, **12**) and each of which stirs in us a facet of longing.

## Longing for the blessings of home

The song is sung by an individual: one who speaks, as always in the psalms, by the Spirit of God, who is the Spirit of Christ. He begins with an exclamation: "How lovely…" (**v 1**). The word translated "lovely" speaks not so much of the objective loveliness of what he will describe (although it is lovely) but about his love for it: in other words, "how beloved" or "how much I love..." So he is saying, *What a dearly-loved place is your dwelling-place, God! I cannot think of anywhere I would rather be.* The "dwelling-place" means the tabernacle, and then the temple of the LORD in Jerusalem. This is the place where the "LORD Almighty"—literally "the LORD of hosts", the covenant God with incomparably large armies—made his presence known on earth.

**Verse 2** intensifies this expression of desire. The inner being of this believer (his "soul", his whole self in its aspect of desire) "yearns" for this place. Both his "heart" (his inner being) and his "flesh" (his bodily existence) "cry out" to be there. The reason is that this place was where "the living God" could be found. The living God is the source of all life that is truly life. The whole person of this believer is entirely oriented—is turned in affection and desire—towards the living God who at that time made himself known in the temple. No facet of the believer's existence looks elsewhere for life or anything that makes life worth living.

As he remembers the courts of the temple, open to the sky, his mind goes to the "sparrow" and the "swallow"—small birds that made their nests there (**v 3a**). Perhaps there is the thought that, for all his infinite power and greatness, the "LORD Almighty" cares for the smallest creature. As Jesus would later say, not a sparrow falls to the ground outside of the Father's care (Matthew 10:29). Here was a place where the weakest and most vulnerable would be loved and cared for: what a lovely place! This thought might have been a comfort to those who had lost a child, whether a young child after birth or a child within the womb. There would be a home for such a little life, as there was a home for the sparrow, for the smallest unborn child is of far greater worth than the sparrow.

The reference to the "altar" (Psalm **84:3**) reminds us that the beauty of this place was, paradoxically, inseparable from the offering of bloody sacrifices for sins. Only because sacrifices were offered on the altar was it possible for sinful men and women to gain some kind of access to the living God. Because of the altar, this believer could address God as "*my* King and *my* God" (**v 3**, my emphasis), the word "my" indicating covenant ties of loyalty. Finally, there would be a perfect sacrifice, offered by the king himself for his people. This great king would be both priest and sacrifice; in him there is full and final forgiveness and true access to God.

**Verse 4** looks backwards (and forwards, perhaps) wistfully. It declares a blessing, the first of the three blessings of the psalm: "Blessed are those who dwell in your house" (the temple). These men and women are constantly taken up with glad and heartfelt praise.

All these longings find their fulfilment in Jesus Christ, the One who is "greater than the temple" (Matthew 12:6). He is the sacrifice for sinners offered on the altar (Hebrews 9:28). He is the place where God tabernacled upon earth (John 1:14). He is the One in whom access to God the Father is found by sinners on earth (Ephesians 2:18). He is the One in whom the life of the living God has appeared (John 1:18). Now, by his Spirit, the church of Jesus Christ is the temple of the living God (1 Corinthians 3:16). As Hans-Joachim Kraus writes:

> "Psalm 84 finds its [New Testament] fulfilment [in Christ]. In Jesus of Nazareth has life appeared (1 John 1:2). Here God has taken residence (John 1:14). The congregation of Jesus Christ, in which the exalted Lord is present, is the counterpart of the Old Testament sanctuary. At the same time, however, the Old Testament psalm points to the 'new Jerusalem' of a final and indissoluble communion with God [see Revelation 21:3-4 and verse 10 onwards]." (*Psalms*, Volume 2, page 171)

When we pray Psalm **84:1-4** through the lens of fulfilment in Christ, we express and we deepen in our own hearts the same yearning that is in the heart of Jesus for his church, and above all for the new Jerusalem that will come down from heaven to earth and be the dwelling-place of Jesus with his people for all eternity. We have natural desires to "go home"—particularly after a period away or at the end of a long and difficult day. But no dwelling-place in this age can finally be our home, no matter how many memories it may hold or how happy it may be. The longing of the believer ought to be to go home in the final sense of living with Jesus in the new Jerusalem, which is the new heavens and the new earth. How lovely that will be, and how much we set our love on that wonderful place of care and security and beauty!

## Looking for the blessings of pilgrimage

But if there is a blessedness in *being* home (**v 1-4**), there is also a blessedness in *going* home, during the pilgrimage journey. This is the theme of **verses 5-7**, with the second ascription of blessedness (**v 5**). Here is someone (literally "Blessed is the man whose...") who finds "strength" (or "refuge") in the God who dwells in Zion. In their "heart" (or "mind") is "pilgrimage". The word translated "pilgrimage" (NIV) is literally "highways"; in the context this is the highways that lead to Zion, which is why some English translations have "the highways to Zion" (e.g. ESV). The NIV's "hearts ... set on pilgrimage" captures this sense, albeit a little loosely.

The point is that here are those who, because their love is fixed upon Zion, cannot stop thinking about the journey to Zion. Because they *love* home, they want every step of their lives to be a part of the *journey* home. They are not wandering aimlessly through this life; they are deliberately, intentionally and consciously heading for home. Like a pilgrim walking up to Jerusalem for one of the great old-covenant festivals, they walk through life with their hearts set on their beautiful destination.

> Believers are not wandering aimlessly through this life; they are deliberately, intentionally and consciously heading for home.

It will not be an easy journey. They will sometimes find themselves journeying through "the Valley of Baka" (**v 6**). This is an unknown place in Old Testament history, although the word "Baka" may be linked to the Hebrew word for weeping or sadness. But it is clear from the context that it is a dry and lifeless place; this is why it is significant to say that "they make it a place of springs" and it is covered with surprising "pools" from the "autumn rains" (**v 6**). This is a poetic way of saying that when someone whose heart is filled with love for Zion travels through the dry and lifeless valleys, he or she makes that very tough and sad place into one of life-giving waters. A place and time that is in its very nature hostile to life will be turned into a place where there is life, simply because walking through it is someone in whose heart are the highways to Zion!

Such people will "go from strength to strength" on the journey, until, at the end of the pilgrimage, "each appears before God in Zion" (**v 7**). Although outwardly they and we will decay as we age, or become ill, or are persecuted, or are crushed by the miseries of sin and sin's consequences in a broken world, inwardly we shall experience a wonderful daily renewal by the Spirit of God (2 Corinthians 3:18). This blessing for the journey home is as wonderful, in its way, as the blessings to be ours when we arrive home. Singing this psalm will stir in us this longing for home in such a way that we are able to view all of life as a highway heading to the new Jerusalem, where we shall dwell with God because of Jesus our Saviour.

## Longing for the Messiah

Psalm **84:8-9** comes as a surprise. Suddenly, and for no obvious reason, the song-leader prays—and by implication invites us, too, to pray—for the Messiah. The one called "our shield" is the same as the one called "your anointed one", which is "messiah" in Hebrew and later "Christ" in Greek. This, in Old Testament history, was a king—every king—in David's line. But, as God's people went on singing this during and after the exile, when there was no such king, it became clear that they were singing about a future King—great David's greater Son. The prayer is that God will "look with favour" on the Messiah—that he will shower his favour and blessing upon him. Why? Because all the blessings of Zion, and of the journey to Zion, are to be found only because of, and in union with, the anointed king. The old-covenant believer prayed for God's "favour" on the king. We know that favour rested in its divine fullness upon Jesus, the beloved Son of God and David's greater Son. We pray this prayer now: that the favour of God may rest on the people of the anointed One, the church of Jesus Christ.

The key word in **verses 10-11** is "good". The word "better" in the English translations of the start of **verse 10** is literally "more *good* than" (so the Hebrew word "good" appears here too). Goodness, or blessing, is to be found in the "courts" of God in a way that dwarfs into insignificance all the goodness that can be found elsewhere (**v 10**); time warps around the temple, for a day of true blessing there is worth incomparably more than all the so-called blessings to be found outside of the Christ, who is the fulfilment of the temple. But the word "good" means more than just pleasure or enjoyment: as the end of **verse 10** makes clear, it is inseparable from moral goodness; it is the opposite of "the tents of the wicked".

The covenant God is "a sun and shield" in Zion precisely because Zion is the place of the anointed king, the Messiah, who is God's "shield" for us (**v 9**). The LORD "bestows *favour*" (**v 11**, my emphasis) upon us because he answers the prayer that he look with "*favour*" on his anointed king (**v 9**). All the blessings of God come to the people of the king precisely and only because they are first poured out without limit upon Christ our King. He is the One "whose way of life is blameless" and from whom God withholds "no good thing". In him, and in him alone, every spiritual blessing of true goodness is to be found (Ephesians 1:3). He is the One who, in his truly human earthly walk, trusted unflinchingly in the LORD Almighty (Psalm **84:12**); he is therefore the pre-eminent recipient of the Father's blessing, and the One in and through whom all that blessing is poured out upon us, his people.

The promise that "no good thing does he withhold from those whose way of life is blameless" (**v 11**) has been a precious promise to many suffering believers down the centuries. It is true for all who are in Christ, the blameless One, that nothing God gives to us is anything other than good. This is very hard to believe when we suffer sometimes inexplicable and often very painful hurts. It cannot have been easy for Jesus of Nazareth to believe it. And yet it is true; it was true for him, and it is true for us. God our heavenly Father will never give to us anything except what he knows, in his infinite wisdom and kindness, to be what is truly the best for us. We will often not understand how this can be so; and yet it is. To trust this promise will bring surprising springs of life-giving water to us as we go through the Valley of Baka with our hearts set on the day when the dwelling-place of God will, at last, be our dwelling-place too.

## Questions for reflection

1. How could you make sure that each step of your life is a step towards the new creation?
2. In what respects do you need to ask the Holy Spirit to renew and strengthen you on the way?
3. How can you encourage other Christians to keep going in their walk with God?

PART TWO

## The longing to belong

Where do you belong? Where do you really want to belong? The longing to belong has deep roots in our humanness. From the desire to have a safe place in a stable family (a source of misery to so many who do not) to the yearning for citizenship in a desirable country (for which refugees will make costly sacrifices to secure it), we all long to belong somewhere. "I wish I had been born somewhere else," says someone. "If only I could fit in," says another.

Psalm 87 encapsulates the most wonderful news in the world: the offer of a new birth certificate that attests and guarantees that we are citizens in the most desirable place on earth.

## A song of Zion

This wonderful song of Zion was sung, and perhaps written, at a time when Zion had little or no visible glory. Its place in Book III of the Psalms suggests an appropriateness for the time of exile in Babylon. Immediately preceding it, Psalm 86 is an old "of David" psalm probably placed here as a reminder of the troubles of the anointed king—troubles now being experienced by his exiled people. Following it, Psalm 88 is a deep lament, and Psalm 89 celebrates the covenant with David's line but then bewails the breaking of that covenant (or so it seems) by the ending of the monarchy at the time of the Babylonian exile.

It is therefore very remarkable, and surprising, to find Psalm 87's joyful celebration of Zion placed just here. Calvin wrote:

> "The miserable and distressing condition in which the [old covenant] Church was placed after the Babylonish captivity, might be apt to sink the minds of the godly into despondency; and accordingly, the Holy Spirit here promises her restoration in a wonderful … manner, so that nothing would be more desirable than to be reckoned among the number of her members."
>
> (*Commentary on the Book of Psalms*, Volume 3, page 393)

This is therefore a song for us to sing when we are despondent about the visible distress of Christ's church today.

## Founded on unchanging love

This city is "founded"—the word speaks of security—"on the holy mountain" (Psalm **87:1**). A mountain, in biblical imagery as in physical reality, is a stable place. The "holy" mountain means the mountain that is set apart to belong to God. In the ancient Near East, people sometimes spoke of a storybook mountain of the gods and goddesses in this way, rather as the Greeks and Romans later spoke of Mount Olympus; sometimes it was called "the mountain in the far north" (or "Mount Zaphon"). But in the Old Testament, God takes the high ground on which Jerusalem is built and dignifies it with this significance. It is the place where God declares his covenant with David and his line of kings (2:6), the anointed messiahs of Old Testament history that would culminate in the final Messiah.

**87:1** is echoed at the end of **verse 5**: "and the Most High himself will *establish* her" (my emphasis). So the psalm twice has this emphasis on the stability of the city, founded and established by God.

The church of Christ is "founded" securely on this covenant promise of God to Christ. It is therefore the place (or people) that "the LORD loves" (**v 2**): "loves" is in the present tense, signifying an unchanging love. (VanGemeren comments that the use of the Hebrew participle here "bears out the constancy of his love for Zion"—*The Expositor's Bible Commentary,* page 655.) The "gates" of an ancient city were not just the entrances through the walls but the focus of business, government and justice. So "the gates of Zion" speaks of all of Zion, rather as we might say "the Kremlin" as shorthand for all of Moscow, or even all of Russia.

The church of Christ ("Zion") owes its unshakeable stability to the unchanging covenant love of God for its King, and therefore for all of its people. It is not secure because its people are strong or impressive, for we are (for the most part) neither. No, our security as the church of

Christ rests not on our goodness, our morality, our power or our skill but entirely upon the unmerited loving promise of God to us in Christ. God the Father loves the Lord Jesus Christ with an unbreakable love, and has so loved him from all eternity; that love has been extended to us as men and women in Christ. If we are in Christ, we belong to a city whose architect and builder is God (Hebrews 11:10).

It is precisely because the church of Christ rests upon the gracious love of God that it can be the wonderful assembly now celebrated in Psalm **87:3-6**. For if it rested upon any human achievements or privileges, it would be a very different, and much narrower, body.

## Marked by glorious diversity

Diversity and inclusivity are watchwords of today's liberal culture. "We are an inclusive church," some proclaim. Often by that they mean that they accept moral standards that deviate from those of the Bible. But this leads to a diversity that comes under the judgment of God. The church should indeed be marked by diversity, but this should come from the inclusivity of the gospel. For Zion is the spiritual home for people who live all over the world. This is the glory of Zion.

There is a sandwich pattern to **verses 3-7**. In **verse 3** and **verse 7** the words "of you" and "in you" are the same in the Hebrew. **Verse 4** and **verse 6** both end with the words, literally, "This one was born there"—in Zion. And **verse 5**, at the centre, celebrates that "this one and that one were *born in her*".

**Verse 3** is the headline to this section. At the time of exile, and indeed after the exile, you could not honestly say that "glorious things" were *visible* in Zion. The city had been utterly destroyed, the temple had been razed to the ground, and the monarchy had ended. A second temple was built after the exile, but it was much less impressive than Solomon's temple (see Haggai 2:3), for this was "the day of small things" (Zechariah 4:10). No, Zion looked no more impressive then than the church of Christ looks today. But "glorious things" were nevertheless "said" of her in prophecy and celebrated in this Spirit-inspired song; as John Newton translated it, "Glorious things of thee are *spoken*, Zion, city of our God" (my emphasis).

What are these glorious things? Psalm **87:4-6** tell us. The splendour of Zion—the glory of the church of Jesus Christ—will, perhaps surprisingly, be the strange and wonderful list of the men and women who will be given citizenship in it. For the church of Jesus Christ will be (and is already in anticipation) the only truly worldwide people on earth.

> The splendour of Zion will be the strange and wonderful list of the men and women who have been given citizenship in it.

**Verse 4** gives representative examples of the kinds of men and women who will be enrolled as citizens of Zion. First, there are two ancient enemies. "Rahab" was the name of a storybook monster in the old stories about the creation of the world; Rahab was a monster of chaos rampaging around the world. The Old Testament writers took these pagan stories and used Rahab as a mocking nickname for the ancient nation of Egypt—the Egypt of the time of the Exodus, and later the local superpower in which the people of God were tempted to trust and with which they were tempted to make an alliance (for example Exodus 89:10; Isaiah 30:7; 51:9-10; Job 26:12). Babylon was, of course, the oppressive power which had taken the people into exile. In this imagery and these historical memories of the exodus and then the exile, both were places that spoke of intense hostility to the covenant God of Israel. But in Psalm **87:4** we discover that one day men and women from both of these places, who had been enemies of God, would bow the knee to God's anointed king and be recorded as men and women who now belonged to the kingdom they had once mocked. While by nature they were once God's enemies, now they would be reconciled to him (see Romans 5:9-11).

Second, there is what we may call an ancient irritant. "Philistia" described the region where the old Philistines had lived, who had been such a long-running sore for the people of God in the days of King Saul and King David. Men and women who had irritated the people of God through successive raids upon their land would now acknowledge the king who ruled in the line of monarchs that they had so vexed.

Then there is "Tyre". Tyre was a rich merchant-trading city: the place where people worshipped wealth, career and worldly success. These men and women had not perhaps thought of themselves as hostile to the people of God; and yet, by their successful worship of wealth just to the north of the promised land, they perpetrated a long-running seduction, luring the people of God away from an undivided devotion to the covenant God. These too, who seemed to have it all, would abandon their worship of wealth and come into Zion.

Finally there is "Cush". Cush was perhaps somewhere in upper Egypt or Ethiopia: a distant place inhabited by men and women of a different colour of skin and a very different ethnicity. This was, in Geoffrey Grogan's phrase, "the fringe of Israel's world" (Grogan, *Psalms*, page 153). These people, who had seemed so impossibly distant geographically and culturally from the God of the covenant and his people, would bow the knee to God's anointed king.

Of all these multiethnic and such very different people it will be said, "This one was born in Zion" (Psalm **87:4**). They were, by nature, born in Egypt, Babylon, Philistia, Tyre or Cush—but they will be given not just a visa to visit Zion but citizenship in Zion. In fact, they will be given a new birth certificate. We may imagine one of them putting on her gravestone "Born in Tyre; born again in Zion"; another of them might inscribe on his "Born in Cush; born again in Zion". When the vicious Assyrian emperors deported conquered peoples, they would resettle them in slavery and would write of them statements such as, "I counted them among the Assyrians". In a far better way the God of Israel, the God and Father of Jesus, writes of you and me—and writes of this wonderful mixture of undeserving men and women—*I counted them among my family, my people; I gave them a new birth certificate upon which it is written, "Born again in Zion", with all the privileges that entails.*

In **verses 5** and **6** there is a tremendous emphasis on the new birth of this astonishing variety of people; on "this one and that one [who] were born in her". There is a sense of wonder as the poet looks at each one in his prophetic imagination: *What, him, a citizen of Zion?! What, her, enrolled in Zion?!*

Yes: enrolled they were, and enrolled we are. They are enrolled through the personal decree of the Father's love, as **verse 6** makes clear. God himself writes their names—our names—in the "register" of the citizens of Zion. "This one [insert your name with awe and wonder!] was born in Zion." *But,* we respond, *I thought I was born in Babylon, a child of Adam, tainted by sin, far from God, deserving of God's wrath, and without hope in the world* (Ephesians 2:3,12). *No,* says the Father in love, *You were born again in Zion, the people of Jesus my beloved Son. Now you are his, and therefore my child for ever.* There is a wonderful sense in which God the Father wrote your name and mine in the register of Zion from all eternity; and yet there is also a sense in which, on the day we first placed our faith in Jesus as our Lord our Saviour and were born again, he wrote our name in the register, as a registrar might write out a birth certificate for a newborn baby.

For centuries—perhaps about half a millennium—believers sang this song of Zion with almost no evidence that it could ever be true. **Ruth** the Moabite had come into Zion, as had **Rahab** the prostitute of Jericho and some in Nineveh in the time of Jonah. But for the most part, Zion was very far from being the glorious place of which this song sings. In a way, this psalm is almost an **exposition** of the promise given to David (itself an echo of the covenant with Abraham) in Psalm 86:9: "All the nations you have made will come and worship before you, LORD".

And then, quite suddenly, in the twinkling of an eye in historical terms, Zion began to be visibly glorious. From the day of **Pentecost** onwards, men and women all over the world began to be born again into Zion—into the people of Jesus Christ. Men and women speaking different languages, inhabiting very varied cultures and from all social classes began to be given citizenship in Zion, as by the Spirit of Christ they were born from above and their names were entered in the Lamb's **book of life**. And, for all her problems, the worldwide church of Christ is a glorious place. How often I have looked around at a Christian gathering and thought to myself, "Apart from the work of Jesus Christ, there is no possible way in which such a varied mixture of men and women could possibly be united in joy. This is indeed the remaking of a broken world."

## The source of all our joy

And so the psalm ends, very appropriately, with great joy—with a wonderful gathering of very surprising men and women making music and singing the great truth that in Zion are found all the fountains that feed their joy (Psalm **87:7**). Everything that makes life worth living comes from membership of Zion. Everything. We do not sing that some of what rejoices our hearts comes from what we may be proud of in this life—our nationality, or education, or career success, or family—and that there is a little room at the end for a measure of joy that we find in belonging to the church of Christ. No! All the fountains that feed my life and give me joy come from being a member, by new birth, of the church of Jesus Christ. Those things that the world counts precious—that I once counted precious—I now count as rubbish for the sake of "the surpassing worth of knowing Christ Jesus my Lord" (Philippians 3:7-11); and instead, I make this the motto of my life:

*Glorious things of thee are spoken,*
*Zion, city of our God;*
*He whose word cannot be broken*
*Formed thee for his own abode;*
*On the Rock of Ages founded,*
*What can shake thy sure repose?*

*With salvation's walls surrounded,*
*Thou may'st smile at all thy foes.*

*See the streams of living waters,*
*Springing from eternal love,*
*Well supply thy sons and daughters,*
*And all fear of want remove;*
*Who can faint while such a river*
*Ever flows their thirst t'assuage?*
*Grace, which like the Lord, the giver,*
*Never fails from age to age.*

("Glorious things of thee are spoken", John Newton)

## Questions for reflection

1. Does it surprise you that God's inclusion of diverse people in his kingdom is said to be an expression of glory?
2. What steps could you take to reach out to more diverse people in and through your church?
3. How do you respond to the idea that all joy comes from being part of God's church?

PSALMS 90 AND 91

# 11. TOTAL SECURITY

Book IV (Psalms 90 – 106) has a different feel to Book III. Most of the psalms here have no superscription. There is little or nothing about the human king in David's line. The major emphasis is on the security and assurance that comes to the people of God from knowing that the covenant God is the ultimate king, whose sovereign faithfulness guarantees all the promises of the covenant.

There is a pushing back, deeper into Israel's history, to before the covenant with David that appears to be broken (Psalm 89)—to the story of God's faithfulness, right back to Abraham and then in the time of Moses. And there is a pushing up, beyond the hope for an earthly messiah to the sovereign God in heaven, who guarantees this hope. When Jesus, the believing Israelite, first sang these psalms, they must have been to him a deep reassurance that his heavenly Father reigned in covenantal faithfulness and would finally bring about the end of the exile (106:47)—as indeed he did, through Jesus himself (see Matthew 1:1-18). They reassure Christ's exiled church (see 1 Peter 1:1) in much the same way—showing us that we will finally be gathered, in and with Christ, into our inheritance, which is now kept in heaven for us (1 Peter 1:4) and which will one day to descend from heaven to earth (Revelation 21).

## Establish the work of our hands!

Do you long to achieve something worthwhile for Jesus? For your life to count for something? Not to be a complete nobody? We all yearn for that (or we ought to). The big surprise at the end of Psalm 90 is that we are authorised to ask God to "establish the work of our hands" (**v 17**)—to make what we do last for eternity.

Although this psalm is often, rightly, used at funerals, it is relevant to any time of weakness and discouragement in our walk with the Lord.

Who sang this song? First, this is a prayer of Moses. It is the only psalm headed "A prayer of Moses". He is called a "man of God", which means a prophet in the Old Testament and then a pastor-teacher in the New Testament. Moses appears seven times in Book IV (Psalm **90:1**; 99:6; 103:7; 105:26; 106:16, 23, 32); outside Book IV, he appears only once (77:21). It makes perfect sense that Moses needed to pray this psalm. Between his waiting in Midian after fleeing Egypt (and perhaps ruing the seemingly lost opportunity to lead the people of God, Exodus 2:11-22) and his final moments on Mount Pisgah, when he could not lead the people into the promised land (Deuteronomy 34), Moses knew many times of frustration and disappointment in his service of God. But although this might have been the prayer of Moses alone, most of it is spoken in the plural, as if Moses was leading the people of Israel in prayer at a time of corporate frustration. Perhaps the most likely occasion would have been during the plague of snakes in Numbers 21, when the people asked Moses to "pray that the LORD will take the snakes away from us" (Numbers 21:7); perhaps he led them in the prayer of this psalm .

As well as being originally a prayer of Moses (who of course lived centuries before the exile from the land to the verge of which he had led God's people) this psalm comes at the head of Book IV—immediately, that is, after the strong context of Babylonian exile that dominates Book III. Second, then, this is a prayer at the time of exile—for both during and after the exile, believers badly needed encouragement to see that their service of God was not utterly futile, as it must have seemed to be.

Third, this is a prayer of Jesus. Surely the Lord must have meditated on this psalm and prayed that the Father would establish the work of his hands at the many times when his **ministry** was frustrating and shadowed with failure (for example, in John 6:66; 12:37).

If Jesus needed to pray this psalm, we his people most certainly need to pray it for ourselves. But we cannot pray the final verse until we have prayed the first 16 verses. Psalm **90:1-16** is like the safety filter to enable us to pray **verse 17** safely. Without **verses 1-16**, the prayer that God will make my discipleship a success would become a dangerous and egotistical prayer.

## Settled affection and sober reality

Much of the psalm will focus on our transience. But we begin centred on God. The first word of **verses 1-2** is "Lord" and the last is "God" (in English as in Hebrew). Whether we have been taken off to exile or we live in the promised land, our weak and transient existence is rooted in the unchanging home ("dwelling-place") that is God. Before God called creation into being, and before time itself began, God is, and is the home of all who belong to him. A child in a family that moved house many times once said to his mother, "Mum, *you* are where home is". So it is with our God. He is unchangeably the same, unchanging in his essence, consistent in his providence, unalterable in his affections, not swayed or moved by passions. It is in and with him that we live, amid "the changes and chances of this fleeting world", as the Anglican Book of Common Prayer puts it.

It is moving to think of the Lord Jesus, who had "nowhere to lay his head" (Luke 9:58), praying this psalm and saying to his Father, *You are my dwelling-place through all generations*. We too can pray this, with even greater new-covenant richness, for our home is with the Father and the Son, who come, by the Spirit, to make their home with us (John 14:23). The security of the remembrance that the eternal God is our home prepares us for the sober realism of what will follow.

You and I become restless and discontented because we make the mistake of thinking that this world is our home. But we should not! The Creator, who formed us from dust (Genesis 2:7), has woven together in each mother's womb an organism of the most wonderful complexity, with astonishing abilities, held together by nerves, sinews, ligaments, neural pathways and a countless multitude of integrated ties. Dust is disintegrated matter. When the Creator declared, with perfect justice, that we would return to dust (Genesis 3:19), he decreed that human existence would always be shadowed by death. We—who in our integration can think, imagine, talk, love, make, desire and delight—will one day be taken apart cell by cell, atom by atom, and returned to dust. One day, the Creator will say to you and to me, "Return to dust, you mortals"; and on that day we will die. Death is God's final "No!" to human pride (see James 4:13-14). "I saw pale kings," wrote John Keats in *La Belle Dame Sans Merci*, "and princes too. Pale warriors, death-pale were they all." For no matter how great kings and princes think they are, they all die.

In Psalm **90:4-6** we join Moses in meditating on the mystery of time. We pass through time like a frail plant in the hot Middle-Eastern climate, blossoming perhaps with strength and beauty, but then suddenly—all too suddenly—withering. Mays writes of how,

> "Time is the medium of our mortality," writes Mays, "and so [it is] the favourite focus of our folly ... The young think they are immortal, the old despair because their time is over."
>
> (*Psalms*, page 295)

We say that time is on our side; but time is never on our side for it is shadowed always by death.

We need this sober realism about our frailty, our mortality, our terrible transience. We may be blighted by the great expectations loaded upon us, perhaps in childhood or early adulthood; perhaps our parents had hoped—and let us know that they had hoped—that we would succeed in particular ways. Maybe they wanted us to be the successes—in exams, or music, or sport, or jobs—that they had failed to be or never had the opportunity to be. How sad we feel when we begin to realise we shall never achieve what they have expected for us or what we hoped for ourselves.

But there is worse to come than mere transience.

## Sad wisdom and sure faith

In **verse 12**, we pray with Moses "that we may gain a heart of wisdom". **Verses 7-12** teach us that wisdom. The terrible words "Return ... you mortals!" (**v 3**) go back to the judgment of God upon sinners in Genesis 3:19: "for dust you are and to dust you will return". And so in Psalm **90:7-9** Moses leads us in prayer to acknowledge that the reason we are transient is the righteous "anger", "indignation", and "wrath" of God against our "iniquities [and] secret sins".

We live for "days", but every day is shadowed by the wrath of God. At the end "we finish our years with a moan" (**v 9**)—a whimper. We sometimes say of someone who dies in old age, "They were tired; they were ready to go". However great someone's achievements may be, the deathbed is not a place for pride. Even if we live a long life (the "seventy years" that was a very good life expectancy in the ancient world), or a very long life ("eighty"), there is no such thing as a perfect day; each day, even the very happiest and best, contains some shadow of "trouble and sorrow"—even if it is only an anxiety that it will not last. The word translated "the best of them" (**v 10**) means something like pride, pageantry, bright energy. But it will not—it cannot—last.

However great someone's achievements may be, the deathbed is not a place for pride.

Why is life shadowed by death? Because we are sinners in a world under sin. "We are mortal because God is angry, and God is angry because we are sinful" (Michael Wilcock, *The Message of Psalms*, Volume 2). And this is still true after Christ, insofar as our *bodily* existence is concerned. We have forgiveness in Christ; there is no condemnation for those who are in Christ (Romans 8:1); God is no longer angry with us. But we still wait for the redemption of our *bodies*, which are "dead" (that is, mortal, dying) because of sin (Romans 8:10, 23). It is not true that Christians do not face death; we do still have to face death, and dying, and sickness, and weakness, and frailty, and ageing—unless the Lord Jesus returns first.

**Verses 11** and **12** teach us to pray that we may grasp deeply this sober truth. We need to understand from our frailty and our mortality that God's anger against sinners is very hot and great. We need to "number our days"—never to forget that we are forgiven sinners who must wait until resurrection day for the redemption of our bodies. A foolish heart lives as if we were immortal; a heart of wisdom remembers every day that we are transient because of our sin. Then, and only then, will we be humbled under the mighty hand of God.

The psalm that began with our eternal home has taken us down to the depths of our fragility and our guilt. It will end with God's grace. The prayers of **verses 13-17** claim the promises of the covenant. In **verse 13** we have the only use in this psalm of the covenant name of God: "Lord". The question "How long?" echoes the same question in 89:46, at the end of Book III. The question that lies behind this question is the question of the covenant: will the covenant God be faithful to his covenant—the precious covenant that seems (by the end of Psalm 89) to be in tatters? The title "your servants" at the end of **90:13** is a covenant designation; it means "those who serve you as covenant servants". In **verse 14** we pray for the Lord's "unfailing love"—*chesed*. We do not pray that God will be nice to us; we pray that he will fulfil his covenant promise of unfailing love. All those covenant promises, in the covenants made to Noah, to Abraham, to Moses, and to David, find their grand "Yes!" in Jesus Christ (2 Corinthians 1:20). Ultimately, Moses leads the people of God in these verses to pray for the coming of the Christ who will fulfil the covenant promises.

In Psalm **90:15** Moses prays with confidence that the gladness that will come in the future is a joy that more than cancels out all the sorrows and miseries of living in a world under sin; and it will so do. At present we have "days" drifting wearily on into "years" of affliction. But when

Christ comes, the gracious deeds of God—his "splendour"—will be shown in wonder and majesty to all his people (**v 16**).

The prayer of **verse 17** is therefore a prayer to be prayed corporately, by the people of God. It is not so much a prayer for "my" personal success in discipleship as a prayer for the shared discipleship of all the discouraged people of God. And it is to be prayed in Christ. Jesus Christ supremely prayed **verse 17**. The Father heard his prayer. The prophecy that Jesus would one day see the fruit of his suffering and be satisfied (Isaiah 53:11) will be gloriously fulfilled, as he sees a countless multitude, with their sins paid for by his finished work, coming into the new heavens and the new earth by resurrection. The "work" of Jesus will most certainly be established!

And, precisely because his work will be established, and because the bodily resurrection of Jesus demonstrates this, we too may know that all our work done in his name will bear fruit (1 Corinthians 15:58). All who persevere in patient discipleship may pray that the work of our hands will achieve something enduring. As we trust and rest in God, our dwelling place, we press on in giving our lives for Jesus and his gospel. We seek to bear witness to Jesus among neighbours, work colleagues, friends and family. We do what we can to share the gospel of Jesus with them and live in such a way that it shows the goodness and power of that gospel. Psalm 90 puts into our hands a prayer led by Jesus Christ, a prayer for us to join in, a prayer to pray most especially when we are most deeply pained by the fragility of our lives. Being a disciple of Jesus is hard, but it is worth it!

## Questions for reflection

1. What difference might seeing time from God's point of view make to you?
2. When are you most pained by the fragility of life?
3. What work of your hands do you want to ask God to establish?

# PART TWO

Psalm 90 is a prayer: Moses, the man of God, leads the people in crying out that God will establish the work of our hands (90:17). In many ways Psalm 91 is the God-given answer to the cry of Psalm 90. It is an astonishingly beautiful and reassuring psalm. Promises of safety, victory and honour pour out of it in verse after verse. It is no surprise that it has become a great favourite of many down the centuries.

And yet we must be careful. It is perhaps here, more than anywhere, that we must resist the temptation simply to appropriate all the "nice" bits of Scripture for ourselves, simply because we would like them to be true for us. The really big question—the question upon which every blessing hangs—is this: to whom are these promises given? We need to ask and answer this question honestly before we can decide how we should sing, and respond to, this psalm.

So we need to begin by hearing the psalm on its own terms. It starts with a headline statement (Psalm **91:1**) and a headline response (**v 2**), and continues with a long speech of assurance about what God will do for this person (**v 3-13**), before concluding with a final direct assurance spoken by God about what he will do for this one (**v 14-16**).

## Who will find safety?

"Whoever dwells" (**v 1**, NIV) translates the singular "He who dwells" (see ESV). Literally, what is going to be said is said of one individual. This individual may represent any person who fulfils the conditions of the psalm, but in the first instance we should think of one person.

This verse reads like a tautology, where the second line says the same as the first. We may be tempted to respond, "Of course the one who dwells in the shelter of the Most High will rest in the shadow of the Almighty"; for the Most High is the same as the Almighty, and shelter and shadow speak of the same security. It's like saying, "The one who finds shelter in God finds shelter in God"! But this is to misunderstand how the poetry works. The second line gives emphasis and reinforcement to the first line. It means something like this: *The one who lives in the safe place that the Most High God offers really does rest safely in the shadow of that Almighty God.* That is to say, if someone genuinely seeks safety in this God alone, they will find it; they genuinely will. This is the theme of the psalm.

In **verse 2** we hear this individual responding with faith: *Yes,* they say, *this God is my safe place; I do trust in him.* Four names for God are used in **verses 1-2**. "The Most High" is a very ancient name; we first hear it in Genesis 14:19, where Melchizedek, the priest-king of Salem (later Jerusalem), uses it to bless Abraham. "The Almighty" (Hebrew *Shaddai*) is also a very ancient title (see Genesis 17:1; it appears often in the book of Job). "The LORD" is the covenant name of the God of Abraham, Isaac, and Jacob, and the God of Moses; and "God" is the most general name for the deity. Putting these four together stresses that the person in view here is not placing their trust in some vague self-defined spirituality but in the covenant Creator God of the Bible.

So the headline truth is that true security is to be found—and only to be found—in whole-hearted trust in the God of the Bible; which sounds nice and reassuring and sweetly religious, until we think honestly about our own responses to danger. We are always looking for places to hide. You and I may like the idea of fleeing to God alone for safety. But in reality we seek safety through caring for our health, through exercise; through education, through qualifications; through money, insurance, investments, or pensions; through close human relationships ... and in many other ways. We don't mind adding in a "God-bit" to the security mix, but we do not seek security in God *alone*. There is therefore, right at the start, a problem with appropriating to ourselves the promises of this psalm. This simply is not a description of me or you.

No—this psalm is given, first and foremost, for the reassurance of the king of Israel. There are several reasons for thinking this. One slightly technical reason is that there is an unusual number of words in the vocabulary of the psalm that echo the language of the old "of

David" psalms in Books I and II (for example, "refuge ... fortress"). A second is that the strength of the promises most naturally makes sense for a king leading his people to victory in battle; for example, see the language of triumph over enemies, pictured as terrible creatures, in Psalm **91:13**. (John Eaton speaks for many commentators when he writes, "The individual on whom such promises are lavished could hardly be any but the king"—*Kingship in the Psalms*, page 17.) A third is that when the devil quotes from this psalm in his temptations of the Lord Jesus, he prefaces his quotation with the words "If you are the son of God" (Luke 4:9). The title "son of God" means, in the first instance, the anointed king in David's line (see, for instance, 2 Samuel 7:14; Psalm 2:7). The devil assumes, and Jesus does not disagree, that the promises of this psalm can be appropriated by the one who is the "son of God"—that is, the anointed king. (Jesus does, of course, completely disagree with the use the devil wants to make of the promise; we shall consider that later.)

## Safety is found in God alone

Psalm **91:3-13** is one long, expansive, rich reassurance to this person—to the king: "Surely [God] will save you". The section is broken in **verse 9** by a virtual repetition of **verse 2**, as a reminder that these promises are given to the one who genuinely says, from a single heart, "The LORD is my refuge". Indeed, **verse 9** uses the same word for "dwelling-place" that meant so much to us at the start of Psalm 90.

**91:3-8** speaks both of what the king will be rescued *from* and of *how* he will be rescued. He will be rescued first from the danger of attacks from hostile people ("the fowler", **v 3**) and from dangerous illness ("deadly pestilence"). **Verse 4** uses the image of God as a large and powerful protective bird, covering the king with his strong feathers, so that under God's wings the king will find refuge. This beautiful metaphor is used in a slightly different way in Ruth 2:12. But here (as in Psalm 57:1) it most likely refers to the huge wings of the symbolic cherubim that stretched out over the ark of the covenant in the Most

Holy Place in the temple and supported the mercy seat, the throne of God himself (Tate, *Psalms 51-100*, page 77). In other words, the protection of God is more than a nice picture; it refers to the protection pledged, and honoured, in God's covenant with the king. This covenant reference is supported at the end of **91:4** with the reference to God's "faithfulness" (that is, covenant faithfulness) being like a shield or protective rampart for the king.

**Verses 5-6** speak vividly of protection at all times and from all threats. All times are conveyed first by the simple words "night" and "day", and then by the more intense words "darkness" and "midday". This means "all possible times"—from the most intensely bright to the most deeply dark, and everything in between (the technical term for this is a merism or merismus). The words "terror", "arrow", "pestilence that stalks" and "plague that destroys" may even have demonic overtones, as though the king is being reassured that God will protect him from every kind of danger, even the most darkly supernatural horrors of the world of demons and spirits.

**Verses 7-8** stress the extremity of the danger from which the king will be guarded. Huge numbers will fall in battle around him, but he himself will be kept safe. What he will see in the casualties around him is "the punishment of the wicked"—among whom he is not numbered. This is why he is protected, for he is a man in right relationship with God, as God's son.

It is a remarkable picture, and it continues in **verses 10-13** after the reminder of the commitment of this king in **verse 9**. The "tent" of the king in **verse 10** may possibly be his battle-tent, but is more likely to be a common image of human frailty, so easily destroyed unless it is protected by God. But protected he will be, for the "angels", God's powerful messengers, sent "to serve those who will inherit salvation" (Hebrews 1:14), will be under orders to protect him. They will be his impregnable security detail. They will guard him in "all" his "ways", wherever he goes, whatever he does. They will protect him from harm (Psalm **91:11-12**); and they will ensure that he wins astonishing victories over every possible enemy, symbolised by the power of the lion and the dangerous threat of a poisonous snake (**v 13**).

So, by the time we reach this part of the psalm, we are rejoicing for this believing king who finds his security in God alone and who is assured—deeply and comprehensively—that there is no safer man in the universe. There is no possible danger that can threaten his security or endanger his final victory over all evil.

## An intimate relationship of love

The psalm concludes with an oracle from the lips of God. (This oracle, and that of 95:7b-11, are the only direct oracles in Psalms 90 – 100. That may suggest that Psalms 91 and 95 form a bracket around Psalms 92 – 94. The LORD, the covenant God, declares that this king "loves" him (the word speaks of clinging to him in love, as God does to his people in Deuteronomy 7:7) and acknowledges his name, declaring his allegiance to this covenant God as he has revealed himself (his "name"). Between God and this king there is a relationship of intimate and committed covenant love, as father to son and son to father.

On the basis of this unbreakable loyal love, God the Father declares that he will "rescue" and "protect" this king, his son (Psalm **91:14**). This son will enjoy the privilege of answered prayer (**v 15**), just as God promised to the king in Psalm 2 (v 8: "Ask me…"). He will be given honour, long life and salvation (**91:15-16**).

## Are these promises for us?

And so we come back to the question with which we began: are these wonderful promises for us or not? On the face of it, the sad answer must be "no"! They are for the king in David's line—which means, ultimately, for the greater King who will inherit all the promises to David. Jesus Christ is the man who, through all the dangers of his life on earth, dwelt entirely in the shelter of God his Father, God Most High, the Almighty covenant God. He is the One who always said of his Father, "He is my refuge and my fortress, my God, in whom I trust" (**v 2**).

When the devil quoted from this psalm (**v 11-12**, recorded in Matthew 4:6 and Luke 4:10-11), he was right to imply that these promises were for Jesus the anointed King, the Son of God. So where did the devil go wrong? In twisting the promises of safety by taking them out of their inseparable context of loyal, loving covenant relationship. The moment Jesus might have taken a promise—for example, as the devil suggested, of Psalm **91:11** and **12**—as a magic wand that he could wield autonomously, independent of his Father, he would have broken the bond of loyal love upon which the promise rested. No! This promise is for the Son, who loyally clings to his Father God in devoted worship and whole-hearted love. This Son, and this Son alone, does indeed inherit all the promises of the psalm.

And he had inherited them through death itself. For although the sufferings of the Lord Jesus appeared to give the lie to these promises, the resurrection, ascension, and heavenly enthronement of Jesus speaks the final "Yes!" to them all. This King did indeed trample on the serpent (**v 13**); he is the offspring of the woman who would crush the snake's head (Genesis 3:15), and he did so by his victory at the cross.

But what about us? The wonder—and it is a very great wonder—of the Bible story is that it demonstrates to us that all the blessings of this psalm are indeed ours. They are not ours by nature, for none of us deserves to inherit them. But they are unbreakably ours in Christ, who has, on the basis of his obedience, won for us every spiritual blessing (Ephesians 1:3; Romans 5:12-21). The grand

The blessings of this psalm are not ours by nature, but they are unbreakably ours in Christ.

conclusion to Romans 8 is a kind of New Testament commentary on Psalm 91: "He who did not spare his own Son, but gave him up for us all—how will he not also, *along with him*, graciously give us all things?" (Romans 8:32). The key words are "along with him"; for it is "along with Christ"—in union with Christ, by the Spirit—that every believer may appropriate for himself or herself the astonishing promises of Psalm 91. They are ours in Christ!

In 1956, Jim Elliot and four other missionaries with him were murdered by members of the Amazonian tribe in Ecuador to whom they were seeking to bring the gospel. Elliot was aged 28. His widow, Elisabeth, wrote his story under a title taken from **verse 1** of this psalm: *Shadow of the Almighty*. It was a brave and insightful title for the story of a man who died an untimely and violent death. For to be in the shadow of the Almighty by being a man or woman in Christ does not insulate us from suffering, sickness or even from violent death. It means something deeper than this, as it did for the Lord Jesus: it means the assurance of bodily resurrection. The fulfilment of the promises of this psalm in the life of Jesus came after his sufferings and death; in his bodily resurrection we see him rescued from every attack and saved out of all suffering. This psalm never exempted Jesus from suffering (as the tempter suggested); but it guaranteed a final rescue from all trials. It is the same for us who suffer with our Lord that we may be glorified with him (Romans 8:17).

## Questions for reflection

1. What would it look like for you to dwell in God's shelter, take refuge in him, and love him—like Jesus?
2. Which of the promises in the psalm means the most to you at the moment?
3. What is the problem with appropriating these promises without looking to Jesus?

PSALMS 95 AND 107

# 12. JUDGMENT AND RESCUE

In this chapter we consider one more psalm from Book IV, and then the first psalm of Book V—a psalm that is intimately linked with the close of Book IV.

After Psalms 90 and 91, which introduce Book IV, Psalms 92 – 100 would appear to be a subsection. All are anonymous. The refrain "The LORD reigns" comes several times (93:1; 96:10; 97:1; 99:1), and there are other references to God being king (for example, **95:3**; 98:6). We are taking just one of these psalms: Psalm 95. This psalm is well-known to those who belong to churches where the so-called **canticles** are sung, among which it is known, from its first word in the Latin, as the *Venite* ("O Come"—see, for example, the Order of Service for Morning Prayer in the Anglican Book of Common Prayer).

Hebrews 3 and 4 preaches a strong exhortation on the basis of part of this psalm.

It is a short psalm in two clear parts, the first itself divided in two. Psalm **95:1-7c** calls us (twice) to worship and give us two reasons for so doing. Then verses **7d-11** call us to listen to the voice of God and heed his warning.

## Join the celebration

The first exhortation comes in **verses 1** and **2**. We hear a voice—we do not know whose voice—exhorting the people of God to join with them in enthusiastic songs. The word "come" has the sense of "Come on now, join me". The verses invite us—exhort us—to join in a shared noisy celebration of God. The words "sing for joy", "shout aloud", "thanksgiving", and "music and song" conjure up a picture of a glad people making a lot of very happy noise. They (we) are to do this singing to "the LORD", the covenant God, who is called "the Rock of our salvation" (**v 1**). The word "Rock" refers to "a high rock that is difficult to access and therefore a potentially secure place of refuge" (Goldingay, *Psalms*, Volume 3, page 754). This God is so high—so safely and inaccessibly high—that no evil power can reach him. And if we are with him, we too will be rescued and made safe. To "come before him" (**v 2**) is literally to "come before his face"; it means being in his personal presence.

Why would we want to join this noisy exuberance? **Verses 3-5** give the answer. It's because of creation. The LORD, the covenant God of **verse 1**, is "the great God ... above all gods". The universe is peopled with many gods and goddesses, created by human imagination; these are real in people's thoughts and worship, but they lack any objective reality. If people ceased to exist, these gods and goddesses would cease to exist. But the covenant God of the Bible is above all these. He is "the great King" (**v 3**). Other nations called their rulers "the great king"—for example, this boastful title is used of the Assyrian emperor in 2 Kings 18:19 when he besieges King Hezekiah in Jerusalem. But there is only one truly great King, and he is the God of the Bible.

Psalm **95:4-5** spells out his kingship over the whole of the created order with a pair of merisms—that is, a form of words by which the totality of something is conveyed by means of two extremes. (For example, in Genesis 1:1, "the heavens and the earth" means "the very highest things and the very lowest things, and everything in between".) So here we have "the depths [literally "remote parts"] of the earth" and "the mountain peaks" (Psalm **95:4**)—the very low stuff and the very high stuff and everything in between. There is no part of the created order so low that it lies outside the Creator's authority, and no region so high that it can stand above his power. Then in **verse 5** we have "the sea" and "the dry land". The "sea" in Bible imagery speaks both of the literal sea and of the whole aspect of creation that is marked by chaos, darkness and evil; even this does not lie outside the power of the Creator.

The voice of this leader of the people of God exhorts us to join a noisy celebration because there is one true God, and only one, who is the unrivalled Creator of all things. There is not an opposite power of evil that rivals his authority, for he made all things and controls all things, without exception. This is extraordinarily good news. If the world was the battleground in which different gods and goddesses slogged it out to see who could gain control, we would indeed live in a frightening place. But it is not: the LORD, the covenant God of the Bible, is the one-and-only great God.

## Bowing down together

We now hear this same voice summoning us to bow down (**v 6**). The word "Come" here means something like "Come in", as if the invitation is to come into the temple, the place of God's presence. In place of—or, perhaps better, alongside—the jubilant enthusiasm, there is a deeply humble bowing down. The words "bow down", "worship" and "kneel" have this in common: the movement is vertical and always downwards! Here we see this exultant people kneeling, prostrating themselves in deep humility; they (and we) are to see no contradiction between joyful singing and a deep humbling. Shared singing can carry us away in the excitement of a gig or concert; but this kind of shared singing moves our hearts and bodies to a willing submission to the God whom we praise.

The reason that supports this second exhortation is different from the reason that was given for the first. After **verses 1-2** the reason given was that the LORD is the Creator of all things (**v 3-5**). Now it is that he is "*our* Maker" (my emphasis)—that is, the Maker of Israel, the people of God. In a special way he created, formed and put together the people of God. Perhaps supremely, he did this in the exodus from Egypt, when he called out a people for himself to live in covenant relationship with him.

**Verse 7** adapts the familiar covenant strapline: "I will be their God and they will be my people" (Exodus 6:7; Ezekiel 36:28; Jeremiah 7:23, 30:22, 31:33). On the lips of the people this becomes "He is our God and we are [his] people". We bow because he has shaped us to belong to him in that personal relationship of covenant. But the verse goes on to speak of God not only as the Maker of Israel but as the Pastor, or Shepherd, of Israel. We are his "flock", and therefore he is our Shepherd.

By the time we get to the third line of Psalm **95:7**, we may be ready to stop singing. We have heard a double exhortation and twin reasons. We have been urged to sing exuberantly because God is the sole Creator of all things. And we have been pressed to bow humbly because this same Creator God is the Maker and Pastor of the people of God.

We learn from this that in our thoughts and our hearts we should hold together the realities that God is the Creator of all things and that God is the Creator and Pastor of the church. The God whom we worship when we sing and bow down corporately in church is the God who made and shaped and controls the whole world. He is not a local deity who belongs to us. We belong to him, and he rules the world. This gives to our corporate worship a sense both of gladness (**v 1-2**) *and* deep reverence (**v 6**).

> We need to learn to hold together in our meetings an exultant gladness and a deep humility.

Further, we need to learn to hold together in our meetings an exultant gladness and a deep humility. This is not easy. It is, perhaps, easy to have an infectious exuberance, a catching noisy gladness that puffs us up and makes us feel good. It may also be simple to have a reverential bowing-down that is devoid of gladness. Neither alone is the authentic worship of the people of God. Both parts are necessary.

But the real shock comes in the final part of the psalm. When I was young, some of the churches I had to attend used to omit **verses 7d-11** because, presumably, they were felt to be too down-beat for a Christian meeting. How wrong that was! For they may be sobering, but they are very important.

## Obeying together

"Today," cries this same voice (**v 7**), because the day when the people of God hear the word of God is always "today". There is an existential immediacy to this. It is never a matter for yesterday or for tomorrow, such that I can leave it behind or put it on the back burner for today. No, it is always "today"—it is always urgent to listen, no matter how many times I may have heard in the past and no matter how often I may come to hear again in the future. It is now that matters.

The people who have been called to make a lot of noise (**v 1-2**) are now summoned solemnly to shut their mouths and open their ears: "Today if … you … hear his voice" (**v 7**). This summons echoes a great theme in Deuteronomy (e.g. Deuteronomy 6:3-4 with its repeated "Hear!").

The summons is supported by a sober warning. In **verse 8** the psalmist says, effectively, *Think back to that place that came to be nicknamed "Strife" (Meribah) and what happened there (Exodus 17:1-7). Think back to that later place that we called "Testing" (Massah) and what happened there (Numbers 20:1-13).* In those places the people of God hardened their hearts against God. Both soon after the exodus (Exodus 17) and much later (Numbers 20), they resisted God's word. They may have gone through the outward motions of corporate worship, perhaps even with a lot of noisy singing, but their hearts were far from God (see Isaiah 29:13).

Psalm **95:9** recounts how, in those places, the hearers' forefathers "tested" God. The word "tested" is linked to the word Massah (**v 8**): so God is saying, *They Massah-ed me.* Even though they had seen God's faithfulness and rescue in the exodus from Egypt, the crossing of the Red Sea, and later his provision for them in the wilderness, they did not, would not, trust him.

The consequence of their hard hearts was desperately serious (**v 10-11**). God was rightly and hotly angry with them. For "forty years"—a whole generation—he turned away from them and declared solemnly that none of them (except **Caleb** and **Joshua**) would enter the promised land, his place of "rest" (Numbers 14:20-24).

And there the psalm ends. It is a surprising and sobering conclusion to a psalm that began so cheerfully.

Hebrews 3:7 – 4:13 takes Psalm 95 as its preaching text, and the writer to the Hebrews preaches this same warning to new-covenant people. For the "rest" that was prefigured in the promised land spoke of a greater and deeper eternal rest that is the destiny of the true people of God. But the true people of God will be marked by a humble, obedient hearing of the word of God, believing the gospel they hear there and living a life of gospel-trusting obedience. If that great change of heart and consequent new direction is not in any way evident in them, they ought to heed this warning and beware.

During Jesus of Nazareth's earthly life, he would almost certainly have heard a leader in the synagogue reading this psalm to the people, exhorting them—and him—to join in exultant worship, to bow with reverent fear and to heed the word of God with obedient faith. Jesus responded with perfect faith to that exhortation. And now, as we hear this psalm, there is perhaps a sense in which we hear his voice as the leader of the people of God, exhorting us, encouraging us, teaching us and warning us. Let us hear and heed his voice.

The placing together of **verses 1-7c** and **verses 7d-11** in this psalm in such a striking way teaches us something of enduring importance. It is all too easy to enjoy a Christian meeting—to enter exuberantly into the singing and glad belonging—as it was all too easy for an old-covenant Israelite to do the same with their gatherings. But that is not true worship. True worship, expressed corporately in joyful song and humble prayer, is marked by an eager attentiveness to the word of God and a careful obedience to that word from the heart. Let us be very careful to hear and to heed all eleven verses of this psalm!

## Questions for reflection

1. Do you find it easier to be deeply humble or loudly joyful before God? How could you foster both?
2. How do you respond to the warning in verses 7d-11?
3. How might you help others to worship in the ways portrayed in Psalm 95?

# PART TWO

## What does it mean to be loved by God?

We often say, sometimes rather lightly, that "God loves you". But what does that mean? Just suppose that God really does love you, with an unchanging love—that he has always loved you, that he loves you now, and that he will love you until eternity. Imagine that he can never love you more than he loves you today, and he will never love you less. It sounds wonderful, if it is true.

This is what the New Testament teaches is true of all who belong to Christ. We know that nothing can separate us from the love of God in Christ Jesus our Lord (Romans 8:39). The love we are told is ours is the fulfilment of the faithful covenant love of God for his people in the Old Testament, for every promise of the old covenant finds its "Yes!" in Christ (2 Corinthians 1:20).

So, let us suppose it is true. What happens when you set your story—the story of your life as it is actually lived—alongside this assertion about the love of God? Does it seem to be true? Or would it be fairer to say that our experience suggests that God loves us more on some days than on others? We have good times and bad times: can it really be true that God loves us as much on the darker days as on the brighter ones?

The final verse of Psalm 107 invites us, if we are "wise", to listen carefully to the psalm because it will help us to "ponder the loving deeds [literally, 'the deeds of unchanging covenant love'] of the LORD" (Psalm **107:43**). Pondering what this psalm sets before us will be a tremendous help to us in the ups and downs of our lives.

## When exiles are gathered

Psalm 107 marks the beginning of Book V of the Psalms (107 – 150). After the great "kingship of God" psalms (Psalms 92 – 100), Book IV concludes with two older psalms "of David" (Psalms 101 and 103) and one "of an afflicted person" (Psalm 102). All three reaffirm "the ongoing significance of Davidic kingship" (O. Palmer Robertson, *The Flow of the Psalms*, page 149). The book concludes with three long "Hallelujah" psalms, each with the refrain "Praise the LORD!" (Psalms 104 – 106). These focus on creation (Psalm 104) and then the long history of God's faithfulness (Psalm 105) and Israel's unfaithfulness (Psalm 106). It is the unfaithfulness of the people of God that leads to deserved exile—and so Psalm 106 concludes with a prayer to "gather us from the nations"; that is, bring us back from exile (106:47). It is this prayer that is answered in Psalm 107, which begins Book V.

This suggests that Book V was first compiled from a mixture of contemporary and older psalms after the return of some of the Jews from exile. For, as Eveson points out, "In contrast to the previous book, many of the psalms of book five suggest that the exile is over and a new beginning is dawning" (*Psalms*, Volume 2, page 247).

## Four stories, one story

After a headline introduction (**107:1-3**), the body of the psalm consists of four very similar stories of trouble and rescue (**v 4-9**, **10-16**, **17-22**, **23-32**), after which there is a rather different section (**v 33-42**) and a concluding verse (**v 43**).

**Verse 1** gives the headline: we are to "give thanks" to the covenant God ("the LORD") because he is "good"; which is to say that his "love"—his covenant steadfast love—lasts for ever. That great word "love" (Hebrew *chesed*) reappears in **verses 8**, **15**, **21**, **31** and finally **verse 43** (as "loving deeds"); it is the grand theme of the psalm.

As we immerse ourselves in the dramas of the psalm, we must remember that it is all about God's unchanging covenant love and is intended to stir thankfulness in us. The words of **verse 1** appear in other places—for example 106:1; 136 (in every verse!); and also Jeremiah 33:10-11, where the context is explicitly the return from exile. Psalm **107:1** is like a return-from-exile motto.

**Verses 2-3** expand that headline. We are going to learn of the goodness and love of God, as the people who are "redeemed" (from slavery in Egypt much earlier in Israel's history) and "gathered" (from exile) tell their story. What we are about to hear, then, is what it means to be a redeemed and gathered people.

The four stories (**v 4-9**, **10-16**, **17-22**, **23-32**) each begin with *distress* that provokes *prayer*, which is *answered* and issues in *joy and thanksgiving*. Although some English translations begin each of these with the word "some", these are not four separate stories, as though there were four different groups speaking in turn. The KJV and NASB correctly translate the word as "they", for these are four stories told by the *same* redeemed and gathered people; they tell the one story of God's rescue in four vivid and complementary ways.

## Lost in a wasteland world

We are taken first (**v 4-5**) to a desperate people: they are wandering, lost, hungry, thirsty and with no "city" in which to "settle". This experience of being lost and unsatisfied in a desert world was felt acutely by the people of God in those wilderness-wandering years between the exodus and the entry to the promised land—and, in particular, until they had a "city", Jerusalem, as the focus of their inheritance. Exile in Babylon felt much the same: far from home, far from the beloved "city" of Zion. But we can track forwards too, to the experience of the Lord Jesus Christ, first in the desert, being "hungry" and tempted (Matthew 4:1-2), and finally on the cross, with a deep and unsatisfied thirst (John 19:28). For us, it is a vivid expression of that dissatisfaction that afflicts all who are under the just judgment of God, and even those who are forgiven but yet await the final redemption of our bodies (Romans 8:23).

God answers the cry of Psalm **107:6** by leading the people "to a city where they could settle" (**v 7**). Notice the repeated mention of the "city". Coming to this city stirs thankfulness in them; they understand that the covenant God, who satisfies the thirsty and fills the hungry, is the God of unchanging love (**v 8-9**). Jesus knew this God, his Father, as the God of unchanging love. He made this Father known as he fed the hungry, and he is, in his own person, the Way, who leads his people to a city—to the New Jerusalem coming down out of heaven to earth.

## Trapped in a dark world

As in a movie of shifting scenes, we move next to the same people, not now "lost in too wide a world" but "trapped in too small a one", as Derek Kidner puts it (*Psalms*, Volume 2, page 385). For they (and we) are prisoners in a dark dungeon enduring a sentence of forced labour (**v 10-12**). The words "utter darkness" mean the shadow of death. This, unlike the first scene, is explicitly because they "rebelled" against God and would not trust his "plans". Forced labour was the bitter experience of the Hebrew slaves in the Egypt of the Pharaohs; it drove them to cry out for rescue (Exodus 2:22-25). Exile in Babylon was a kind of imprisonment and forced labour, perhaps literally for some but metaphorically for all. God warned them that if they were unfaithful to the covenant, this is what would happen (for example, Leviticus 26:33; Deuteronomy 28:47-48). As Jesus bore the punishment of our sins, he, too, knew what it was to be surrounded by a dark world: to be watched, hated, bound as a prisoner and to hang in supernatural darkness and the shadow of death. And we, too, know what it is to endure slavery to sin—to experience sin as a power that traps us and will not let us go, and that makes life dark and miserable.

Again, "they" cry for help (Psalm **107:13**), and the LORD brings them out of darkness and breaks their chains (**v 16**, echoing Isaiah 45:2). He brought ancient Israel out of the darkness of slavery into the promised land; he brought the Israel of the psalmist's day out of the slavery of exile back into the land; and he broke the iron chains of death that bound the Lord Jesus and brought him out of the darkness of the tomb, for he came "to shine on those living in darkness and in the shadow of death" (Luke 1:79). And so, when the Son sets us free from slavery to sin, we too will be free indeed (John 8:36). In this way the Father makes known to us, as he made known to them, his unchanging love—by bringing us out of a dark slavery and into freedom.

## Weak in a sick world

In scene three, we watch the same people becoming desperately ill (Psalm **107:17-18**). Again, as in scene two, this is because of rebellion. Sin brought death into the world, and every sickness is the shadow of death; all sickness is the result of sin. (To clarify: individual sicknesses may not be the results of particular sins, although they may be; but overall, had there been no sin, there would be no sickness.) The ancient Hebrews knew what it was to suffer "the diseases of Egypt"; those in exile were often very weak. The Lord Jesus knew what it was to bear our sorrows and to suffer the shadow of our sins even during his life, before he finally bore the full penalty for our sins on the cross. We, too, know what it is to be sick, to age, to be frail, to walk through the valley of the shadow of death. Even as those who are forgiven in Christ, our bodies are still mortal and live in the shadow of death (Romans 8:10).

Again "they" cry out (Psalm **107:19**); again God rescues (**v 20**); and again, they give joyful thanks (**v 21-22**).

## Scared in a dangerous world

In scene four we are meant to feel acutely how small we are, and how powerfully dangerous is the world in which we live. We picture a boat, so small, so vulnerable, on the mighty waters in a perfect storm (**v 23-27**). It is a frightening scene. As an old proverb puts it, "If you don't know how to pray, try going to sea". The sea here is both literal and metaphorical, for in Bible poetry the sea is often a symbol of the overwhelming and supernatural powers of chaos and evil, of death and the devil and demons, of all the powers in the universe that threaten us and are far too strong for us.

The ancient Hebrews knew the power of a sea that formed an evil and impregnable barrier between them and safety (the Red Sea). Isaiah describes the Jerusalem that will endure exile as the "afflicted city, lashed by storms" (Isaiah 54:11). The life of the Lord Jesus was threatened by a storm, stirred up no doubt by evil and supernatural forces on the Sea of Galilee. We too know what it is to feel ourselves very small, very weak and utterly incapable of taking on the strong powers of chaos that disorder our lives and families.

Again "they" pray (**v 28**), and again God answers (**v 29-30**); he stills the storm, as (most famously and dramatically) he did through the words of Jesus in Galilee (Mark 4:35-41). So again, they give thanks (Psalm **107:31-32**).

An old commentator, A.F. Kirkpatrick, wrote:

> "Israel has been on the point of perishing in the great desert of the world, imprisoned for its transgressions in the gloomy dungeon of exile, sick unto death through its own sin, all but swallowed up in the vast sea of the nations."
>
> (*The Book of Psalms*, page 637-8)

These historical experiences of Israel foreshadow the sufferings of the Lord Jesus and the experience of his people in every age. We know the love of God by his rescue from this plight in all its fourfold awfulness.

## The final surprise

The surprise at this point in the psalm is that next we do not have a fifth scene following the same pattern. Instead, we find God taking his people through both hard times (**v 33-34**, **39-40**) and good times (**v 35-37**, **41**). Notice that it is God who does both. The bad times do not just happen: God allows them. Both the bad times and the good times are the consistent outworking of his unfailing love. This is why the wise need to "ponder" these things: for every one of the events described, both hard and good, are "the loving deeds of the LORD" (**v 43**).

In terms of Old Testament history, we have here a catalogue of covenant curses and covenant blessings (see Deuteronomy 28). The good times are the blessings of covenant faithfulness; the bad times are judgments on covenant rebellion. So the true surprise is that God perseveres with a naturally unfaithful people to bring them into a place of blessing. He uses suffering to humble them and to lead them to repentance, that he may bless them. Even the Lord Jesus, who knew no sin, was made perfect (in the sense of living as a human in perfect obedience to his Father) by what he suffered (2 Corinthians 5:21; Hebrews 2:10). As the Lord Jesus heard and sang this psalm in his earthly life, he too would have pondered the loving deeds of his Father and understood that the process by which even he, who never sinned, would be made perfect had necessarily to include passing through valleys of tears.

Our Christlikeness, not our comfort, is God's aim.

If that was true of him—the perfect man who suffered that we might be forgiven—it will most certainly be true for us. God has promised that he will make each one of his people like the Lord Jesus in character (Romans 8:29). This is the "good" that he is always working for in those who love him (Romans 8:28). We sometimes wish—I often wish—that it did not have to hurt so much. But our Christlikeness, not our comfort is God's aim. He has promised to do it, that we may be blessed, in becoming more like Jesus, with whom we will be in the end. And, however much it may hurt in this life, we shall see then that it has been abundantly worth it.

The ups and downs of life are not evidence that God's love has strengthened or weakened. Because we are in Christ, who fully and finally satisfied God's law, each one is the consistent outworking of his unchanging love. God really does love you—and that is always cause for giving joyful thanks to him.

## Questions for reflection

1. What have you learned in this psalm about the love of God?
2. Does anything that God does in this psalm surprise you?
3. Looking back on your own past, where can you see God's loving deeds?

PSALMS 109 AND 110

# 13. A BETRAYAL AND A PROMISE

Although Book V would seem to have been compiled after the exile, the Spirit-inspired editors have included two little groups of older psalms of David (108 – 110 and 138 – 145: though four of the "songs of ascents"—122, 124, 131 and 133—are also of David). We will enjoy two of these here. The first focuses on the betrayal of King David: a betrayal that foreshadows a deeper betrayal many centuries later. In the second, God gives a wonderful promise to King David: a promise that is fulfilled in great David's greater son. Each, as we shall see, is quoted in the New Testament.

## A difficult psalm

As we embark on learning to pray the psalms, we find that some are easier than others. And Psalm 109 is a difficult psalm to pray. But not infrequently we come across the problem that this psalm presents us with: we struggle when the psalmist prays for his enemies to be punished, and we wonder how we can ever join in this prayer, or if we should join in at all. I have chosen Psalm 109 because it is a particularly acute example of this problem. Other examples would include Psalm 69:24-28; Psalm 104:35; and parts of Psalms 137 and 139 (see chapter 15).

Psalm 109 feels like praying...

*Dear God, my loving heavenly Father, I want to pray about so-and-so, who is causing me problems at work. Please may he/she die soon. May his/her children become wandering beggars. May no one take pity on them. Please do that for me. Thank you, loving heavenly Father. In Jesus' name, Amen.*

Clearly we do not want to utter a vindictive prayer like that! And, in truth, prayers like Psalm 109 are not at all like that; they are very, very different, and, with care, we can include them in our praying of the psalms.

There are at least five reasons why we should not simply omit them from our prayers.

1. Such prayers are woven into the fabric of many psalms in such a way that removing them destroys the whole fabric of the Psalter.
2. We must not fall for the shallow and erroneous idea that these prayers are part of a bad Old Testament, whereas, as Christians, we follow a much nicer New Testament. After all, many of the things we most applaud in the New Testament are quotations from the Old (for example, "Love your neighbour as yourself", Leviticus 19:18; and "If your enemy is hungry, give him food to eat", Proverbs 25:21-22 and quoted in Romans 12). Equally, the New Testament contains some very strong negative statements, every bit as strong as the Old (for example, 1 Corinthians 16:22).
3. Once we begin to pick and choose which parts of the psalms we will pray, the psalms as a whole have ceased to be our guide; for it is then we who select what we like to pray.
4. Christian history strongly supports the practice of praying all the psalms.
5. The New Testament explicitly quotes with approval a number of the prayers we find so problematical in the psalms. (Most notably, Acts 1:16-20 quotes with approval from Psalm 69 and Psalm 109. For a fuller discussion, see chapter 8 of my book *Teaching Psalms*, Volume 1, especially page 129.)

The psalm begins by describing the crisis faced by David (Psalm **109:1-5**). After that, David prays strongly against his opponents, and particularly one betrayer (**v 6-20**), before praying urgently for himself (**v 21-29**) and concluding with praise (**v 30-31**).

The psalm begins and ends with praise (**v 1**, **30**). Far from being a problem, we are meant to find in the verses between a truth that will move us to glad praise of God.

## Prayer in crisis

The issue at the heart of the psalm is what is *said* about David. Will he be condemned or will he be vindicated? God is "silent", and David longs for him to speak (**v 1**) for there are plenty of other people who have "opened their mouths" against him (**v 2**). They are "wicked" in their character, motivated by "hatred", and "they accuse" David falsely (**v 4**) despite the fact that he has shown them "friendship" and done to them nothing but "good" (**v 2-5**).

Knowing David's life story as we do, the person of whom he is speaking may be Doeg the Edomite, who betrayed David to Saul (1 Samuel 21; 22:9); Ahitophel, who joined the rebellion of David's son Absalom (2 Samuel 16 – 17); or Shimei, who cursed David (2 Samuel 16:5-8). We cannot know. But the point is that David is being accused of wrongdoing and urgently needs to be vindicated; for if the king is not justified, he will be condemned.

## Prayer against the betrayer

Note that Psalm **109:6-20** is not a curse but a prayer. David prays to God to "appoint" a witness to stand "at his right hand" (this is law-court language) to testify against this false and treacherous witness (**v 6-7**). In **verse 6**, "someone evil" (in the first part of the verse) means much the same as the "accuser" in the second half of the verse; so "appoint someone evil" means to appoint someone who is hostile to them—a prosecuting attorney who will condemn them.

These prayers are sometimes loosely called "imprecations" and the psalms in which they occur are called "imprecatory psalms". This comes from the Latin word *imprecare,* meaning "to curse". Yet this is precisely what they are not. David here and the psalmists elsewhere do not seek to unleash a curse on their enemies; rather, they pray to God about their enemies. That is very different, for it leaves the outcome in God's hands. The king here heeds the teaching of the Old Testament in the words of God: "It is mine to avenge; I will repay" (Deuteronomy 32:35, which is quoted in Romans 12:19). "I will repay," says the LORD, and therefore you and I (and David) must not. By using law-court language, David prays that he, the king accused of wrongdoing, will be vindicated, while the false witness will be convicted of the falsity of his accusations; for unless the false witness is convicted, the king will be falsely condemned.

In Psalm **109:8** we discover that this man has a "place of leadership". He is not just any old Israelite—he is a senior figure in David's government. And therefore what he is doing is not just a personal slight against David; it is treason against the king. High treason is perhaps the most serious crime in any nation's law code, for it threatens the fabric of a whole nation; the anointed king, the "Messiah", was the one under whose protection the people hoped to live safely (Lamentations 4:20). If David's enemy succeeds, the whole nation will be threatened. We need to feel the intensity of the seriousness of this crime.

In Psalm **109:9-15** David prays against this man's family. This is probably the part we find most difficult, because, in our individualistic Western culture, we cannot see why (even if the man himself is guilty) his wife and children should be punished. But we need to understand what underlies this prayer. David prays that this man's whole family will be "blotted out" and be no more. Why? The answer is that the default convictions and behaviour of the man's family will line up with the behaviour of the man himself. Like father, like son and like daughter—that is the normal way things work. The spirit of treachery that motivates this man is like a terrible virus infecting his family and all who are influenced by him. Just as a life-threatening virus must be blotted out if the rest of us are to be safe, so all who share this man's heart must be removed.

Even as we consider this general truth, we must remember how the Bible repeatedly gives us glimpses of glorious exceptions. The Moabites were ancient enemies of the people of God, and yet Ruth was converted and came under the wings of the God of Israel for refuge (Ruth 2:12). There were physical descendants of the Pharaohs who came into the people of God (see, for instance, Exodus 12:38; 1 Chronicles 4:17-18). This is wonderful. But they had to break their corporate solidarity first, to save themselves from the corrupt family or culture by which they had been shaped (see Acts 2:40). What David prays in Psalm **109:9-15** is that all who share this treacherous heart will be defeated and removed. It is a necessary prayer, even if it leaves unspoken the wonderful possibility of conversion.

**Verses 16-19** have a visibly fair appropriateness about them, for the punishment for which David prays perfectly fits the crime of which this man is guilty. The word "kindness" (**v 16**) is the same word we know as "steadfast love" (*chesed*); this man forfeits steadfast love because he has never shown it. He loved to curse others, so that cursing became a part of his character; and so he will, David prays, be cursed by God (**v 17-19**).

**Verse 20** stresses that this punishment will be from the LORD, and not from King David. Those who falsely accuse God's anointed king and speak evil of him attack all God's people; and God promised back in the days of Abraham that those who cursed Abraham's people would be cursed by God himself (Genesis 12:3). David therefore prays that God will do precisely what God has already said he will do.

## Prayer for vindication

In Psalm **109:21-29** the king prays again for his vindication. He asks it "for [God's] name's sake", because the honour of God depends upon the vindication of God's king. He is in desperate straits, fading away and very close to death. He longs for blessing (**v 28**) and for vindication (**v 29**), so that the final verdict will be given in his favour and against his false accusers.

## The king's praise

David ends by affirming that in the midst of the great "throng of worshippers"—all God's gathered people—he will lead them in praise of the good God who "stands at the right hand" (law-court language again) "of the needy, to save their lives from those who would condemn them" (**v 30-31**). Note how David praises God not only because he will vindicate David himself, the king, but because God's vindication of the king is the guarantee that God will justify—declare to be righteous—every man and woman who belongs to the king.

King David is right to pray that, as the king of God's chosen people, he will not be condemned by false accusation. He is right because the wellbeing and peace of all the people depend upon his vindication. He is right because this betrayer threatens the whole fabric of the people of God. This psalm is not about a personal vendetta between two individuals; it is about a traitor who puts a knife to the throat of the king: the king who is the only hope of all the people.

Weeks after Jesus' death and resurrection, when the apostle Peter spoke about Judas Iscariot, he rightly quoted from two psalms, one of which was this one: "May another take his place of leadership" (**v 8**; Acts 1:20). Whoever it was who betrayed King David all those centuries before, it was a terrible foreshadowing of Judas. He had "a place of leadership" in the apostolic band and betrayed his master with a kiss. The master who had shown him nothing but friendship was rewarded with lies and treachery. Judas' terrible fate (see Acts 1:18) is a warning that Psalm 109 is true.

But it still leaves us with the question: can we pray it? We might understand how the Lord Jesus can pray it; for he who gave his life in love for sinners is the only one who can, with utterly pure motives, pray simultaneously that the Father will forgive those who crucify him for they are ignorant of what they do (Luke 23:34), and that the Father will give to Judas Iscariot the terrible judgment that must be, and is rightly, his.

But what about us? Stephen, the first Christian martyr, prayed that God would forgive those who stoned him (Acts 7:60). We are to pray for those who persecute us; we are to bless them and not to curse (Matthew 5:44; Romans 12:14). So where does a psalm like this fit in with that? There is a sense in which, whenever we pray the words "your kingdom come" in the Lord's prayer, we are praying for the final judgment; we are asking the Father to bring in the kingdom, knowing as we do that, on that day all who are finally hardened in their hearts and are therefore impenitent will be condemned. It is terrible to ask this; and yet it is necessary to ask this. For unless this final judgment comes, the new heavens and the new earth will still be spoiled by sin, and the Lord Jesus will still not receive the honour he is due. Only a final and definitive judgment will suffice to bring in "a new heaven and a new earth, where righteousness dwells" (2 Peter 3:13), and where we will see "every tongue acknowledge that Jesus Christ is Lord, to the glory of God the Father" (Philippians 2:11).

We cannot and must not name names with confidence—we should not pray for a particular person to be condemned—for we do not know who will be finally impenitent. Had we watched the apostolic band respond to Jesus' arrest and trial, we might have assumed that Simon Peter would be condemned, as he repeatedly denied his master; and, again, we would have been wonderfully wrong. Had we been first-generation Christians, we would have thought that Saul of Tarsus, as he ravaged the church, would be condemned, and we would have been wonderfully wrong. But we can pray, led by Jesus, that all treachery against Jesus and his people will finally be brought to an end. This psalm shows us how to pray for that.

John Calvin wrote that King David is a type, so that...

"everything that is expressed in the Psalm must properly be applied to Christ, the Head of the Church, and to all the faithful

> inasmuch as they are his members; so that when unjustly treated and tormented by their enemies, they may apply to God to help, to whom vengeance belongs."
>
> (*Commentary on the Book of Psalms,* Volume 4, page 268)

There is more to be said about this; in particular, there is a deep truth that when—quite wonderfully—a persecutor repents, as Saul of Tarsus did, their sins are indeed paid for at the cross. So the prayer of this psalm is always answered, whether in the judgment on the persecutor or in the wounds of the Saviour who pays for them. (See my book *Teaching Psalms*, Volume 1, pages 132-133.)

## Questions for reflection

1. When people treat you badly, do you retaliate or do you ask God for help?
2. When might you be likely to pray for God to judge? Do you think you should pray for this more?
3. How does reflecting on the cross change the way you read this psalm?

## PART TWO

It is all very well to say that God's king will win. But how will he win? Will it be by overcoming human power with a stronger power, overwhelming his opponents and consigning them to oblivion? Or in some other way?

If you are a follower of Jesus, this matters hugely—for the Jesus who you follow does not seem to many to be a winner. To most people, it seems frankly absurd to suggest that Jesus Christ will conquer the world. Psalm 110 will help us to grasp just why this claim is believable. It is a psalm that is quoted or alluded to an extraordinary number of times in the New Testament, like a section of a web page choc-a-bloc with hyperlinks to other parts of the web.

God's king will win. But how will he win? This matters hugely.

This is the third and last of this little "of David" collection near the start of Book V. Psalm 108 is a composite of two earlier psalms of David and focuses on the king's victory in war. In Psalm 109, as we have seen, the king is in dire straits, being betrayed and in imminent danger of being condemned through treachery and false witness; he appeals urgently to God, the judge, to vindicate him (109:31). But will he be vindicated? This is the question in our minds as we come to Psalm 110.

This short and famous psalm comes in two clear sections. Each section begins with a statement that God in heaven makes about his king. Psalm **110:1-3** begins with God speaking to the king and making him a promise. Then **verses 4-7** begin with God swearing an oath concerning the king.

### Victory through changed lives

The first thing we notice is that the king needs victory because he has many enemies. The "enemies" appear in **verse 1**, and then in

**verse 2** the king is described as ruling "in the midst of his enemies", which suggests the enemies are all around him. This is just what we knew to expect from the start of Psalm 2, in which all the powerful people in the world, who disagree about almost everything, nevertheless say in unison that the one thing they all agree about is that they will not be ruled by the covenant God in heaven ("the LORD") or by his anointed king on earth (Psalm 2:1-3).

In the Old Testament David's enemies, and later the enemies of his successors, were nations such as Philistia, Moab, Edom, Ammon, Assyria and Babylon. But these were just representatives of a universally rebellious human race. All of us by nature refuse to have God's king rule over us. We are determined to make our own decisions about our jobs, our careers, our sexual relationships, our possessions, our money, our rights. The idea that our (supposed) freedom could be constrained by some external power telling us what to do sounds abhorrent.

In the face of a hostile world, God solemnly makes a declaration to the king. The words translated "the LORD says" are literally "an **oracle** of the LORD". The only other use of that weighty word "oracle" in the Psalms is in 36:1 ("I have a *message* from God", my emphasis). Here in **110:1**, God in heaven speaks to "my lord", which means "my master"; it soon becomes clear that "my lord" is the human king in David's line.

The covenant God in heaven declares to the king that he is to "sit at my right hand". This is symbolic rather than literal—to "sit at [the] right hand" means to enjoy a posture of power and authority given by the one at whose right hand someone sits. It is, in our idiom, to be God's "right-hand man". The empty "seat" below the wings of the cherubim in the Most Holy Place was, in Old Testament symbolism, the throne on which the invisible God sat to rule the world—he is described as "enthroned between the cherubim" (for example 1 Samuel 4:4).

The king in David's line does not physically sit on this throne, but the throne on which he sits is the place from which he exercises the authority of God. It was even said of Solomon that he sat on the throne of the LORD (1 Chronicles 29:23). Psalm 80 speaks of God raising up a man at his right hand (Psalm 80:17). Jeremiah, looking forward to the new covenant, prophesied about the day when a leader would be raised up who would be "one of their own" (that is, human), whom God would "bring ... near" so that he dwelled "close" to God (Jeremiah 30:21).

From this throne, the king can place his feet upon the necks of his enemies, so that they become "a footstool for your feet" (Psalm **110:1**). When Joshua conquered five kings, he told his army commanders to "come here and put your feet on the necks of these kings" as a vivid sign of their defeat and Joshua's victory (Joshua 10:24). This king of Psalm 110 will be that kind of conqueror. That is what it means to sit at God's right hand.

Further, his power will spread. He "will extend [his] mighty sceptre [the symbol of his power] from Zion" (Psalm **110:2**), the place of the covenant with David (2 Samuel 5:7). He will inherit the promises to David made in 2 Samuel 7 and echoed in Psalm 2.

But how will all this happen? Psalm **110:3** is the key. His army will be "willing" as they go with him to battle. They will not be reluctant conscripts but men whose hearts have been deeply changed so that, from the bottom of their hearts, come what may—whatever sufferings they may be called upon to endure and however the battle goes—their willingness to serve their king will never be in doubt. They will be a very fine army, "arrayed in holy splendour", their shining garments speaking of a distinctiveness and a holiness of life and heart that sets them apart from others. They will be "young men"—in the language of battle, full of youthful vigour. The idiom of "dew from the morning's womb" conjures up a picture of fresh energy—these are lively volunteers. Charles Spurgeon wrote of the "great numbers" of converts who would "hasten with cheerfulness to **own his sway**, appearing at the Gospel call as it were spontaneously, just as the dew comes forth in the morning" (*Psalms*, Volume 2, page 130). It is by this *willing* army that the king will conquer.

## Victory through priestly work

In **verse 4** we have another solemn promise of God. In **verse 1** the solemnity was signalled by the word "oracle"; here it comes from the words "has sworn and will not change his mind". In one sense, God never changes his mind; but there are things that God has chosen to change as men and women respond in one way or another, all under his sovereign direction. He chooses to make blessing conditional on faith; when he grants faith, he changes his attitude towards some-one from curse to blessing (as he did, for example, for Nineveh in the time of Jonah—Jonah 3:9-10). In that sense, God may be said to change his mind. But here in Psalm **110:4** is something utterly unchangeable. Men and women may do and say whatever we wish; God in heaven has decided that what he is about to say is, and will always remain, true; and what he solemnly promises is that the king will be "a priest".

He will be a priest-king: one who combines in his person the office of king (to rule people for God) and the office of priest (to intercede or mediate with God for people). Further, he is to be a priest "for ever". His priesthood will not end when he retires or dies; his mediation—the work he does in speaking on behalf of his people before God—will never end. It is permanent, final, unchangeable.

And he will be a priest for ever "in the order of Melchizedek". We read of Melchizedek (literally, "king of righteousness") in Genesis 14, right back very near the start of the story of the people of God. The priests who came later as part of the covenant God made with Moses were in the line of **Aaron**. But this priest in Psalm 110 is in the line of Melchizedek. In a most surprising twist to the story in Genesis 14, that ancient priest-king of the city of Salem (later Jeru-salem) blessed Abraham (then called Abram), and Abram gave him an offering, a **tithe**. And so the great **patriarch** acknowledged that this priest-king foreshadowed in his unique person someone who would be greater than Abraham—who would have the greatness to bless Abraham and to whom it was right that Abraham gave a tithe. Melchizedek, as priest-king, ruled a people (as king) and gave to his people the astonishing privilege of access to God (by his priestly role). Hebrews 7 explains all this.

And here in Psalm 110, the king in David's line is promised that he will be a priest-king of the kind foreshadowed all those centuries before by Melchizedek.

At this point, we need to put together the priesthood of the king (**v 4**) with the appearance of his willing army in **verse 3**; for it is by his priesthood that he will, in new-covenant fulfilment, grant to his people forgiveness of sins, give them access to God, and change their hearts. And he will do these things for ever.

No wonder the psalm concludes with a portrait of triumph (**v 5-7**). The sovereign God ("The Lord"—Hebrew *Adonai*) will be at his right hand. Never mind that he is at God's right hand; if we take this literally rather than symbolically, we will be in all sorts of trouble! No, when we hear that God will be at his right hand, we understand that God in heaven will be so closely allied to him that he is bound to conquer. The rebellious "kings" of Psalm 2 will be crushed when this king is rightly angry ("the day of his wrath", **110:5**). All the rebellious "nations" and "rulers of the whole earth" will have their power utterly broken (**v 6**). As he leads his troops in a victory charge after his fleeing foes, he stops—in the image of **verse 7**—to drink a refreshing draught of water; and in the end he will lift his head high in final victory. In ancient and easily understood battle language, this king wins—and he wins big!

## The king who is the priest

We tend to think that kingship is more important than priesthood, but perhaps it should be the other way around. It is because this king is a priest that everything else follows; for kingship is exercised on behalf of God over people, whereas priesthood is exercised towards God on behalf of people. Only because this king would offer a sacrifice to atone for the sins of his people can he lead a people whose hearts will be transformed deep within, so that they form a huge and invincible army of men and women determined to, and given grace to, overcome evil with good. Such an army, which does not answer evil with evil, will finally be unstoppable, for it follows the King who, on the cross, offered himself as the final sacrifice, and thereby overcame evil with good.

## Fulfilment and response

Like so many Old Testament pictures, the description of the one spoken of here is rather like how King Saul's armour proved for David: it is simply too big for any Old Testament character. We must wait until Jesus of Nazareth comes to see this King-Priest walk the earth, announcing the kingdom of God in his own person, offering himself as the sacrifice as he, our great High Priest, makes atonement for the sins of all who will trust in him.

The description here is like King Saul's armour proved for David: simply too big for any Old Testament character.

No wonder the New Testament keeps quoting and alluding to this psalm. Whenever we hear of Jesus "sitting at the right hand" of God, it is this psalm being quoted (for instance, Acts 2:34-35). Hebrews 5 – 7 expounds his priesthood after the order of Melchizedek. Again and again, his final victory is spoken of in ways that echo Psalm 110 (for instance, 1 Corinthians 15:25).

So how should we respond?

1. *We should be warned.* We are fools (see Psalm 2) if we persist in rebellion against this King, for God has solemnly and unchangingly declared that he will win. To those who condemned him, Jesus said, "You *will* see the Son of Man sitting at the right hand of God" (Matthew 26:64, my emphasis).

2. *We should be willing*. What a joy to be a willing soldier of the Lord Jesus Christ, gladly and freely to offer him our lives, our energies, our service!

3. *We should be assured*. Perhaps the deepest effect of this psalm is a rich assurance: all over the world, God is changing hearts through the priestly ministry of Jesus and bringing men and women gladly into his kingly service. Our lives are now "where Christ is, seated at the right hand of God"; this is where our life is "hid" in absolute safety (Colossians 3:1-3). One day we too will, as it were, drink a refreshing victory drink from the brook and have our heads held high as we share in his final victory over all evil.

## Questions for reflection

1. "It is by this willing army that the king will conquer." Christians are part of God's army. How might that imagery change the way you go about your day?
2. Why is it important that Jesus is both Priest and King?
3. After reading this psalm, what do you want to say to God?

PSALMS 122 AND 126 - 128

# 14. GOING UP TO ZION

One of the most delightful collections in the Psalter is the so-called songs of ascents. Psalms 120 – 134 are all headed (in the NIV) "A song of ascents". Almost certainly this was a collection of songs to be sung by pilgrims as they went up to Jerusalem, perhaps after the return from exile (for Book V as a whole was clearly put together during or after the exile—see Psalm 137), for the great old-covenant festivals like the Passover. Some are older songs (Psalms 122, 124, 131 and 133 are "of David" and Psalm 127 is "of Solomon"), but they have been incorporated into this collection.

Jerusalem is on relatively high ground, but the reason you go "up" to Jerusalem is not because of this. Even if you were to start at the top of the (much higher) Mount Hermon, you would still go "up" to Jerusalem, not because of its altitude but on account of its significance. In the days of the old covenant, when the temple stood there and God's presence dwelled within it, Jerusalem was the most important place on earth. This was where God's "feet" touched earth; where sinners could have some sort of access to God by sacrifice; where God's king ruled over God's people.

All this has been fulfilled in the Lord Jesus Christ, who is in every way the fulfilment of what the temple foreshadowed. He is the One greater than the temple, the great High Priest, the perfect sacrifice for sins and the King in David's line. Both when he walked on earth and now in his presence with his church, by his Spirit, he is "Jerusalem" or "Zion". When we transpose these songs into a new-covenant key, they are about Jesus Christ and his church.

"Jerusalem" today, in its Bible significance, is no longer a place in what we call the Middle East. It is fulfilled in Jesus (Matthew 12:6; John 2:12-22), partially seen in the local church (1 Corinthians 3:16; 1 Peter 2:5) and to be consummated when the perfected church of Christ dwells in the new Jerusalem, which will fill the new creation (Hebrews 12:22; Revelation 21:2).

It is possible that some at least of this collection of psalms are grouped into threesomes. So we shall break our usual pattern of considering just two psalms in a chapter and consider two of these threesomes.

## A city of peace

Where is peace to be found? Countless men and women—and perhaps you yourself—long for peace, for harmony within yourself and harmony with those among whom you live.

Division and unity is one overarching theme of the songs of ascents. The collection begins with a song that laments the misery of having to live in a world riven by strife. The psalmist is in great "distress" (Psalm 120:1) because he or she is surrounded by "deceitful tongues"—for truth is the first casualty of war—and by "those who hate peace" and are "for war" (v 6-7).

It is a miserable picture and we know just what the psalmist means; for we too live in this same broken world. In so many marriages there is deceit and strife. In too many families, there are broken relationships between children and parents and bitter rivalry between siblings. In our local neighbourhood, our workplace, our region or our country strife or the threat of strife is an ever-present and painful reality. And it hurts so much. Psalm 120 helps us to feel the misery of living in such a world. And, of course, you and I are part of the problem; we are not just victims of the warlike sins of others.

Psalms 120 – 122 fit together as a threesome. If Psalm 120 bewails the brokenness of the world, Psalm 121 is a song for the journey to a better place, as the pilgrims set out on their travels to Jerusalem, seeking the help that comes from the LORD, the covenant God. And then Psalm 122 is a song for arrival.

This threesome also fits into the whole collection of songs of ascents, which begins with strife but will eventually come to its conclusion on a note of blessed harmony in Psalms 133 and 134, where God's people have gathered in unity in the temple. It is with this framework of war and peace in mind that we join our pilgrim in Psalm 122: he (or she—but for the sake of simplicity, we will call our pilgrim "he") arrives in Jerusalem to join the gathering.

## A city of wonder, security and unity

In **verses 1-5** it is as if the pilgrim uses David's song as he stands on the edge of the city exclaiming in wonder at what he has found! (If "of David" means this was originally written by David, then there is presumably a sense in which what he says is prophetic, since the temple was not built until after his death.) There is an infectious sense here of delight. When people first suggested going on pilgrimage, "I rejoiced" (**v 1**), most especially because they were going "to the house of the LORD". They would soon arrive at the temple, where sinners could come close to the living God without being burnt alive because their sins could be covered by sacrifice and forgiveness could be found. This was the place where the priests, who offered the sacrifices, functioned as mediators between sinful people and the holy God.

It is hard for us to feel the authentic wonder that a true old-covenant believer would feel about the temple. But it is good to try, for it will help us to translate that wonder into the awe and astonished delight we should feel about Jesus Christ. Every sensation of relieved joy felt by this believer can be amplified in your heart and mine as we meditate on sins forgiven by the sacrifice of Jesus, and access into the very presence of God the Father through the high-priestly mediation of Jesus.

It is this sense of wonder that our pilgrim expresses as he says, with his fellow pilgrims, that "our feet are standing in your gates, Jerusalem" (**v 2**). This is not a cold GPS readout ("We're in Jerusalem now");

this is amazement: *How astonishing! How deeply wonderful! We are in Jerusalem now!*

Paul uses that language of "standing" when he speaks of our standing in the grace of God (Romans 5:2). We used to "stand" in a terrible place, under the just judgment of God; but now we "stand" in a new place, a new sphere—the grace of God. John Newton captured this in his hymn "Glorious things of thee are spoken" when he wrote the lines,

*Saviour, if of Zion's city*
*I through grace a member am…*

When they look around the city, the pilgrims observe that it is "closely compacted together" (Psalm **122:3**). This does not mean that it has what we would call a high housing density, like Singapore! No, it means that it is bound or held together firmly: it is well-built, solid, firm. It has no fractures, no gaps in the walls through which an enemy might come. It is not a city divided against itself, like Berlin before 1989. It is a safe and impregnable city with foundations and walls that are earthquake-proof and attack-resistant. It is a city of solidity, of glory, of weight, of substance, of great stone buildings and fine stone walls. The psalmist feels safe here. The city of God is the world's only really safe place.

The city of God is the world's only really safe place.

Next, having looked with wonder at the strength of the city, our pilgrim notices who goes up there, and why. "The tribes" (**v 4**) are the twelve tribes of the sons of Jacob, who spent much of Old Testament history fighting one another! By the time this song was sung after the exile, most of the tribes had scattered and disappeared from history. So these are remarkable words to sing, because here he sees the twelve tribes, in the mind's eye, all going up together "to praise the name of the LORD". If these endlessly quarrelling tribes are to be united, what will unite them? The only solid answer is a shared praise and worship for the same God. Who or what we worship will shape to whom or where we belong. In the final analysis we belong with those who worship what we worship; we are rivals of those who devote their energies to other goals. Our problem is that we naturally worship ourselves, and we create idols for ourselves, shaped and chosen by us. I worship the idols, or projects, or dreams that I choose; and you worship the gods and goals that you choose. From that point on, we are bound to be at war, or at least on the way to war. Human society can never enjoy a stable harmony while rival gods, and therefore rival worships, try to coexist. There may of course be a fragile "live and let live" that enables us to rub along together without all-out war; but it will never—can never—be stable.

What this pilgrim sees, with the eyes of faith, is a city that is the focus of a worldwide, shared worship and praise. This is why it is a stable and secure city. The safety of the city rests upon the shared worship of its citizens and pilgrims. Today the church of Christ is at its best when it is united under the scriptural authority of Christ its Head. What we think of as "freedom" so often just means our liberty to depart from the stability that comes from glad submission to Christ.

## A city ruled by the king

As the pilgrims look around Jerusalem, their gaze is riveted by the government! They see "thrones for judgment" (**v 5**)—a vivid image for the places where decisions are taken, justice is administered and authority is exercised. These "thrones" belong to "the house of David". Their authority comes from the anointed king in David's line. It is because all the citizens, and all the pilgrims, bow down in obedience to the same authority—a good and godly authority—that harmony endures. This city is the place where the Anointed One, the Christ, rules.

What our pilgrims saw, in their **reverie** of faith, was a wonderful city. This was where God dwelt, where safety was to be found, where human warfare was subdued and transformed into shared worship, where the Christ ruled. But it was a reverie. When the psalmist opened his eyes and took a sober look at the historical reality of Old Testament Jerusalem, he must have seen something very, very different. Far from being "closely compacted together", the Jerusalem of Old Testament history was all too often riven with divisions, beset by weakness and ruined by sin. Far from being a place of unity, it was, again and again, a place of strife and warfare. Did everyone gladly bow down before the good authority of the Davidic king? No! The reality was that Jerusalem was in many ways the opposite of what it was meant to be. From time to time there were glimpses of God's purposes for it; but, by and large, it was a terrible disappointment.

The most terrible, acute disappointment came many years after this, when the man to whom all the prophecies pointed came to Jerusalem. Far from bowing before his good authority, its people falsely accused him, hated him, condemned him and crucified him. As Jesus entered Jerusalem, he wept over it and said:

> "If you, even you, had only known on this day what would bring you peace—but now it is hidden from your eyes. The days will come upon you when your enemies will build an embankment against you and encircle you and hem you in on every side. They will dash you to the ground, you and the children within your walls. They will not leave one stone on another, because you did not recognise the time of God's coming to you." (Luke 19:41-44)

The Jerusalem celebrated in Psalm **122:1-5** was not fulfilled in the historical Jerusalem of Old Testament history. It was a Jerusalem seen only with the eyes of faith. It still is. It will not reach its fulfilment until the Lord Jesus Christ, who has died, has been raised and has ascended to heaven, builds his worldwide church and then returns from heaven to gather together his church to dwell in the perfect heavenly Jerusalem when it comes down from heaven to earth. Then, and only then, will the perfect presence of God, the flawless security, the boundless harmony and the glad submission to the rule of God's King be seen for all eternity. It is that heavenly Jerusalem we see most clearly anticipated in the language of this psalm. And it is precisely because the reality fell so far short of the prophecies that the psalm ends as it does—with the exhortation to pray.

## Longing for the new Jerusalem

*Pray!* says the song as it closes. *Pray! Pray! Pray!* "Pray for the peace of Jerusalem" (**v 6**), because we do not yet see this perfect harmony. Pray for the security of Jerusalem (**v 7**), because it is not yet safe. The peace and security that have been celebrated in **verses 1-5** needs to be prayed for, and prayed for urgently. Commenting on the link between the name "Jerusalem" and the Hebrew word for "peace" (*shalom*, or *salem*), Geoffrey Grogan comments that "the psalmist seems to be praying that it will live up to its name" (*Psalms*, page 201).

This is not an exhortation to pray for peace in the Middle East. It is good to pray for peace in the Middle East, just as it is good to pray for peace in the Far East or the Americas or Africa or Europe. But this psalm is not about that. This psalm exhorts us to pray for the church of Jesus Christ. Inspired by the beautiful vision of **verses 1-5**, we are to pray that it will be realised in the church. We are to pray that it will increasingly be true of our own local church. We are to pray that our local church will be a place where God is present in his forgiving grace, where men and women scarred by a dangerous world can find safety and where divided peoples see barriers fall as they bow together before the loving authority of Jesus Christ, the King in David's line.

This is what our "family and friends" so badly need (**v 8**); for their sake, we need to pray that each local church will be the place they need—a place where they too can find God the Father through Jesus the Son, where they find reconciliation with God and with the people from whom they are estranged, where they too can join with others in bowing gladly to the authority of Jesus the King. As we pray for this—and as, by God's grace and our commitment to their health (**v 9**), our churches become more and more like this—we shall become a house of the LORD, where the people will come to "praise the name of the LORD" (**v 4**).

## Questions for reflection

1. How does reading Psalms 120 and 121 change the way you read Psalm 122?
2. As you read the description of Jerusalem—which is really a description of the heavenly Jerusalem, the new creation—which phrase do you find the most comforting or inspiring?
3. Why is it so important to pray for the church?

## PART TWO

We will now consider three very short psalms (Psalms 126 – 128), each of which speaks of Zion in some way as a project. The fascinatingly different imagery of these psalms sheds great light for us on the work of the gospel in building local churches.

### The fortunes of Zion

Psalm **126:1-3** looks back to a time when God "restored the fortunes" of Zion (**v 1**). That phrase came to be used especially of the return from exile, but it can refer to any time when God worked in power to rescue the people of God and establish them afresh. The song-writer looks back to that wonderful time. It was a period of dreamlike wonder (**v 1**), just as we might say "It was a dream holiday". It was a time of happy "laughter" and wonderful "songs of joy" (**v 2**). People far and wide heard about it and said to one another that the LORD, the God of Israel, had done these "great things for them". The song-writer agrees: *Yes*, he says, *the LORD did indeed do great things for us; we were so very happy* (**v 3**).

Let us pause here. To join in this song is to sign up to an emotional mindset in which the thing that give us the deepest joy in the world is the restoration of Zion. The psalm depicts a world in which people care more for Zion than for their individual or personal prosperity. So in new-covenant terms, the psalm is the expression of a heart that cares more deeply and passionately about the cause of Christ and the church of Christ than it does for its own success, comfort, good name or health. We should long for the church of Christ to be united under Scripture, to be marked by godliness of life, to be earnest about evan-gelism, to be filled with costly love for one another and for a needy world—to be, in short, a shining witness to the goodness of Jesus. To long for that is quite a challenge. It is no light or easy thing to sing **verses 1-3**. Most of us cannot sing this with a good conscience unless and until God has done some deep work in our hearts, because most of us, by nature, care more for ourselves than we do for the church of Jesus Christ. I want the LORD to restore *my* fortunes; I care less about whether or not he restores the fortunes of "Zion", the church.

So let us enter imaginatively into that feelings-world of this believer, so that we feel with them the joy, express with them the laughter and dream with them the dreams of a restored Zion. And then let us pray that we would sing or speak these words today in their new-covenant meaning and find welling up in our hearts such a deep delight in the prosperity of the church of Christ, expressed in our own local church, that it overwhelms all our purely personal joys or cares.

## A harvest sown in tears

It is perhaps surprising that **verses 4-6** follow, rather than precede, **verses 1-3**; for **verses 4-6** are a passionate prayer for a yet-to-be-restored Zion, and we might expect the joy in a restored Zion to come later. Yet this order is realistic. That is, past restorations of Zion—whether the rescues in Old Testament history (such as in the days of King Hezekiah, 2 Kings 18:1 – 19:21) or in the New Testament age (beginning with the Day of Pentecost, Acts 2)—are not yet the final restoration of Zion. In our day we may look back, in many of our countries, to days when the church of Christ was honoured and influential, and lament the present desolate state of the church. This psalm, then, is for us.

For in Psalm **126:4**, we are led to pray, "Restore our fortunes". We cry to the Lord for the same mercy that he has shown his church in the past to be shown again in our day. The Negev is the dry region south of Jerusalem towards the Dead Sea, in which there are many stream beds. These stream beds, or wadis, are bone dry for much of the year; but when the rains come, they can very suddenly fill to overflowing. So the "streams in the Negev" is a picture of sudden, even unexpected, blessing. When the waters come to a desert area, buried seeds that have lain dormant for a long time suddenly germinate and sprout. *Please do this for your church*, we pray, crying to the Lord for the watering of his Spirit that alone can give new life.

**Verse 5** speaks of Zion as a project like a harvest. The mention of "streams" naturally brings to mind the germination and sprouting of seeds, and therefore the sowing that is necessary first. **Verse 5** puts it simply: there are those who "sow". As Jesus uses this imagery, they "sow" the word of God, which is the seed of the Zion harvest. They sow "in tears", for sowing is hard and often thankless work. But here is the promise: they "will reap with songs of joy". There will be a harvest from Zion seed-sowing. And when that harvest comes, there will be "songs of joy" like the songs that greeted an earlier time of blessing in **verse 2**.

**Verse 6** wonderfully intensifies the simple contrast of **verse 5**. In **verse 5** they "sow with tears"; in **verse 6** they "go out weeping, carrying seed to sow". The sixth-century bishop Augustine of Hippo conjured up for his hearers this vivid image:

> "When the farmer goes out with the plough, carrying seed, is not the wind sometimes biting, and does not sometimes the rain deter him? He looks to the sky, sees it overcast, shivers with cold, but nevertheless goes out and sows. For he fears lest while he is watching the foul weather, and waiting for sunshine, the time may pass, and he may not have anything to reap."
>
> (*Expositions on the Psalms (Nicene and Post-Nicene Fathers*, volume 8), page 605—I have updated the translation)

Gospel work is like this. It means sleepless nights, it involves enduring mockery, it calls for financial sacrifice, it requires much hard work with very little to show for it, and it prompts rejection from hard-hearted people. There will be many tears in authentic Zion work; if there are no tears, we must question whether the work is genuine.

> Gospel work requires much hard work. But there will be a harvest. Never doubt that.

So why is it worth the tears? Again, the second half of **verse 6** intensifies the simple second part of **verse 5**:

they "will return with songs of joy, carrying sheaves with them". Before in **verse 6**, they carried seeds and they wept; now they carry sheaves of corn and they sing! There will be a harvest. Never doubt that. This is a psalm to sing when we are discouraged in the work of the gospel—when the ground seems dry, the response negligible, the cost just too great, the tears too many. Our weeping is a necessary precursor to harvest joy. Zion—the true Zion, the church of Jesus—is a harvest which is sown in tears and reaped with songs of joy. The tears come first, but the joy does come. We may be given some foretaste of that reaping and joy in this age, perhaps with a measure of revival—or we may not. But the harvest will come.

Sometimes a sceptical voice will say of some impractical project, "It will all end in tears". The Christian must not say this. Rather, we say of our gospel work, "It will most surely begin in tears; but it will just as surely end in great joy".

## A city built while we sleep

In Psalm 127, the picture changes from a harvest sown and reaped to a city being built. In the context of the songs of ascents, the "house" and the "city" of **verse 1** most naturally refer to the temple and Jerusalem or Zion. It is the building of God's "house" and God's "city"—ultimately the church of Jesus Christ (see, for instance, 1 Peter 2:4-5)—that is the subject that begins this psalm. There are "builders" and there are "guards". Various humans are involved in the project, much as there were for Solomon's temple and the second temple after the exile and the wall-builders under Nehemiah (1 Kings 5 – 6; Nehemiah 3). There they are, building away, watching away. But—and this is the point of Psalm **127:1**—the true builder and the true guard is the LORD himself. This is his project before it is ours.

The anxiety evident in **verse 2** is the worry that comes from believing, in our hearts, that this is really our project and our responsibility. If that is the case, then I cannot really afford to take a break, let alone sleep. I must get up early and go to bed very late, and in between I must toil away trying to bear this crushing burden of responsibility. But it is all pointless, "in vain"; for I can work as hard as anyone ever worked, but all to no avail. I can do gospel work morning, noon and night, seeking to build the church of Jesus Christ. But unless God himself is at work, *nothing* will happen. It's all pointless, fruitless and crushingly destructive of my life.

This is not the way to view the work. "He grants sleep" (**v 2**). Sleep is his gift. Sleep is an expression of faith. When I sleep, when I take a **Sabbath** break, when I go on holiday, when I do something that refreshes my life, I am saying by my actions that I genuinely believe the Zion project—the church project—is God's project and not mine. God is the builder; God is the watchman. I can sleep precisely because God does not (see Psalm 121:3-4). The believing builders do build and the believing watchmen do watch; there is work to be done! But they also sleep and rest, because they know that the project ultimately depends upon God.

## A family nurtured by God

The third metaphor for Zion is a family. I am not sure why the metaphor changes in the middle of Psalm 127; but suddenly, from the world of building a house and guarding a city, we are in the world of children! Perhaps this follows the pattern of the book of Nehemiah. Nehemiah comes to the ruined post-exilic Jerusalem, and first he rebuilds the wall. After that, we read that "the city was large and spacious, but there were few people in it" (Nehemiah 7:4). Then the focus shifts from the walls to the people who will dwell within them. In a similar way, Psalm 127 begins with the building of the city and seems to go on to the need for it to be populated.

We tend to read **verses 3-5**, and then Psalm 128, as if their primary application is to our marriages and our very natural desire to have children. But, while everything said here is true about our marriages (it is good to want children and to rejoice when God blesses us with children), the context very strongly suggests that the scope here is not so much individual nuclear families as families that populate the people of Zion.

The key idea in **127:3-5** is usefulness, and the central theme of Psalm 128 is fruitfulness. So in **127:3-5** we have a picture of a family in which a man fathers children who are described as "arrows" in his "quiver", and who will prove useful "in court": that is to say, these children will fight the good fight of the faith. They will be useful citizens of Zion. It is not so much that they will bring joy to their parents' hearts (although they may) but that they will be effective fighters of the good fight.

In a similar way, Psalm 128 uses the language of fruitfulness. We see a wife described as "a fruitful vine" (**v 3**—perhaps not our first choice of metaphor!), with children "like olive shoots" sitting around the kitchen table. In biblical imagery, "fruit" speaks of godliness—of lives that mirror the qualities of God's own character to build a society of justice, kindness and love. Here in this believing family is a wonderful picture of church growth by the conception and nurture of children who will gladly grow in godliness and be—in our terms—Christlike members of the church of Christ.

This context of Zion comes through again very strongly at the end of the psalm. This man is promised blessing "from *Zion*": that he will see "the prosperity of *Jerusalem*" and, as he lives into old age to see his children's children, that there will be "peace" coming upon "*Israel*" (**v 5-6**, my emphasis). This is not about our nuclear-family hopes; this is the growth of the people of God, and ultimately the church of Jesus Christ. And there is a sense in which this God-fearing man, both in **127:3-5** and throughout Psalm 128, is fulfilled in Jesus Christ himself, to whom are given many, many spiritual children, who will be made like him and who will populate the new Jerusalem.

So, while we are not wrong to pray that God will give us the blessing of children, the context of these psalms encourages us to raise our sights beyond this, to the grand vista of the church of Jesus Christ populated by more and more spiritual children, made God's by new birth. Again, it is good to want children; but these psalms remind us that there is something far greater than that—the growth of Christ's church. It is always sad to so focus on the former that we do not go to work for the latter.

## Putting the three pictures together

Let us draw the threads of these three psalms together. If we are followers of Jesus, we are called to be involved in the great work of building and growing Zion, the church of Jesus. That is a wonderful work and a tremendous privilege. But we need to hold in our hearts the burden of these three pictures. For this is a harvest for which we are called to sow in tears, trusting that there will one day be a joyful harvest. And this is a building project of which God is the builder and watchman; it is not finally our responsibility. We may—we must—rest and sleep as a sign that we really trust it to be God's work. And this is a family for whom every conception—physical or spiritual—is from God, and all godly nurture comes as the unmerited blessing of God alone.

The church of Christ is the most deeply wonderful project in the world. There is no higher cause to which we can devote our love and our energies. It is worth considering what that means for each of us in the particular local churches to which we belong. Your local fellowship may not look very impressive; indeed often our local churches look rather unimpressive. But in truth, a building is being constructed, by God but through our labours, that will shine with glory in eternity. What a privilege and a joy to be a part of that!

## Questions for reflection

1. How do these psalms help you reflect on the gospel work you or those you know are doing?
2. How might they alter your priorities?
3. How do you think God could use you to contribute to the growth of the church?

PSALMS 137 AND 139

# 15. PAIN AND COMFORT IN EXILE

After the songs of ascent (Psalms 120 – 134) there are three rather different psalms (Psalms 135 – 137) before the final "of David" collection (Psalms 138 – 145) and then the "Hallelujah Chorus" to close the Psalter (Psalm 146 – 150). In this chapter, we take two very famous psalms: one in which great pain is voiced and the other (the first of that last "of David" group) that speaks of a deep comfort.

## A song to sing when you can't sing

Do you ever feel the mismatch between what we sing in church and the harsh reality in the world outside—and, perhaps, in your own life? If you don't, you probably should. For mismatch there is, and that dissonance is perhaps increasing as our churches become more and more marginalised. We sing that Jesus is king of all the world, that only in Jesus there is the forgiveness we need, that God will rescue a broken world through Jesus, that good will triumph, and that there will be a new heavens and new earth in which there will be no sin or sorrow and nothing that spoils. In the real world outside, these things seem utterly absurd. They don't really match the weak, divided, compromised churches we so often lament. And sometimes the circumstances we ourselves face also suggest that good may well not triumph.

Psalm 137 is a song to sing when we don't feel we can sing the songs we want to sing. We have here a song sung by those who felt they could not sing.

## Babylon then and now

We do not know when Psalm 137 was first written and sung. But it bears the marks of eye-witness memory, of one who knew what it was to be an exile in Babylon (e.g. 2 Kings 25; Jeremiah 52; Lamentations; Daniel 1). And Babylon soon became more than a historical designation of an empire. After Babylon fell, two of the rulers of the Persian Empire were still called "King of Babylon" by the Old Testament writers (see Ezra 5:13; Nehemiah 13:6). Before long, Babylon became a symbol of the city of the world—that is, any society that was hostile to God and the people of God. That symbolism reached its climax in Revelation 18. It remains powerful imagery even today. For example, in 1975 Kenneth Anger wrote his book *Hollywood Babylon*, exposing the dark secrets of Hollywood. So, when we hear "Babylon" in this psalm, we should not confine our thoughts to the ancient neo-Babylonian Empire. This is what the apostle John simply called "the world"—society organised in hostility to God.

Although some translations take Psalm **137:1-3** as the first paragraph, I am going to take **verses 1-4** as our first section. These four verses are plural and corporate ("we"); but in **verse 5** we hear the beginnings of an individual voice ("I").

We join the exiled believers by the riverside. **Verses 1-4** begin with "the rivers of Babylon" (the network of rivers and irrigation canals for which Babylon was famous—Leslie Allen writes of "an intricate canal system intersecting the southern Babylonian plain"—*Psalms 101-150*, page 307) and end with "a foreign land". We are emphatically away from home. Ezekiel had some of his early visions by one of these rivers (Ezekiel 3:15); Ezra gathered his returning exiles by another (Ezra 8:21).

Picture the scene. A group of believers gather by the river with their musical instruments, presumably to pray and to sing "the songs of Zion" to encourage one another in their faith in the God of the covenant. Perhaps they sing from Psalm 46, where Zion is by a river and it is promised that she will not fall. Or maybe Psalm 48, where

Zion's beauty is praised, and foreign enemies flee in terror at the very sight of her grandeur. Maybe their songs include Psalm 50:2 with that memorable phrase "Zion, perfect in beauty". Whatever songs they had on their songlist, some of them probably celebrated the glory of Zion in the purposes of God.

And then a group of Babylonians draw near. They see these exiles from Jerusalem, and they begin to mock them: *Were you singing? We didn't quite catch the words. Could you sing those songs again?* It is so painful. There is a Hebrew word-play between the word "tormentors" (Psalm **137:3**) and the word "hung (up)" in **v 2**: *We hung up our harps*, God's people say, *and they tormented us for doing so.*

*Oh, you won't sing?* we can imagine the Babylonian mockers asking: *I wonder why not*. The answer is all too obvious. How can the believers sing about the impregnability of Zion when it has been destroyed; about the glory of Zion's God when he has been disgraced;about the worldwide rule of Zion's king when he is no more; about the prosperity of Zion when it is shattered? No, the mismatch is too great. And so they hang up their harps on the branches of the trees, and they hang their heads in despair.

The songs of Zion appear so utterly absurd—so evidently wishful-thinking and make-believe. The Jews themselves took those words "perfect in beauty" from Psalm 50:2 and used them in Lamentations: "Is this the city that was called perfection of beauty?" (Lamentations 2:15) Not now it isn't. Not any more. Later believers like Simeon and Anna (Luke 2:25-38) must have sung this psalm and felt its sadness. Jesus himself would have sung it and grieved for the people of God. His disciples might very appropriately have sung it on Good Friday, when the One who was the fulfilment of Zion was destroyed on the cross.

It is the same today, for we too are "exiles, scattered" (1 Peter 1:1). We look at the reality of the church of Jesus Christ, and it is very hard to sing, and go on singing, about the glories of that church as they are promised in the word of God. It is very, very tempting to hang up our harps, to hang our heads in shame and to abandon all attempts at gospel proclamation. Psalm **137:1-4** helps us weep with this pain and to feel the force of this temptation.

## Deep love

An unnamed individual comes to the front of the discouraged believers in **verse 5** and begins to speak or sing. He or she pledges, most movingly and courageously, that they will never forget Jerusalem. If they do, they call upon themselves the worst curse that a musician can utter: that they will lose their ability to play an instrument and to sing (**v 6**). For this singer, Jerusalem is and will always be their "highest joy". It is a poignant moment. With a lovely irony, they say that if they cannot sing of Zion, they will not sing at all, for there is true joy to be found nowhere else.

But how would the others respond? I guess there would have been different reactions. Some would be overcome with silent shame over what had happened, and sorrow over how far they were from the promised land. But surely others felt keenly a constant temptation to throw in their lot with Babylon—to abandon the old superstitions about Jerusalem, to embrace the new and shiny gods of Babylon, and to make a life for themselves in their new home. It is not hard to imagine how that could happen. At the start it was miserable, but then, gradually over the generations, they would get used to living in Babylon. They would get along. They would fit in with Babylon's values. They would "go native", accept Babylon's values and begin to imitate Babylon's behaviour.

This singer believes the promises even when there is nothing to show for them in the present.

But this singer believes the promises even when there is nothing to show for them in the present. They count the promises more precious than gold. *Babylon is visible, audible, tangible, delightful, and it is all around me,* they sing; *but I rest my joy on the promises of God about Zion.*

Implicitly, what this individual says is a call to each man, woman and child in the group to join them in this pledge of loyalty to Zion. Who was this person? We do not know. But we know by whose Spirit they spoke, for all the psalms are spoken and sung by the Spirit of God, who is the Spirit of the Christ who was to come. The day came when Jesus of Nazareth sang this song, and as the synagogue came to **verses 5** and **6**, he was the man upon whose lips these words of courageous loyalty reached their climax.

To join in **verses 5-6** is to join our voices and pledge our allegiance with the loyal courage of Jesus Christ. It takes an act of the will to speak these words—to make the "I" that was Jesus the "I" that is me, so that "I", the singer of the psalm today, pledge myself to count the church of Jesus Christ as my highest joy. It takes an act of the will to say—and mean—that I cannot imagine finding true joy anywhere other than in the church. That is quite a thing to say!

The apostle Peter writes with wonder to believers who love Jesus even though they haven't seen him (1 Peter 1:8); in a similar way, there is a small miracle when believers trust that the church, the bride of Jesus, has a destiny far brighter than the shiniest wonders of "Babylon" today. We haven't yet seen the bride (the church) in her glory, but we know that one day she will shine in glorious robes (see Revelation 19:7-8)—while Babylon ceases to look like anything at all (Revelation 18:1-3, 21-24).

But there is more. And it is the final part of the psalm that most sticks in our gullets, until we properly understand it.

## Deep confidence

The focus in the final verses is on the enemies whose hostility took the people of God into exile. Psalm **137:7** is about the Edomites, and **verses 8-9** about the Babylonians.

The Edomites were the enemy close at hand. They were cousins of the Israelites, the descendants of Jacob's brother Esau. They lived to the east of Israel. On the day when the Babylonians finally destroyed Jerusalem, what were the Edomites doing? They were cheering the Babylonians on! *Go on! Well done! Tear it down, tear it right down to its foundations!* they shouted (**v 7**). Literally their cry meant "Strip it naked, expose it, as an assailant might do to a woman" (the Hebrew uses the same word for this horrifying action).

Four short texts in the Old Testament help fill out this picture. First, in Lamentations 4:21-22 we learn that the Edomites would suffer the same "stripping naked" (same word) that they helped perpetrate against Jerusalem. Second and third, Ezekiel twice speaks of their vengefulness and ancient hostility towards Judah (Ezekiel 25:12; 35:5). And fourth, the short prophecy of Obadiah is all about what the Edomites did.

The prayer in Psalm **137:7** is actually quite restrained: "*Remember*, LORD, what the Edomites did" (my emphasis). The psalmist entrusts the destiny of Edom to the Lord's wise and just hands. But implicit in this prayer is the belief that God will not let Edom's treachery pass without any just punishment. If an Edomite turns away from Edom and comes into God's people Israel (as Ruth the Moabite turned from Moab), they will be saved; but if they persist in their Edomite allegiance, God will remember the treachery with which they align themselves.

Hostility to the church of Christ is perhaps most painful when it comes from close at hand: from those we might reasonably expect to be our friends, and at times from within the visible institution of the "church" itself. When that happens, we are called, both by this psalm and by the New Testament (for instance, 2 Timothy 4:14) to entrust it all to God, who sees and knows.

The second enemy is Babylon: the epitome of hostility.

Psalm **137:9** is often quoted as an example of the vengeful violence of the Old Testament. It is a horrifying verse. But it is, in fact, not vengeful, and it is necessary (see the discussion of Psalm 109 in chapter 13 of this book, on pages 203-210). It is not a curse but a declaration of something that is true. It is an expression of confidence that, as and when Babylon finally falls, those who bring about its downfall are doing the will of God and are—in that **objective** sense—"happy" (that is, "blessed"). This is not about some horrible **subjective** enjoyment of inflicting suffering; it is about doing the will of God.

The point about Babylon is that they are "doomed to destruction". Although they are called "Daughter Babylon"—which means something like "refined, delicate, fashionable, beautiful, prosperous, clean"—God has decreed that they will be destroyed. We find prophecies to this effect, for example, in Isaiah 47 and Jeremiah 50 – 51. This psalm affirms our confidence that God will do what he has said he will do.

But what about the children in Psalm **137:9**? One old (and anti-Semitic) scholar wrote that **verse 9** is an expression "of ancient Judaism that knew how to hate and avenge" (quoted in Othmar Keel, *The Symbolism of the Biblical World*, page 9). But this is not so—there was nothing specific to Judaism about this reality of conflict. In ancient warfare, if you wanted properly and finally to conquer a foe, you left the old people alone, but you made sure to get rid of the young men (because they could fight and father children), the young women (because they could bear children), and the children (because they would grow up to fight and continue the existence of this hostile people). Sad to say, the ripping open of pregnant women was a commonplace of ancient warfare (see, for instance, 2 Kings 8:12; Luke 19:44)—because a victorious invader would not want their enemy to have a future. Othmar Keel, in his scholarly work *The Symbolism of the Biblical World*, suggests that the word "infants" here may be metaphorical, just as "daughter" is metaphorical in "Daughter Babylon" (page 9). In our less vivid way of speaking, he writes, we might say, "Happy is he who puts an end to your self-renewing domination". It means the same thing.

So the point of Psalm **137:9** is that one day Babylon will finally be no more. It is chilling; but it is necessary. If the children of Babylon live, then Babylon lives and will rise again. But the day will come when Babylon will not rise again. We see this final defeat most clearly in Revelation 18:21-24 with its assuring refrain "never ... again". One day evil will be no more. One day hostility to God and his people will be no more.

This is a wonderful hope. It is sobering, for God's coming judgment will be terrible—and final. But it is necessary and good. Knowing that this final judgment will come, and that one day Babylon will be no more, will encourage us to keep singing the praises of the God and Father of the Lord Jesus Christ and of Jesus himself, by the Spirit. In the language of Psalm 137, we will not hang up our harps. Judgment is not something to be embarrassed about; it is a sober truth to make us glad and to strengthen our resolve to keep telling people the only gospel that offers rescue from that judgment.

Only Jesus, the Lamb who died for sinners, can lead his church in the singing of this psalm. For only in him is to be found such intense grief at the desolate state of his people (**verses 1-4**; see Luke 19:41-44), only in him do we hear such single-hearted joy in his people (Psalm **137:5-6**), and only in him is there such a holy and pure resolve that one day Babylon, with Edom, will be no more (**v 7-9**).

## Questions for reflection

1. When have you felt unable to sing songs of joy?
2. How would the experience of being separated from God and his church compare to that?
3. How does it feel to know that the joy of being among God's people will last for ever and that hostility to God will come to an end?

## PART TWO

In Psalm 137 we were encouraged to join with Christ in voicing loyal confidence in the context of deep sorrow. Next, in Psalm 139 we will see that our being "in Christ" is the key to singing it.

### Life in the presence of God

Are you conscious, moment by moment, of living life in the presence of God? Too often I am not. The Reformers used the Latin phrase *coram Deo* to describe the idea. This psalm will help us learn to live like this; and it will make all the difference to our lives.

Parts of this psalm are great favourites; they appear on **devotional** calendars and Instagram pics, and we love them. But there are two parts we are apt to omit. First, we tremble when we reach **verses 19-22**, and we wish that that section were not there; these verses seem to break the heartwarming devotional flow. And we also forget that it is headed "Of David". We need to remember, as ever, that this was first a psalm of David—and therefore also later a psalm of Jesus; and we must understand how it was sung by the king before it can be sung by us, as men and women united to the king by faith. As we shall see, that will help us know how to sing **verses 19-22**.

Structurally, the 24 verses of the psalm come in four equal sections of six verses. In each of these sections the final two verses (**v 5-6**, **11-12**, **17-18**, **23-24**) stand somewhat apart from the previous four and help us grasp how we ought to respond to the first part of the section.

In addition the words "searched" and "know" in **verse 1** are echoed in the final prayer of **verses 23-24** ("*search* me" and "*know* my heart"). This rounds off the psalm and helps to define its theme.

### His intimate knowledge of me

God's knowledge dominates this first section. The words "searched ... know" (**v 1**), "know ... perceive" (**v 2**), "discern ... are familiar with" (**v 3**), "know" (**v 4**), and "such knowledge" (**v 6**) set the theme. This psalm is not simply speaking about the doctrine we call God's omniscience: the truth that God knows all things. God does know all things, but here it is the king speaking of God's personal and relational knowledge of *himself*: God does not just know *about* him but knows *him*. God knows his king intimately because he is the LORD, the covenant God, and is in covenant relationship with the king. He knows the king's movements, he knows the king's thoughts, he knows the king's "going out" (public life) and "lying down" (private life), and he knows what the king will say and why ("completely").

There is between the covenant God and his covenant king in David's line an extraordinary intimacy of knowledge. In **verses 5-6** the king responds with awe and wonder at being known with such depth of personal relationship by God. It is an astonishing knowledge, not just because of its **cognitive** content (what God knows about him) but because of the closeness of relationship it creates.

This relationship between the Father God and the king, who was often called God's "Son" (e.g. Psalm 2:7), reaches its fulfilment in the Lord Jesus Christ, who could say of himself, "No one knows the Son except the Father, and no one knows the Father except the Son" (Matthew 11:27). Supremely it is Jesus who sings Psalm **139:1-6** with awe and wonder at how deeply the Father knows him.

But—and this is wonder upon wonders!—Jesus the Son went on to say in Matthew 11:27, "No one knows the Father except the Son and those to whom the Son chooses to reveal him". In Christ the beloved Son, each and every believer comes to be "known by God" (see Galatians 4:9) with this intimate personal knowledge, and to know God with the privileged relationship of sharing in Jesus' sonship, as those who are now sons and daughters of God. So there is this difference between the searching truth that God knows everything and therefore knows everything about everyone (including the thoughts and intentions of our hearts), and the relationship that means God knows all who are in Christ with a deep knowledge of commitment and relationship. He knows all about each of us; but he knows us in Christ *relationally*.

Perhaps there is a small (though imperfect) analogy between the knowledge that someone has of their fiancé(e) before they get married and the much deeper knowledge they have after getting married.

God's knowledge of his children is a wonder we should meditate on with awe. It is also a warning, that the most terrifying words a person can hear from Jesus on the last day would be "I never *knew* you. Away from me" (Matthew 7:23).

## His unbreakable presence with me

Just as Psalm **139:1-6** is not about God's omniscience—but rather about personal knowledge of his Christ and, by extension, of all who are in him—so **verses 7-12** are not simply about God's omnipresence. It is true that God is fully present in each and every place, and indeed at each and every moment of time. But these verses are not about that. This again is about a personal presence. David sings of God's "Spirit", who is his personal "presence" (**v 7**). David is not simply saying that he cannot find any place in the universe where God is not; he is saying he cannot find any place in the universe where God is not *with him*.

*Suppose*, says David, using a dramatic literary technique, *just suppose I were to try to run away from the God who is in covenant with me. What would happen* (**v 7**)? In **verses 8-10** he takes two pairs of extremes to highlight the extent of his mental experiment. First, in **verse 8** he imagines going up as high as it would be possible to go—"to the heavens"—and then going down, down, down to "the depths", which means the depths of the chaotic sea, the place where the entrances to Sheol (the place of the dead) are to be found. David's answer: *Whether I go as high as is possible or as low as is imaginable (and everywhere in between), you will be there with me.* (This is another example of merism.)

Then, in **verses 9-10**, David says, *Suppose I go to the very far east* ("the wings of the dawn"—to the eastern horizon, where the sun rises) *or to the very far west* ("the far side of the [Mediterranean] sea"), *or anywhere in between*; even there "your hand will guide me, your right hand will hold me fast". So this is not just about God being there; it is about God being there for *him*—being personally present to hold and guard him. The personal presence of the covenant God guarantees the king's safety.

In **verses 11-12** the king meditates on this comforting truth. Sometimes he feels himself in darkness and fears that he will be hidden in darkness, with no more hope of light. That is a fearful anxiety. But, wonderfully, even in the deepest darkness the God who is light, who shines "like the day", will be there. No darkness can overcome the God who is life and light; and this God is pledged in unbreakable covenant with the king.

What a comfort this must have been to the Lord Jesus! As he dwelt in a land of deep darkness, and as finally he plunged into the shadow of death upon the cross, even there he could be confident that God would watch over him and bring him through the sleep of death into resurrection life.

In Christ, and in Christ alone, the loving presence of God our heavenly Father is unbreakably, unshakeably with us however dark the valley of death into which we may be led. For nothing in all creation, not even the deep darkness of death itself, "will be able to separate us from the love of God that is in Christ Jesus our Lord" (Romans 8:39).

## His creative wisdom in shaping me

Psalm **139:13-18** is full of creative words: "created ... knit ... together" (**v 13**), "made ... your works" (**v 14**), "made ... woven together" (**v 15**), "unformed body ... days ordained for me" (**v 16**). There is a precious general truth here: that it is God who knits together each and every human being in the image of God, from conception. But I think the more focused and particular truth that we find here concerns not all human beings but precisely Christ and those in Christ. Let me explain.

Long before David was anointed king by the prophet Samuel (1 Samuel 16), God knit him together, cell by cell, in the womb of Jesse's wife.

David was the handiwork of God, the man made to be the one who imaged God's own heart. He was shaped for the kingship and every day of his reign was written beforehand in God's book (Psalm **139:16**). For David, those days included days of sin as well as days of faith. But God's careful, painstaking shaping of David anticipated a greater, more wonderful, shaping within the virgin womb of Mary, as a tiny embryo was formed and, cell by cell, a fully human man was formed who was yet fully divine. This knitting-together was the greatest miracle in the whole of human history. Jesus of Nazareth was shaped and knitted together, prepared lovingly by the Father: the **incarnate** Son of God, who would work the Father's will in every way. Every day and night of the life of Jesus on earth was written in the Father's book before it came to be. This is why the prophets could write so fully about him centuries before, for they were inspired by the Spirit of the God who had shaped and ordained those days before they came to be. What infinite skill and what amazing wisdom must have been expended in the shaping of Jesus, the incarnate **Word**!

In **verses 17-18**, as David meditates on his own creation, he speaks of how "precious" are these "thoughts" of God: the thoughts and intentions of God that have been written into his life in every particular on each and every day. What a "vast" repository of wisdom there must be to shape this one human life like this. God's thoughts must be more than "the grains of sand"!

I am not to regret that I am not someone else. In Christ, God has shaped me just as he purposed for me to be.

And yet—and again this is an astonishing truth—in Christ each man and woman may say of themselves, "I too am God's personal loving handiwork; I too have been created by God, in Christ Jesus, so that I may do precisely the good works God has prepared in advance for me to do (Ephesians 2:10). I am not to regret that I am not someone else, that I didn't have different parents or a changed upbringing; for, however flawed it seems to me, and however painful, I may trust that, in Christ, God has shaped me just as he has purposed for me to be."

## A prayer that boomerangs

In the final section, Psalm **139:19-24**, we see that, for the psalmist...

> "the LORD'S enemies are his enemies. For the psalmist there can be no moral or spiritual neutrality. He knows whose side he is on." (Robert Davidson, *The Vitality of Worship*, page 449)

If I think that I, with my mixed motives and vengeful heart, am meant to pray **verses 19-22**, I have made a big mistake; for, on my lips, these words would indeed be terrible. Only on the lips of the king—ultimately the perfect King, the Lord Jesus—can these words possibly be prayed. For Jesus is God's beloved and loving Son, and his appointed King—and therefore hostility to Jesus is enmity towards the Father. By definition, the enemies of Jesus are the enemies of God. And therefore it is right and pure for him to pray that these enemies—if they persist in their inveterate hostility—be removed from the earth, so that there will no longer be rebellion. In Christ, and in Christ alone, we may (with very great caution) join in with this prayer that wickedness will finally be destroyed.

Of course, in the heart of David, and in the heart of a believer with a Spirit-guided conscience, such a prayer boomerangs and causes us to look at our own hearts. I think this is why, in the final two verses, the king leads his people in praying: I am to pray that the God who searches hearts will search my own heart (**v 23**), to know and test what is there, and to ensure that any thought or imagination that is "offensive" to God will be removed and I will be led "in the way everlasting" (**v 24**). As we close this psalm, Jesus leads us to open ourselves afresh to the God who searches and knows us (**v 1**), that he may again search and know us (**v 23**).

In Christ, as you and I pray this psalm, we bring to mind the amazingly intimate knowledge that God has—personal knowledge of each of us in all the depths of our thoughts and hopes and fears and imaginations. We are deeply assured again that, in Christ, there is no place in the universe, be it ever so dark, that can separate us from the Father's love and care. We treasure the infinite wisdom with which our heavenly Creator Father knit us together and ordained for us every day and night of our life on earth. And we open ourselves afresh to his searching eyes of love, that he may purify us and lead us in the way to everlasting life, where all evil will finally be ended.

## Questions for reflection

1. How could you remind yourself day by day that you are living in the presence of God?
2. What difference does it make to the way you read this psalm, knowing that it is first and foremost about God's king?
3. What "offensive way" do you want to ask God to remove from your heart, your mind or your life?

PSALMS 145 AND 148

# 16. THE FINAL HALLELUJAH

For our final two psalms, we take first the last "of David" psalm in the Psalter—a psalm in which our king leads us in the praise that is so energetically expressed in the final five psalms—and then we look at one of those final five, as an example of the kind of final praise given for us to sing.

## The king's call to praise

The trouble with praise is that when someone exhorts me to praise, I often don't want to. You can tell me to praise God till you are blue in the face; but, however much you beat me over the head with your exhortations, nothing you can say will change my heart from a heart of grumbling or low spirits or sadness into a heart from which praise flows out in glad exuberance. In fact, you will probably just make me feel worse. As I listen to you, it confirms something I have always suspected: that I am a failure in praise, as I am a failure in so many other parts of my Christian life.

Now, on the face of it, Psalm 145 does exactly that: it exhorts me to pledge myself to praise. In **verses 1-2** there are three words for praise: "exalt", "praise" and "extol". They are **synonyms**, and putting them all together conjures up the picture of praise that is unreserved. Further, this is to be unbroken praise, for it happens "every day". And it is unending praise, "for ever and ever" (said twice). So, if we say these verses, we find ourselves pledging to offer God unreserved, unbroken and unending praise. How can you and I do that? We can't.

And yet praise is very important. If God is not praised, then God is not made known to a needy world; for it is by praise that we tell others about God. When we tell people how good and great God is, we are praising him. Truly to know God is to praise him. Praise is not the icing on the believer's cake—it is the necessary condition of the true God being known. What is more, if my life is not marked and shaped by praise, I will be in grave spiritual danger of being lured away to the worship of some other god—a worship that promises me a greater joy in life but will deliver nothing, or worse.

> There are many ups and downs in the Psalter, but there is a gradual movement towards praise.

So praise matters. There are many ups and downs in the Psalter as the tone shifts from lament to praise and back again to lament. There is no simple unbroken trajectory. But, taking the picture of the Psalter as a whole, there is a gradual movement towards praise. By the time we reach the final five psalms, praise dominates with overflowing exuberance.

## Learning to praise

So the question is: how are we to learn to praise? This psalm gives us a wonderful answer. The key is to remember that it is a psalm of David—it is, in fact, the final psalm of David in the final arrangement of the Psalter. It is a particularly important psalm of David. The first person to speak **verses 1-2**—that is, to pledge unreserved, unbroken, and unending praise to God—is the king. It was part of Old Testament corporate worship that the king should lead the people in praise as their representative head. That is what David is doing here.

Of course King David did not succeed in keeping this pledge. There were days—especially the terrible day when he slept with Bathsheba, and the days following that disaster—when his life most certainly did not make God known. And, ultimately, he failed to praise "for ever and ever" because he died!

David's pledge here calls—as does so much of the later part of the Psalter—"for a praise that was yet to be given" (Claus Westermann, *Praise and Lament in the Psalms*, page 161). These psalms kept calling for this wonderful praise, but no Israelite succeeded in giving it until, centuries later, a boy sang the psalms in the synagogue. And—as he grew up as a child, a youth and a young man—every time he heard the call to praise, there was an answering cry in his believing heart: *Yes! Yes, I will praise. Yes, with every deed I do and every word I speak, I will make the Father known* (John 1:18). With complete consistency, with integrity, with perseverance and with perfection, Jesus Christ gave the praise that is pledged at the start of this psalm. (This is why Hebrews 2:12 quotes something very similar from Psalm 22:22: "I will declare your name ... I will praise you".)

Still today, Jesus the King praises God the Father-King: the King praises the King. Or, to put it more accurately, the divine-human King leads his people in praise of God the Father-King. This is such a relief to us. Having feared that we may be asked to dredge out of our reluctant hearts a praise of which we are not capable, we learn now that we are not being asked to take the microphone to lead the praise: no, we are invited to join the choir of Jesus and to join in the praise that he is already leading.

There are two main themes of praise in the body of the psalm. These two motifs shape the reasons why Jesus our King leads us in praise of the Father.

## Praise his goodness

Psalm **145:3-13a** combines greatness and goodness. As we shall see, it is precisely this combination that is beyond the wisdom of human beings to fathom. In **verse 3**, David speaks of an unfathomable greatness; and then greatness dominates **verses 4-6**. Look at the words: "mighty acts" (**v 4**); "glorious splendour of your majesty ... your wonderful works" (**v 5**); "the power of your awesome works ... your great deeds" (**v 6**). The word translated "wonderful" speaks here (as elsewhere in the Old Testament) of things that are beyond our understanding and beyond our control; it speaks of powerful understanding or wise strength.

Then **verses 7-9** shift the focus to goodness. David sings of God's "abundant goodness ... righteousness" (**v 7**); he does what is right and good. **Verse 8**, with its list of "gracious ... compassionate ... slow to anger ... rich in love", echoes the most-quoted description of God in the Old Testament. First spoken when God forgave his people's sin in the episode of the golden calf (Exodus 34:6), this description echoes around the Old Testament: this covenant God is unfailingly good. And then again in Psalm **145:9**, God is described as "good to all ... he has compassion".

From **verses 10** to **13a** the focus shifts back to power: notice the words "kingdom ... might ... mighty acts ... kingdom ... everlasting kingdom ... dominion". As the old hymn puts it:

*O worship the King, all glorious above,*
*O gratefully sing his power and his love.*

It is sometimes hard to see God in this way: as simultaneously all-powerful and all-good. If he is all-powerful, why would he make a world in which bad things happen? So, if he is all-good, he can't be all-powerful. We therefore either compromise on his goodness, and think he must be a morally mixed-up deity; or we compromise on his power, and assume there are things he cannot control. David quite unselfconsciously praises God for the fact that in his infinite wisdom and power he is both all-powerful and all-good. He praises God for precisely the two attributes that our "problem of evil" says cannot simultaneously be true! No doubt David struggled with this. Certainly those who set this psalm in Book V—after the exile, when most of the promises of God seemed not to be true—must have thought carefully about this. They didn't hold to these things because they were less sophisticated than us or not as observant of the world. No, they knew as well as we do that bad things happen to good people, and good things to bad people (to put it bluntly).

No doubt Jesus himself was tempted to doubt that his Father was all-good and all-powerful. And yet, when the towns in which he had invested much of his energy refused to repent (Matthew 11:20-23), here is his response: "I praise you, Father, Lord of heaven and earth, because you have hidden these things from the wise and learned, and revealed them to little children" (v 25-26). He knew his Father to be "Lord of heaven and earth"—no compromise on his sovereignty there! And he also knew him to be wise and good.

The epitome of this problem is seen at the crucifixion, which was the single most evil deed ever done by human beings and yet, at the same time, was decreed and willed by God for his wonderful and good purpose of rescuing his people (Acts 2:23). As the poet William Cowper put it:

*God moves in a mysterious way,*
*His wonders to perform …*

*Deep in unfathomable mines*
*Of never-failing skill*
*He treasures up his bright designs*
*And works his sovereign will.*

*Judge not the Lord by feeble sense,*
*But trust him for his grace;*
*Behind a frowning providence*
*He hides a smiling face.*

This truth leads David naturally on to his second theme: the goodness of God is a faithful goodness.

## Praise his faithfulness

Notice how similar Psalm **145:13b** and **17** are. Each says that the LORD is "faithful in all he does". He is "trustworthy" in keeping his promises. This (near) refrain subdivides the section from **verses 13b-20**.

First, there is faithfulness to the world. The people to whom God is faithful are "*all* who fall … *all* who are bowed down … the eyes of *all* … *every* living thing". Here is a faithfulness to all of humankind, and indeed every living being including animals, birds, fish and even blades of grass. There is here an indiscriminate generosity to all without distinction: to the wicked and the righteous, to the complex and the simple, to the rational and the sub-rational, to the sentient and the insentient—to every living thing.

The covenant referred to here is God's promise to Noah, sealed by the rainbow, to maintain the good order of the universe: the days and nights, the seasons, the harvests and so on (Genesis 9:9-11). Then, God promised never to let this world become hell on earth. Evil may be terrible, but it will always be restrained in this age. After darkness, the sun will rise. After winter, spring will come. After drought, rains will fall. This is because God, the heavenly Father, "causes his sun to rise on the evil and the good, and sends rain on the righteous and the unrighteous" (Matthew 5:45). Every day of life is a day of God's common grace to all. He made this promise to Noah; he keeps it.

But there is another faithfulness, to another covenant; a yet-deeper faithfulness because a greater covenant is kept. The promise that began in Genesis 12 through the covenant with Abraham, which was sustained for centuries and fulfilled in Jesus Christ, is the promise that one day there will be a new heavens and new earth, which will be governed by Jesus Christ, the seed of Abraham, and by all his people in him.

So the focus here is on the covenant God's nearness "to all who call on him … in truth" (Psalm **145:18**), "those who fear him" (**v 19**), and "all who love him" (**v 20**): that is to say, his people. And, no matter how kind he has been to everybody, in the end this covenant will triumph. Those who persist in wicked hostility to this good Creator will finally be destroyed (**v 20b**). Until that day, though, every day is a day of gospel invitation and grace.

The Lord Jesus made the Father known as the One who is unfailingly faithful to every living being in the whole created order, but above all as the One who demonstrates his unfailing reliability to all who trust him through Jesus.

## Join the choir

And so the king gives his invitation (**v 21**). He repeats his own pledge that his own "mouth will speak in praise of the LORD". He has done that. Jesus fulfilled that perfectly when he came to make the Father known, and as—by his Spirit, through his gospel messengers—he continues to make the Father known (John 17:26). And so he calls out, "Let every creature praise his holy name for ever and ever" (Psalm **145:21b**). This is where we come in—not to initiate the praise, for Jesus has done that, and not to lead the praise, for Jesus is doing that, but to join the choir.

And so we come back to the problem of praise. You and I know that simply being exhorted to praise doesn't work. A human being trying to jolly me along and arouse me to praise doesn't get to my heart. But when a man or woman is born again by the Spirit of God, who is the Spirit of Christ, something wells up in their hearts, and they find themselves beginning to be willing to join in the great chorus of praise to the Father that Jesus leads. Their King leads them, as a member of his people, in singing the praises of God the Father-King. Precisely because the Spirit of our great Praise-Leader indwells our hearts, our joining in comes from the deepest depths of our human personhood. We praise because the Spirit of Jesus really makes us want to join the praise!

## Questions for reflection

1. Where have you seen God's goodness, faithfulness and power—in this psalm, in the life of Jesus, and in your life?
2. How could you remind yourself to praise God more often?
3. What impact might your praise have on those around you?

## PART TWO

In the Psalter, Psalms 146 – 150 are a kind of answer to the king's call to praise, for they give just the sorts of praise to which the king himself has pledged himself to.

John Calvin famously said that the universe is the theatre of God's glory (*Institutes* 1.5.1). In the visible universe we see, shining forth, the outflow of the nature and character of God, as is hinted at in another great creation psalm: "he wraps himself in light" (Psalm 104:2). "Light" here is a shorthand for the whole visible universe. It is as though the visible universe is a kind of "visibility cloak" (the opposite of an invisibility cloak!) which the invisible God wears to make himself visible.

But it is not quite so simple as that. Simple observation of the world will yield some beautiful, ordered, amazing wonders that we are glad to acknowledge as speaking of the Creator. But it will also yield some ugly things—some dark and evil realities. What are we to make of them? Are we just to pick and choose the aspects of creation we would like to select to represent the Creator? Surely that will not do!

Psalm 148 will help us gain a proper perspective on creation. It answers the question: what will it take for the universe unambiguously and harmoniously to reflect and proclaim the glory of God and to sing his praises?

### The Hallelujah Chorus

Psalms 146 – 150 each begin and end with the word "Hallelujah", translated as "Praise the LORD" in the NIV. "Hallelujah" is a plural imperative Hebrew word. It means something like this: *Come on, all of you (plural): I want you to praise the LORD, the covenant God, the God of the Bible.* It is not so much an exclamation of praise as a call to praise.

The focus of Psalm 148 is a call to the whole created order to give unambiguous praise to the God who made it. It is a deceptively simple psalm, and it is readily misunderstood.

The psalm falls into two unequal parts. First, in **verses 1-6**, there is a call to high things in creation to praise God. Then in **verses 7-13** the appeal is made to lower, earthly things to praise God. We could think of a great choir on two levels. First, the conductor looks up to the balcony and motions to the high choir to praise. Then they turn their gaze to the lower-level choir and calls on them to praise. And then at the end there is a surprising conclusion (**v 14**) that turns out to be the key to the whole psalm!

## Unreachable creation needs to praise God

As the psalm begins, we hear a call in several parts (**v 1-4**) and then the reason or motivation behind the call (**v 5-6**). After the headline summary in **verse 1** ("the heavens ... the heights"), the call begins (using imagery typical of biblical poetry) at the top, with supernatural creatures (**v 2**). The "angels" in their vast "heavenly hosts" are rational creatures. They are supernatural spirits, lower than God (for they are not divine) and yet greater than humans. They can decide whether or not to praise, and it seems that some rebelled (Jude 6). It seems that the devil and his evil spirits are fallen angels.

It may be that this call for praise implies that there is something lacking in the supernatural realm. The New Testament speaks of the devil as "the prince of the power of the air" (Ephesians 2:2 ESV) and of a spiritual battle in heavenly places, in which there are "cosmic powers over this present darkness ... the spiritual forces of evil in the heavenly places" (Ephesians 6:12 ESV). So this is not a superfluous cry: praise him, *all* his angels!

We then move down (as it were) to inanimate heavenly objects (Psalm **148:3-4**). The "sun", "moon" and "shining stars" are to praise the LORD; and so are the "highest heavens" and "waters above the skies". In the **cosmology** of the Bible's poetry, the sky is like a ceiling (the "firmament" of Genesis 1:7; 7:11 KJV), above which are the containers for things like rain, hail and snow. These are the "waters above the skies" (see also Job 38:22-38). The psalmist is saying that *all* these are to praise God.

The word "heavens" combines two ideas. On the one hand, it may simply mean the sky "up there". On the other, it is a poetic and easily understandable way of speaking of places that are out of our reach, above and beyond us, and ultimately of "God's space"—the realm where God dwells in unapproachable light. God is not materially up there in the clouds; but it is a way of helping us grasp that God is out of our reach.

We find it very easy to over-exalt the power of unreachable things. In particular, humanity may think—and often has thought—that the sun, moon and stars are powerful deities that must be worshipped because they influence affairs on earth. Everyone who has consulted a horoscope has signed up to this view. In some circles deceased saints, or angels and spirits, can serve a similar function. The Bible will have none of this. No, all these are created bodies, called upon to bow down and give praise to their Creator.

But what can it mean for inanimate objects like the sun, moon and stars to give praise? The two truths given in Psalm **148:5-6** help us to understand. First, they were created; they are not the Creator—they are created bodies. Second, "he established them [and] issued a decree that will never pass away" (**v 6**). Those words "established" and "decree" speak of what theologians call the "order of creation"—that matrix of physical and moral laws that give order to the universe, not only in its material dimension but also in its morality. The heavenly bodies praise God by being what they are and doing what they do: that is, by exhibiting in their regularities and functions the order that God has placed in creation. The sun praises God by shining, by remaining in its place in this solar system, and so on. The moon praises God by orbiting the earth in a regular manner. There is a sense in which, just by being what they are meant to be, created things speak, as it were, the praise of God. In their regularity, they speak of his faithfulness. In their variety, they speak of his creativity. In their wonder, they speak of his beauty. This principle extends to the rest of the created order. And we too, as created human beings, praise God by living in line with the order and purpose for which he has created us.

We praise God by living in line with the order and purpose for which he has created us.

As we overhear this call, it reminds us never to worship the sun, the moon, the stars, spirits, angels or saints (and not to look at horoscopes). And it reminds us to worship the One who made all those things, and who set each in its place in his awesome creation.

## Down-to-earth creation needs to praise God

But what about down here? The next section of the psalm (**v 7-13**) is a little longer, and its length points to a problem. It begins with three pairs of verses covering what we call the biosphere.

**Verses 7-8** call wild things to praise God. The "great sea creatures" living in the "ocean depths" (**v 7**) probably refer not so much to whales and sharks and so on, but rather, to the storybook sea monsters or dragons common in ancient stories about the gods, and taken up by the Old Testament to speak of spiritual forces of evil. The most famous is Leviathan, mentioned in Job 41, which provides a dramatic way of speaking of the devil in all his terror.

Along with this wild supernatural power of darkness, there are the wild weather phenomena of "lightning and hail, snow and clouds, stormy winds" (Psalm **148:8**). All these terrifying and extreme events are under the control of the God whom they are to praise, for they too "do his bidding". There is no second god, no rival power. Even in their frightening effects, these strange things never do anything except what the Creator bids them to do. In the strangest of ways, they praise him by doing what they do!

In **verse 9** we move to inanimate things: "hills" (small) and "mountains" (big); and trees, both small ("fruit trees") and large ("cedars"). Then in **verse 10** the psalmist speaks to sub-rational creatures: "wild animals" and domesticated farm animals ("cattle"), small creepy-crawly flying insects and large flying birds. These too praise God by being what they are created to be and doing what they are created to do.

Whereas in the high choir the general movement was from higher to lower, here the general movement is from lower to higher, in significance if not in **topography** (compare how the creation of humankind is the pinnacle of God's creation in Genesis 1). In Psalm **148:11-12** we reach the climax: human stuff ought to praise God. Humankind is described first in terms of powerful people ("kings ... princes ... rulers", **v 11**) and then in terms of all people: young and old, men and women (**v 12**). All human beings—whether powerful or weak, old or young, male or female, all without exception are called upon to praise God. Ultimately (as we saw in Psalm 122) only the shared glad praise of the Creator will unite humankind.

**148:13** gives the reason for praise to the low choir, just as **verses 5-6** gave the reason to the high choir. It is a very simple reason, and perhaps it is meant to apply to both sections of the choir: God the Creator is incomparably great. There is no exaltation that can compare with his incomparable greatness, for only the Creator has created. His "splendour" is "above the earth [the low choir] and the heavens [the high choir]". From the highest angels down to the weather systems in the sky... from the lowest order of inanimate being to the very highest, to humankind... the call comes: you should all praise your Creator!

But it is humankind who are the problem. Whatever may or may not be happening with spirits and demons, we know for certain that human beings do not, and will not, heed this call to praise. For, as Paul so graphically puts it in Romans 1:21-32, we have exchanged the proper worship of the Creator for a twisted worship of created things. It is as if the human section of the choir turns away from the conductor and begins singing praise to other sections of the choir, whether it be other human beings (worshipped as gods and goddesses) or animals (the sacred cow), heavenly bodies (the worship of the sun) or idols made of material substances.

This is why we need the surprise of the final verse.

## We are raised up to praise God

Suddenly, and seemingly out of nowhere in a psalm about creation, in Psalm **148:14** we have reference to God's "faithful servants"—to "Israel, the people close to his heart". Where has that come from?! The answer is in the word "horn". "Horn" in biblical imagery symbolises strength and power, wielded by a ruler. It is used often in the Old Testament about God's anointed king, the messiah who is to come (for example, 1 Samuel 2:10). God will raise up a "horn" for his people when he raises up for them a powerful messiah, who will lead and shape a new humanity: men and women who will heed the call of Psalm **148:11-12**. The old humanity in Adam will never do this, for Adam sinned and all humanity sinned in him, and that is why death and sickness and suffering and all the sadness of a groaning creation came into the world. This is why Zechariah, the father of John the Baptist, knowing that his son is the prophet who will announce the coming Messiah, sings after John's birth, "Praise be to the Lord, the God of Israel, because he has come to his people and redeemed them. He has raised up a horn of salvation for us in the house of his servant David" (Luke 1:68-69)

The term "faithful servants" refers to men and women marked by covenant faithfulness to God. These people—this new humanity under the anointed king—will be "close to his heart". The first of these humans was Jesus Christ himself, who had enjoyed the most intimate relationship possible with the Father from all eternity (John 1:18). But now Jesus—this anointed "horn", this strong Messiah—is recreating the human race so as to exhibit rightly the image of God. These men and women are being remade into the image of Jesus, who is the perfect image of God.

Then—and only then, when this new humanity is completed—will the whole created order be the unambiguous theatre of the glory of

God. This is a wonderful and beautiful psalm. But it is not a comfortable psalm. And it can never be a psalm simply about creation. It must necessarily be about redemption, and therefore about Jesus Christ and the gospel that we must take to a needy world. The most urgent need of the created order is not creation care, worthy and good though that may be; it is the gospel of Jesus Christ the anointed King, the strong "horn", who will raise up a people close to God's heart—a new, redeemed humanity who will take their proper place in the created order, living a life of obedient praise to their Creator. To Jesus, and to this new humanity, the government of the new heavens and the new earth may safely be entrusted, for the mandate to be stewards and guardians of creation will gladly and willingly be heeded. Until then, Christian people will do what they can to be responsible stewards of creation; but they will make it a priority to spread the gospel of Jesus the King. In all our lives—in our creation care, our responsible stewardship, and above all our sharing of the gospel of Jesus—we also join with the praise our Creator so richly deserves, because we've been brought into the new humanity that Jesus died and rose to create, and we can now live lives of glad obedience.

## Questions for reflection

1. How could looking at the created world help you to praise God?
2. How could you take the gospel of Jesus Christ to a needy world?
3. For whom could you pray, asking that they would begin to obey and praise the God who made them?

# GLOSSARY

**Aaron:** Moses' brother and the first priest of God's people.

**Abel:** one of the two sons of Adam and Eve.

**Abraham:** the ancestor of the nation of Israel. God made a binding agreement (covenant) with him, promising to make his family into a great nation through which God would bless all the nations.

**Adversarial:** involving conflict.

**Anna:** a woman who prophesied about Jesus when he was a small child (see Luke 2:36-38).

**Anointed:** specifically chosen by God.

**Anthropomorphism:** speaking about something non-human as if it were a human.

**Apostle:** one appointed directly by the risen Christ to teach about him with authority.

**Applied:** taught in such a way that, as well as explanation, there is also a call to action.

**Ark of the covenant:** a chest made out of wood and gold which was the symbol of God's presence with the Israelites.

**Articles:** rules or statements laid out in a formal list.

**Babylonian exile:** the period between 586 and 538 BC, when the majority of the Jewish population was taken out of their own land and into Babylon.

**Biblical theology:** the study of the Bible, its big themes and storylines, and what they teach us about God.

**Book of life:** mentioned in Revelation 3:5; 13:8; 17:8; 20:12, 15; 21:27. It is a book into which are written the names of everyone who trusts in Christ for salvation.

**Cain:** one of the two sons of Adam and Eve.

**Caleb:** one of the spies sent by Moses into the promised land (see Numbers 13 – 14). Unlike the other spies, he and Joshua were confident that God would give them the land.

**Cameo:** a brief appearance or depiction.

**Canticle:** a type of song whose words are taken directly from the Bible.

**Charismatic movement:** a movement in the church which emphasises the gifts of the Holy Spirit.

**Cherubim:** a type of angel, depicted in carvings on the ark of the covenant.

**Christocentrically:** with Christ at the centre.

**Church fathers:** influential theologians and church leaders in the early church.

**Cognitive:** connected with thinking and knowing—mentally, not emotionally.

**Commentator:** a scholar who writes about a text, generally going through it verse by verse.

**Common grace:** good things which God gives regardless of whether someone is a Christian or not (e.g. rain, oxygen).

**Cosmology:** the study of the universe and its arrangement.

**Covenant:** a binding agreement or promise. The old covenant set out how believers in the Old Testament related to God; Jesus established the **new covenant**, so believers now relate to God through Christ's saving death and resurrection.

**Covenant curse:** the punishment which God promised will result when someone makes an agreement with God and then breaks that agreement.

**Daniel:** an Israelite and a prophet who lived in Babylon during the period when the Israelites were in captivity there.

**Deity:** divine status.

**Devotional:** used in personal worship.

**Doctrine:** a statement of what is true about God.

**Edomites:** people from the nation of Edom, one of Israel's neighbours.

**Endemic:** typical of a particular place or group of people.

**Evangelical:** emphasising the Bible's authority and the need to be personally converted through faith in Jesus' death and resurrection.

**Existential:** to do with human existence and experience.

**Exodus:** literally "way out" or "departure": the time when the people of Israel, led by Moses, left slavery in Egypt and began to travel towards the promised land.

**Exposition:** a detailed explanation.

**Ezekiel:** a prophet in the Old Testament.

**Faith:** wholehearted trust.

**Feast of Tabernacles:** a festival taking place in September or October, when Jews remember the time spent by the Israelites in the wilderness (see Leviticus 23:33-43).

**Fleshly nature:** the natural, sinful state of humanity, without the Spirit of God.

**Golden calf:** the statue which the Israelites made out of gold and worshipped while Moses was on Mount Sinai (see Exodus 32).

**Goliath:** the giant defeated by David in 1 Samuel 17.

**Grace:** unmerited favour. In the Bible, "grace" is usually used to describe how God treats his people. Because God is full of grace, he gives believers eternal life (Ephesians 2:4-8); he also gives them gifts to use to serve his people (Ephesians 4:7, 11-13).

**Harvest home:** a festival celebrating the gathering of the harvest in September.

**Hezekiah:** a king of Judah (see 2 Kings 18 – 20; 2 Chronicles 29 – 32).

**Hittites:** a nation of people who lived near to and around God's people in Old Testament times.

**Hyperbolic:** overexaggerating.

**Imperative:** a command (e.g. "come here," "ask him").

**Imputed:** when a quality belonging to one person is given to another so that it is seen as completely belonging to them.

**Incarnate:** coming as a human being.

**Jacob:** the grandson of Abraham and a key ancestor of the Israelites.

**Job:** a man who experienced great suffering despite having done nothing wrong. His story is told in the book of Job.

**Joshua:** Moses' assistant and successor as leader of God's people.

**Josiah:** a king of Judah (see 2 Kings 22 – 23; 2 Chronicles 34 – 35).

**Judas Iscariot:** one of Jesus' followers, who eventually betrayed him.

**King David:** the second king of Israel, and the most important king in Old Testament history. He also wrote many of the psalms.

**King Saul:** the first king of Israel, whose story is told in the book of 1 Samuel.

**Kingdom of God:** life under Jesus Christ's perfect rule. We enter God's kingdom when we turn to his Son, Jesus, in repentance and faith; we will enjoy the kingdom fully when Jesus returns to this world and establishes his kingdom over the whole earth.

**Legalism:** living by following rules in the belief that keeping these requirements will earn blessing or salvation.

**Liberal theology:** writing or teaching about God which does not view Scripture as being without error.

**Lutheran:** a branch of Christianity that identifies with the teaching of Martin Luther, a key figure in the Reformation.

**Manasseh:** a king of Judah (see 2 Kings 21; 2 Chronicles 33).

**Martyr:** someone who dies as a result of refusing to give up their faith.

**Masculine:** an aspect of grammar in some languages. In Biblical Hebrew, unlike in English, the way a verb is spelled can reveal whether the person doing the action is male or female.

**Meditate:** reflect on.

**Mercy seat:** the top of the ark of the covenant, where God's presence would appear (Exodus 25:17-22). Also called "atonement cover" or "place of propitiation".

**Metaphorically:** using one thing as a symbol for another.

**Melchizedek:** a priest and king whom Abraham meets in Genesis 14.

**Ministry:** the work of someone who cares for others. It includes preaching and teaching about Jesus as well as caring for physical needs.

**Minor key:** a musical term. Music in a minor key tends to sound sad or unsettled.

**Moabites:** people from the nation of Moab, one of Israel's neighbours.

**Moralism:** emphasising and promoting morality and good behaviour. People who are moralistic sometimes end up becoming judgmental about those they think are not behaving correctly.

**Morally liberal:** having the opinion that people should be able to behave however they want, rather than obeying what God says about how we should live.

**Moses:** the leader of God's people at the time when God brought them out of slavery in Egypt. God led his people toward the promised land under Moses' leadership, and also communicated his law (including the Ten Commandments) through Moses.

**Most Holy Place:** the innermost room in the Jerusalem Temple, where the ark of the covenant was kept and God dwelt. Because people are sinful, only the high priest could enter this room, and only once a year.

**Nehemiah:** a leader of God's people during the time when they left captivity in Babylon and were allowed to return to rebuild Jerusalem.

**Objective:** based on facts rather than being influenced by personal feelings.

**Omnipresent:** being present everywhere at once.

**Oracle:** a message from God.

**Own his sway:** recognise his rule.

**Paradigm shift:** total change.

**Paradox:** a combination of two things which seem to contradict one another.

**Party spirit:** being divisive by caring more about the reputation or success of your own "group" than the whole. For instance, if a politician cares more about his or her political party than his nation, they would be displaying "party spirit".

**Passover:** a Jewish festival celebrating the event recorded in the book of Exodus when God rescued his people from slavery in Egypt through sending plagues. The final plague was the death of the firstborn in every family, which could be avoided only by killing a lamb in the firstborn's place so that God's judgment would "pass over" that household (see Exodus 12 – 13).

**Patriarch:** one of the key early ancestors of God's people: Abraham, his son Isaac, and Isaac's son Jacob.

**Paul and Silas:** two early Christian missionaries, who took the message of Jesus around the Mediterranean world.

**Pentecost:** a Jewish feast celebrating God giving his people his law on Mount Sinai (Exodus 19 – 31). On the day of this feast, fifty days after Jesus' resurrection, the Holy Spirit came to the first Christians (Acts 2), so "Pentecost" is how Christians tend to refer to this event.

**Pharisaical:** being fanatical about keeping rules.

**Pharisee:** leaders of a first-century Jewish sect who were extremely strict about keeping God's law, and who added extra laws around God's law to ensure that they wouldn't break it. They tended to focus on external acts of obedience.

**Philistines:** a nation of people who lived near to and around God's people in Old Testament times.

**Pious:** someone who prioritises good religious deeds. The word is often used to mean someone who is proud of their religious devotion and looks down on others as a result.

**Platonic:** following the teachings of the Greek philosopher Plato.

**Poet laureate:** a poet officially appointed by a government, who composes poems for national events and important occasions.

**Preposition:** a word that connects two nouns or pronouns, for example "by", "from", "under", "after".

**Promised land:** the land on the eastern coast of the Mediterranean Sea that God promised Abraham he would give his descendants (Genesis 12:6-8; 13:14-18), and which the Israelites eventually took possession of under the leadership of Joshua.

**Prosperity gospel:** the false teaching that God rewards faith with good health or greater wealth, and that Christians should expect and seek these things.

**Providential:** planned by God in advance.

**Psalter:** the book of Psalms.

**Rahab:** a woman from Jericho who helped the Israelites conquer the city and enter the promised land. See Joshua 2.

**Redemption:** freeing or releasing someone from slavery by buying them for a price. The word is used in the Bible to show how Christ released us from slavery to sin and death.

**Reformer:** one of the first two generations of people in the fifteenth and early sixteenth centuries who preached the gospel of justification by faith, and opposed the Pope and the Roman church.

**Remnant:** a small remaining quantity of something.

**Reverie:** a dreamlike state.

**Ruth:** a woman from Moab who became part of God's people when she followed her mother-in-law. Her story is told in the book of Ruth.

**Sabbath:** the holy day when Jewish people were commanded not to work (see Exodus 20:8-11).

**Samuel:** the prophet who led Israel before the appointment of their first king, Saul.

**Sanctuary:** the innermost part of the temple, also called the Most Holy Place or Holy of Holies, which held the ark of the covenant and was identified with God's presence.

**Saul of Tarsus:** more commonly known as Paul. He persecuted the first Christians, before becoming a Christian himself and taking the gospel across the Mediterranean world.

**Seventh commandment:** "You shall not commit adultery." This is one of the Ten Commandments, found in Exodus 20 v 1-17.

**Simeon:** a man who recognised Jesus as the Messiah and prophesied about him when he was a small child (see Luke 2:25-35).

**Solomon:** the king who succeeded David. He built the temple in Jerusalem and was renowned for his wisdom.

**Sons of Korah:** a family group in the tribe of Levi. They were temple doorkeepers (1 Chronicles 9:19), singers and praise leaders (2 Chronicles 20:19). A descendant of Korah, Heman, was the main musician in the temple under David's kingship (1 Chronicles 6:31-38—Korah is listed as one of Heman's ancestors in verse 37).

**Sovereign:** having supreme authority and complete control.

**Stephen:** a member of the early church who was killed for his beliefs (Acts 6:8 – 7:60).

**Stewardship:** looking after something on behalf of someone else.

**Subjective:** based on personal feelings, tastes or opinions.

**Tabernacle:** the name for the tented temple in which the Israelites worshipped God from the time of Moses until the rule of Solomon.

**Theologians:** those who study and write about God.

**Theologically pluralist:** believing that all beliefs about God are equally valid, instead of seeing Jesus Christ as the only way to God.

**Tithe:** an offering or gift of a tenth of annual earnings.

**Topography:** the arrangement of physical features of a place or area.

**Second Adam:** a name for Jesus, used because Jesus marks the end of the story that began with Adam. Adam was the first created man, and we are all like him; but Jesus brings a new creation, enabling us to have heavenly or spiritual life after death (1 Corinthians 15:42-49). The curse of sin came through Adam, and Jesus was the one to end that curse (Romans 5:14-19).

**Synonyms:** two words that mean the same thing.

**Transcendental:** spiritual; deep and eternal.

**Types and shadows:** when the Old Testament hints at or points towards truths or events which would be made clear in the coming of Jesus.

**Vindication:** being proved to be right.

**Wisdom literature:** a section of the Bible that deals with general truths about life and God. It includes Job, Psalms, Proverbs, Ecclesiastes and Song of Songs.

**Word:** the name used for Jesus in John 1. It refers to the fact that Jesus is the supreme way by which God has communicated with and acted among humans.

**Yahweh:** the name by which God revealed himself to Moses (Exodus 3:13-14). Literally, it means "I am who I am" or "I will be who I will be". Most English-language Bibles translate it as "LORD".

**Zion:** another name for Jerusalem (and, more specifically, the mountain upon which it was built).

# APPENDIX: Psalms in the New Testament

As well as clear and explicit quotations from the psalms, there are countless echoes of language from the psalms in the New Testament. In this appendix I have tried to include the most significant of these, although there are many more that might have been included. It is hard to know where to stop.

| Psalm | | New Testament references |
|---|---|---|
| **2** | *v 1-2* | *Acts 4:25-27; Revelation 19:19* |
| | *v 7* | *Matthew 3:17 = Mark 1:11 = Luke 3:22; Matthew 17:5 = Mark 9:7 = Luke 9:35; Hebrews 1:5; 5:5* |
| | *v 8-9* | *Revelation 2:26-27; 12:5; 19:15* |
| **4** | *v 2, 4* | *Ephesians 4:25-26* |
| **5** | *v 9* | *Romans 3:13* |
| **6** | *v 3* | *John 12:27* |
| | *v 8* | *Matthew 7:23; Luke 13:27* |
| **8** | *v 2* | *Matthew 21:16* |
| | *v 4-6* | *Hebrews 2:6-8; 1 Corinthians 15:27; Ephesians 1:22* |
| **9** | *v 7-8* | *Acts 17:31* |
| **10** | *v 7* | *Romans 3:14* |
| **11** | *v 6* | *Revelation 14:10; 19:20; 20:10; 21:8* |
| **14** | *v 1-3* | *Romans 3:10-12* |
| **16** | *v 8-11* | *Acts 2:25-28; 13:35* |
| **18** | *v 2* | *Luke 1:69* |
| | *v 4* | *Acts 2:24* |
| | *v 49* | *Romans 15:9* |
| **19** | *v 4* | *Romans 10:18* |
| **22** | *v 1* | *Matthew 27:46; Mark 15:34* |
| | *v 5* | *Romans 5:5* |
| | *v 7* | *Matthew 27:39* |
| | *v 9-10* | *Matthew 27:43* |
| | *v 12-13* | *2 Timothy 4:17-18* |
| | *v 18* | *Matthew 7:35; Mark 15:24; Luke 23:34; John 19:24* |
| | *v 22* | *Hebrews 2:12* |

| | | |
|---|---|---|
| **24** | *v 1* | *1 Corinthians 10:26* |
| | *v 4* | *Matthew 5:8* |
| **26** | *v 6* | *Matthew 27:24* |
| **28** | *v 4* | *2 Timothy 4:14; 1 Peter 1:17; Revelation 20:12-13* |
| **29** | *v 3* | *Acts 7:2* |
| **31** | *v 5* | *Luke 23:46; Acts 7:29; 1 Peter 4:19* |
| **32** | *v 1-2* | *Romans 4:7-8* |
| **34** | *v 8* | *1 Peter 2:3* |
| | *v 12-16* | *1 Peter 3:10-12; Hebrews 12:14; 2 Timothy 2:22; Romans 14:19* |
| | *v 20* | *John 19:36* |
| **35** | *v 19* | *John 15:25* |
| **36** | *v 1* | *Romans 3:18* |
| **37** | *v 11* | *Matthew 5:5* |
| **40** | *v 6-8* | *Hebrews 10:5-9* |
| **41** | *v 9* | *John 13:18* |
| **44** | *v 22* | *Romans 8:36* |
| **45** | *v 6-7* | *Hebrews 1:8-9* |
| **48** | *v 2* | *Matthew 5:35* |
| **51** | *v 1-3* | *Luke 18:13* |
| | *v 4* | *Romans 3:4* |
| **68** | *v 18* | *Ephesians 4:8* |
| **69** | *v 4* | *John 15:25* |
| | *v 9* | *Romans 15:3* |
| | *v 21* | *Matthew 27:34, 48; Mark 15:23, 36; Luke 23:36; John 19:28-29* |
| | *v 22-23* | *Romans 11:9-10* |
| | *v 25* | *Acts 1:20* |
| **78** | *v 2* | *Matthew 13:35* |
| | *v 24* | *John 6:31* |
| **79** | *v 3* | *Revelation 16:6* |
| **82** | *v 2* | *John 10:34* |
| **86** | *v 9* | *Revelation 15:4* |
| **89** | *v 26* | *1 Peter 1:17* |
| | *v 27* | *Revelation 1:5* |
| **91** | *v 11-12* | *Matthew 4:6; Luke 4:10-11* |

| | | |
|---|---|---|
| ***93*** | *v 1* | *Revelation 19:6* |
| ***94*** | *v 11* | *1 Corinthians 3:20* |
| ***95*** | *v 7-11* | *Hebrews 3:7-11* |
| ***96*** | *v 13* | *Acts 17:31* |
| ***97*** | *v 1* | *Revelation 19:6* |
| ***98*** | *v 9* | *Acts 17:31* |
| ***99*** | *v 1* | *Revelation 19:6* |
| ***102*** | *v 25-27* | *Hebrews 1:10-12* |
| ***104*** | *v 4* | *Hebrews 1:7* |
| | *v 12* | *Matthew 13:32; Mark 4:32; Luke 13:19* |
| ***105*** | *v 40* | *John 6:31* |
| ***109*** | *v 8* | *Acts 1:20* |
| ***110*** | *v 1* | *Matthew 26:64; Mark 12:36; 14:62; Luke 20:42-43; Acts 2:34-35; Romans 8:34; 1 Corinthians 15:25; Ephesians 1:20; Colossians 3:1; Hebrews 1:3, 13; 8:1; 10:12-13; 12:2* |
| | *v 2* | *Matthew 27:44* |
| | *v 4* | *Hebrews 5:6, 10; 6:20; 7:17, 21* |
| | *v 7* | *Luke 22:69* |
| ***112*** | *v 9* | *2 Corinthians 9:9* |
| ***116*** | *v 3* | *Acts 2:24* |
| | *v 10* | *2 Corinthians 4:13* |
| | *v 11* | *Romans 3:4* |
| ***118*** | *v 6-7* | *Hebrews 13:6;* |
| | *v 22* | *Luke 20:17; Acts 4:11; 1 Peter 2:4, 7* |
| | *v 25-26* | *Matthew 21:9, 52; 23:39; Mark 11:9-10; 12:10-11; Luke 13:35; 19:38; John 12:13* |
| ***125*** | *v 5* | *Galatians 6:16* |
| ***130*** | *v 8* | *Titus 2:14* |
| ***135*** | *v 14* | *Hebrews 10:30* |
| ***140*** | *v 3* | *Romans 3:13* |
| ***146*** | *v 6* | *Acts 4:24; 14:15; 17:24; Revelation 10:6; 14:7* |

# BIBLIOGRAPHY


- Leslie C. Allen, *Psalms 101 – 150,* Word Biblical Commentary series (Thomas Nelson, 2002)
- Robert Alter, *The Art of Biblical Poetry* (Basic Books, 1985)
- Christopher Ash, *Teaching Psalms* (2 volumes: Christian Focus, 2017 and 2018)
- Augustine, *Expositions on the Psalms*: Volume 8 of *Nicene and Post-Nicene Fathers: First Series* (Hendrickson, 2004)
- Andrew A. Bonar, *Christ and His Church in the Book of Psalms* (James Nesbit & Co, 1859)
- John Calvin, *Commentary on the Book of Psalms* (5 volumes. Calvin Translation Society, 1847)
- Peter C. Craigie, *Psalms 1 – 50,* Word Biblical Commentary series (Thomas Nelson, 1983)
- Robert Davidson, *The Vitality of Worship: A Commentary on the Book of Psalms* (Eerdman, 1998)
- John H. Eaton, *Kingship in the Psalms* (SCM Press, 1976)
- Philip Eveson, *Psalms* (2 volumes: Evangelical Press, 2014)
- John Goldingay, *Psalms* (3 volumes: Baker, 2006, 2007, 2008)
- Geoffrey W. Grogan, *Psalms* (Eerdmans, 2008)
- Allan Harman, *Psalms: A Mentor Commentary* (2 volumes: Christian Focus, 2011)

- William L. Holladay, *The Psalms through Three Thousand Years* (Fortress Press, 1996)
- Othmar Keel, *The Symbolism of the Biblical World* (Seabury Press, 1978)
- Derek Kidner, *Psalms* (2 volumes: IVP, 1983)
- A.F. Kirkpatrick, *The Books of Psalms* (Cambridge University Press, 1912)
- Hans-Joachim Kraus, *Psalms* (2 volumes: Fortress Press, 1993, translated from the German 5th edition of 1978)
- Eric Lane, *Psalms* (2 volumes: Christian Focus, 2006)
- James L. Mays, *Psalms* (John Knox Press, 1984)
- O. Palmer Robertson, *The Flow of the Psalms* (P & R, 2015)
- Charles Spurgeon, *Psalms,* Crossway Classic Commentaries series (2 volumes. Crossway, 1993)
- Marvin E. Tate, *Psalms 51 – 100,* Word Biblical Commentary series (Thomas Nelson, 1990)
- Willem A. VanGemeren, *Psalms: Volume 5,* Expositor's Bible Commentary series (Zondervan, 2008)
- Bruce K. Waltke and James M. Houston, *The Psalms as Christian Worship* (Eerdmans, 2010)
- Claus Westermann, *Praise and Lament in the Psalms* (John Knox Press, 1981)
- George Whitefield, *Sermons of George Whitefield* (Crossway, 2012)
- Michael Wilcock, *The Message of Psalms,* The Bible Speaks Today series (2 volumes: IVP, 2001)

# ACKNOWLEDGEMENTS

I am grateful to the Proclamation Trust and to Christian Focus Publications for permission to use and adapt material previously published in my two-volume work *Teaching Psalms*. This in turn was the fruit of several years of teaching Psalms at the Cornhill Training Course in London and preaching Psalms in a variety of churches, and at several conferences. I am grateful to all who listened, questioned, and commented to me, to sharpen and clarify my understanding on many points. I am also thankful to a number of scholars and pastors who have interacted with me at Tyndale House, notably Dr. James Hely Hutchinson and Dr. Kim Phillips. I am grateful also to my excellent editors, Carl Laferton and Katy Morgan, for their encouragement, perceptive comments and painstaking work on the details.

# More For You

## Exodus For You

"The book of Exodus is key to understanding Jesus. It is an exciting story, a historical story and—as it points us to and inspires us to worship Jesus—it is *our* story."

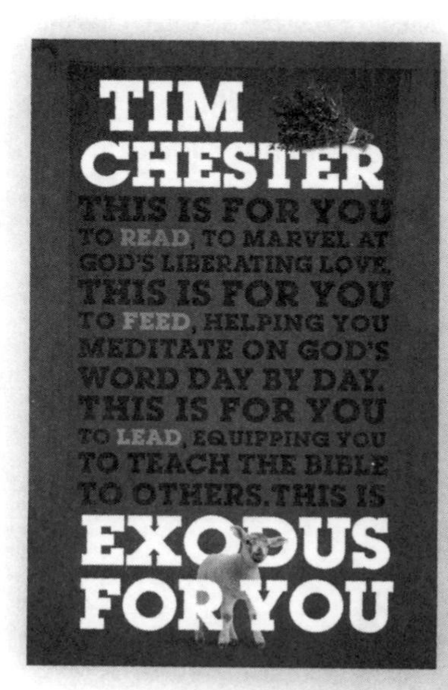

## Galatians For You

"Galatians is all about the gospel—the gospel all of us need throughout all of our lives. It's dynamite, and I pray that its powerful message explodes in your heart as you read this book."

# The Whole Series

- **Exodus For You**
  *Tim Chester*
- **Judges For You**
  *Timothy Keller*
- **1 Samuel For You**
  *Tim Chester*
- **2 Samuel For You**
  *Tim Chester*
- **Psalms For You**
  *Christopher Ash*
- **Daniel For You**
  *David Helm*
- **Micah For You**
  *Stephen Um*
- **Luke 1-12 For You**
  *Mike McKinley*
- **Luke 12-24 For You**
  *Mike McKinley*
- **John 1-12 For You**
  *Josh Moody*
- **John 13-21 For You**
  *Josh Moody*
- **Acts 1-12 For You**
  *Albert Mohler*
- **Acts 13-28 For You**
  *Albert Mohler*
- **Romans 1-7 For You**
  *Timothy Keller*
- **Romans 8-16 For You**
  *Timothy Keller*
- **2 Corinthians For You**
  *Gary Millar*
- **Galatians For You**
  *Timothy Keller*
- **Ephesians For You**
  *Richard Coekin*
- **Philippians For You**
  *Steven Lawson*
- **Colossians & Philemon For You**
  *Mark Meynell*
- **1 & 2 Timothy For You**
  *Phillip Jensen*
- **Titus For You**
  *Tim Chester*
- **James For You**
  *Sam Allberry*
- **1 Peter For You**
  *Juan Sanchez*
- **Revelation For You**
  *Tim Chester*

**BIBLICAL | RELEVANT | ACCESSIBLE**

At The Good Book Company, we are dedicated to helping Christians and local churches grow. We believe that God's growth process always starts with hearing clearly what he has said to us through his timeless word—the Bible.

Ever since we opened our doors in 1991, we have been striving to produce Bible-based resources that bring glory to God. We have grown to become an international provider of user-friendly resources to the Christian community, with believers of all backgrounds and denominations using our books, Bible studies, devotionals, evangelistic resources, and DVD-based courses.

We want to equip ordinary Christians to live for Christ day by day, and churches to grow in their knowledge of God, their love for one another, and the effectiveness of their outreach.

Call us for a discussion of your needs or visit one of our local websites for more information on the resources and services we provide.

Your friends at The Good Book Company